IRAQ

UN Documents of early March 2003

Presented to Parliament
By the Secretary of State for Foreign and Commonwealth Affairs
By Command of Her Majesty
March 2003

Cm 5785   £22.50

© **Crown Copyright 2003**

The text in this document (excluding the Royal Arms and departmental logos) may be reproduced free of charge in any format or medium providing that it is reproduced accurately and not used in a misleading context. The material must be acknowledged as Crown copyright and the title of the document specified.

Any enquiries relating to the copyright in this document should be addressed to The Licensing Division, HMSO, St Clements House, 2-16 Colegate, Norwich NR3 1BQ. Fax: 01603 723000 or e-mail: licensing@cabinet-office.x.gsi.gov.uk

INTRODUCTION

This paper is intended to bring together in an easily accessible form some of the key international documents relevant to the Iraq crisis. It comprises:

Reproduced with the permission of the UN

SECURITY COUNCIL 7 MARCH 2003

Oral introduction of the 12th quarterly report of UNMOVIC

Executive Chairman Dr. Hans Blix

Mr. President,

For nearly three years, I have been coming to the Security Council presenting the quarterly reports of UNMOVIC. They have described our many preparations for the resumption of inspections in Iraq. The 12th quarterly report is the first that describes three months of inspections. They come after four years without inspections. The report was finalized ten days ago and a number of relevant events have taken place since then. Today's statement will supplement the circulated report on these points to bring the Council up-to-date.

Inspection process

Inspections in Iraq resumed on 27 November 2002. In matters relating to process, notably prompt access to sites, we have faced relatively few difficulties and certainly much less than those that were faced by UNSCOM in the period 1991 to 1998. This may well be due to the strong outside pressure.

Some practical matters, which were not settled by the talks, Dr. El-Baradei and I had with the Iraqi side in Vienna prior to inspections or in resolution 1441 (2002), have been resolved at meetings, which we have had in Baghdad. Initial difficulties raised by the Iraqi side about helicopters and aerial surveillance planes operating in the no-fly zones were overcome. This is not to say that the operation of inspections is free from frictions, but at this juncture we are able to perform professional no-notice inspections all over Iraq and to increase aerial surveillance.

American U-2 and French Mirage surveillance aircraft already give us valuable imagery, supplementing satellite pictures and we would expect soon to be able to add night vision capability through an aircraft offered to us by the Russian Federation. We also expect to add low-level, close area surveillance through drones provided by Germany. We are grateful not only to the countries, which place these valuable tools at our disposal, but also to the States, most recently Cyprus, which has agreed to the stationing of aircraft on their territory.

Documents and interviews

Iraq, with a highly developed administrative system, should be able to provide more documentary evidence about its proscribed weapons programmes. Only a few new such documents have come to light so far and been handed over since we began inspections. It was a disappointment that Iraq's Declaration of 7 December did not bring new documentary evidence. I hope that efforts in this respect, including the appointment of a governmental commission, will give significant results. When proscribed items are deemed unaccounted for it is above all credible accounts that is needed - or the proscribed items, if they exist.

Where authentic documents do not become available, interviews with persons, who may have relevant knowledge and experience, may be another way of obtaining evidence. UNMOVIC has names of such persons in its records and they are among the people whom we seek to interview. In the last month, Iraq has provided us with the names of many persons, who may be relevant sources of information, in particular, persons who took part in various phases of the unilateral destruction of biological and chemical weapons, and proscribed missiles in 1991. The provision of names prompts two reflections:

The first is that with such detailed information existing regarding those who took part in the unilateral destruction, surely there must also remain records regarding the quantities and other data concerning the various items destroyed.

The second reflection is that with relevant witnesses available it becomes even more important to be able to conduct interviews in modes and locations, which allow us to be confident that the testimony is given without outside influence. While the Iraqi side seems to have encouraged interviewees not to request the presence of Iraqi officials (so-called minders) or the taping of the interviews, conditions ensuring the absence of undue influences are difficult to attain inside Iraq. Interviews outside the country might provide such assurance. It is our intention to request such interviews shortly. Nevertheless, despite remaining shortcomings, interviews are useful. Since we started requesting interviews, 38 individuals were asked for private interviews, of which 10 accepted under our terms, 7 of these during the last week.

As I noted on 14 February, intelligence authorities have claimed that weapons of mass destruction are moved around Iraq by trucks and, in particular, that there are mobile production units for biological weapons. The Iraqi side states that such activities do not exist. Several inspections have taken place at declared and undeclared sites in relation to mobile production facilities. Food testing mobile laboratories and mobile workshops have been seen, as well as large containers with seed processing equipment. No evidence of proscribed activities have so far been found. Iraq is expected to assist in the development of credible ways to conduct random checks of ground transportation.

Inspectors are also engaged in examining Iraq's programme for Remotely Piloted Vehicles (RPVs). A number of sites have been inspected with data being collected to assess the range and other capabilities of the various models found. Inspections are continuing in this area.

There have been reports, denied from the Iraqi side, that proscribed activities are conducted underground. Iraq should provide information on any underground structure suitable for the production or storage of WMD. During inspections of declared or undeclared facilities, inspection teams have examined building structures for any possible underground facilities. In addition, ground penetrating radar equipment was used in several specific locations. No underground facilities for chemical or biological production or storage were found so far.

I should add that, both for the monitoring of ground transportation and for the inspection of underground facilities, we would need to increase our staff in Iraq. I am not talking about a doubling of the staff. I would rather have twice the amount of high quality information about sites to inspect than twice the number of expert inspectors to send.

Recent developments

On 14 February, I reported to the Council that the Iraqi side had become more active in taking and proposing steps, which potentially might shed new light on unresolved disarmament issues. Even a week ago, when the current quarterly report was finalized, there was still relatively little tangible progress to note. Hence, the cautious formulations in the report before you.

As of today, there is more. While during our meetings in Baghdad, the Iraqi side tried to persuade us that the Al Samoud 2 missiles they have declared fall within the permissible range set by the Security Council, the calculations of an international panel of experts led us to the opposite conclusion. Iraq has since accepted that these missiles and associated items be destroyed and has started the process of destruction under our supervision. The destruction undertaken constitutes a substantial measure of disarmament - indeed, the first since the middle of the 1990s. We are not watching the breaking of toothpicks. Lethal weapons are being destroyed. However, I must add that no destruction has happened today. I hope it's a temporary break.

To date, 34 Al Samoud 2 missiles, including 4 training missiles, 2 combat warheads, 1 launcher and 5 engines have been destroyed under UNMOVIC supervision. Work is continuing to identify and inventory the parts and equipment associated with the Al Samoud 2 programme.

Two 'reconstituted' casting chambers used in the production of solid propellant missiles have been destroyed and the remnants melted or encased in concrete.

The legality of the Al Fatah missile is still under review, pending further investigation and measurement of various parameters of that missile.

More papers on anthrax, VX and missiles have recently been provided. Many have been found to restate what Iraq had already declared, some will require further study and discussion.

There is a significant Iraqi effort underway to clarify a major source of uncertainty as to the quantities of biological and chemical weapons, which were unilaterally destroyed in 1991. A part of this effort concerns a disposal site, which was deemed too dangerous for full investigation in the past. It is now being re-excavated. To date, Iraq has unearthed eight complete bombs comprising two liquid-filled intact R-400 bombs and six other complete bombs. Bomb fragments were also found. Samples have been taken. The investigation of the destruction site could, in the best case, allow the determination of the number of bombs destroyed at that site. It should be followed by a serious and credible effort to determine the separate issue of how many R-400 type bombs were produced. In this, as in other matters, inspection work is moving on and may yield results.

Iraq proposed an investigation using advanced technology to quantify the amount of unilaterally destroyed anthrax dumped at a site. However, even if the use of advanced technology could quantify the amount of anthrax, said to be dumped at the site, the results would still be open to interpretation. Defining the quantity of anthrax destroyed must, of course, be followed by efforts to establish what quantity was actually produced.

With respect to VX, Iraq has recently suggested a similar method to quantify a VX precursor stated to have been unilaterally destroyed in the summer of 1991.

Iraq has also recently informed us that, following the adoption of the presidential decree prohibiting private individuals and mixed companies from engaging in work related to WMD, further legislation on the subject is to be enacted. This appears to be in response to a letter from UNMOVIC requesting clarification of the issue.

What are we to make of these activities? One can hardly avoid the impression that, after a period of somewhat reluctant cooperation, there has been an acceleration of initiatives from the Iraqi side since the end of January.

This is welcome, but the value of these measures must be soberly judged by how many question marks they actually succeed in straightening out. This is not yet clear.

Against this background, the question is now asked whether Iraq has cooperated "immediately, unconditionally and actively" with UNMOVIC, as required under paragraph 9 of resolution 1441 (2002). The answers can be seen from the factual descriptions I have provided. However, if more direct answers are desired, I would say the following:

The Iraqi side has tried on occasion to attach conditions, as it did regarding helicopters and U-2 planes. Iraq has not, however, so far persisted in these or other conditions for the exercise of any of our inspection rights. If it did, we would report it.

It is obvious that, while the numerous initiatives which are now taken by the Iraqi side with a view to resolving some long-standing open disarmament issues, can be seen as "active", or even "proactive", these initiatives 3-4 months into the new resolution cannot be said to constitute "immediate" cooperation. Nor do they necessarily cover all areas of relevance. They are nevertheless welcome and UNMOVIC is responding to them in the hope of solving presently unresolved disarmament issues.

Mr. President,

Members of the Council may relate most of what I have said to resolution 1441 (2002), but UNMOVIC is performing work under several resolutions of the Security Council. The quarterly report before you is submitted in accordance with resolution 1284 (1999), which not only created UNMOVIC but also continues to guide much of our work. Under the time lines set by the resolution, the results of some of this work is to be reported to the Council before the end of this month. Let me be more specific.

Resolution 1284 (1999) instructs UNMOVIC to "address unresolved disarmament issues" and to identify "key remaining disarmament tasks" and the latter are to be submitted for approval by the Council in the context of a work programme. UNMOVIC will be ready to submit a draft work programme this month as required.

UNSCOM and the Amorim Panel did valuable work to identify the disarmament issues, which were still open at the end of 1998. UNMOVIC has used this material as starting points but analysed the data behind it and data and documents post 1998 up to the present time to compile its own list of "unresolved disarmament issues" or, rather, clustered issues. It is the answers to these issues which we seek through our inspection activities.

It is from the list of these clustered issues that UNMOVIC will identify the "key remaining disarmament tasks". As noted in the report before you, this list of clustered issues is ready.

UNMOVIC is only required to submit the work programme with the "key remaining disarmament tasks" to the Council. As I understand that several Council members are interested in the working document with the complete clusters of disarmament issues, we have declassified it and are ready to make it available to members of the Council on request. In this working document, which may still be adjusted in the light of new information, members will get a more up-to-date review of the outstanding issues than in the documents of 1999, which members usually refer to. Each cluster in the working document ends with a number of points indicating what Iraq could do to solve the issue. Hence, Iraq's cooperation could be measured against the successful resolution of issues.

I should note that the working document contains much information and discussion about the issues which existed at the end of 1998 including information which has come to light after 1998. It contains much less information and discussion about the period after 1998, primarily because of paucity of information. Nevertheless, intelligence agencies have expressed the view that proscribed programmes have continued or restarted in this period. It is further contended that proscribed programmes and items are located in underground facilities, as I mentioned, and that proscribed items are being moved around Iraq. The working document contains some suggestions on how these concerns may be tackled.

Mr. President,

Let me conclude by telling you that UNMOVIC is currently drafting the work programme, which resolution 1284 (1999) requires us to submit this month. It will obviously contain our proposed list of key remaining disarmament tasks; it will describe the reinforced system of ongoing monitoring and verification that the Council has asked us to implement; it will also describe the various subsystems which constitute the programme, e.g. for aerial surveillance, for information from governments and suppliers, for sampling, for the checking of road traffic, etc.

How much time would it take to resolve the key remaining disarmament tasks? While cooperation can and is to be immediate, disarmament and at any rate the verification of it cannot be instant. Even with a proactive Iraqi attitude, induced by continued outside pressure, it would still take some time to verify sites and items, analyse documents, interview relevant persons, and draw conclusions. It would not take years, nor weeks, but months. Neither governments nor inspectors would want disarmament inspection to go on forever. However, it must be remembered that in accordance with the governing resolutions, a sustained inspection and monitoring system is to remain in place after verified disarmament to give confidence and to strike an alarm, if signs were seen of the revival of any proscribed weapons programmes.

SECURITY COUNCIL 7 MARCH 2003

**Report by Dr EL-BARADEI,
Director General of the IAEA**

Thank you, Mr. President.

My report to the Council today is an update on the status of the International Atomic Energy Agency's nuclear verification activities in Iraq pursuant to Security Council resolution 1441 (2002) and other relevant resolutions.

Inspection Activities

When I reported last to the Council, on 14 February, I explained that the Agency's inspection activities had moved well beyond the "reconnaissance phase" - that is, re-establishing our knowledge base regarding Iraq's nuclear capabilities - into the "investigative phase", which focuses on the central question before the IAEA relevant to disarmament: whether Iraq has revived or attempted to revive its defunct nuclear weapons programme over the last four years.

At the outset, let me state one general observation: namely, that during the past four years, at the majority of Iraqi sites, industrial capacity has deteriorated substantially, due to the departure of the foreign support that was often present in the late 1980s, the departure of large numbers of skilled Iraqi personnel in the past decade, and the lack of consistent maintenance by Iraq of sophisticated equipment. At only a few inspected sites involved in industrial research, development and manufacturing have the facilities been improved and new personnel been taken on. This overall deterioration in industrial capacity is naturally of direct relevance to Iraq's capability for resuming a nuclear weapons programme.

Inspections

The IAEA has now conducted a total of 218 nuclear inspections at 141 sites, including 21 that had not been inspected before. In addition, IAEA experts have taken part in many joint UNMOVIC-IAEA inspections.

Technical Methods

Technical support for nuclear inspections has continued to expand. The three operational air samplers have collected, from key locations in Iraq, weekly air particulate samples that are being sent to laboratories for analysis. Additional results of water, sediment, vegetation and material sample analyses have been received from the relevant laboratories.

Our vehicle-borne radiation survey team has covered some 2000 kilometres over the past three weeks. Survey access has been gained to over 75 facilities, including military garrisons and camps, weapons factories, truck parks, manufacturing facilities and residential areas.

Interviews

Interviews have continued with relevant Iraqi personnel - at times with individuals and groups in the workplace during the course of unannounced inspections, and on other occasions in pre-arranged meetings with key scientists and other specialists known to have been involved with Iraq's past nuclear programme. The IAEA has continued to conduct interviews even when the conditions were not in accordance with the IAEA's preferred modalities, with a view to gaining as much information as possible - information that could be cross-checked for validity with other sources and which could be helpful in our assessment of areas under investigation.

As you may recall, when we first began to request private, unescorted interviews, the Iraqi interviewees insisted on taping the interviews and keeping the recorded tapes. Recently, upon our insistence, individuals have been consenting to being interviewed without escort and without a taped record. The IAEA has conducted two such private interviews in the last 10 days, and hopes that its ability to conduct private interviews will continue unhindered, including possibly interviews outside Iraq.

I should add that we are looking into further refining the modalities for conducting interviews, to ensure that they are conducted freely, and to alleviate concerns that interviews are being listened to by other Iraqi parties. In our view, interviews outside Iraq may be the best way to ensure that interviews are free. We intend, therefore, to request such interviews shortly. We are also asking other States to enable us to conduct interviews with former Iraqi scientists that now reside in those States.

Specific Issues

In the last few weeks, Iraq has provided a considerable volume of documentation relevant to the issues I reported earlier as being of particular concern, including Iraq's efforts to procure aluminium tubes, its attempted procurement of magnets and magnet production capabilities, and its reported attempt to import uranium. I will touch briefly on the progress made on each of these issues.

Uranium Enrichment

Since my last update to the Council, the primary technical focus of IAEA field activities in Iraq has been on resolving several outstanding issues related to the possible resumption of efforts by Iraq to enrich uranium through the use of centrifuges. For that purpose, the IAEA assembled a specially qualified team of international centrifuge manufacturing experts.

Aluminium tubes

The IAEA has conducted a thorough investigation of Iraq's attempts to purchase large quantities of high-strength aluminium tubes. As previously reported, Iraq has maintained that these aluminium tubes were sought for rocket production. Extensive field investigation and document analysis have failed to uncover any evidence that Iraq intended to use these 81mm tubes for any project other than the reverse engineering of rockets.

The Iraqi decision-making process with regard to the design of these rockets was well documented. Iraq has provided copies of design documents, procurement records, minutes of committee meetings and supporting data and samples. A thorough analysis of this information, together with information gathered from interviews with Iraqi personnel, has allowed the IAEA to develop a coherent picture of attempted purchases and intended usage of the 81mm aluminium tubes, as well as the rationale behind the changes in the tolerances.

Drawing on this information, the IAEA has learned that the original tolerances for the 81mm tubes were set prior to 1987, and were based on physical measurements taken from a small number of imported rockets in Iraq's possession. Initial attempts to reverse engineer the rockets met with little success. Tolerances were adjusted during the following years as part of ongoing efforts to revitalize the project and improve operational efficiency. The project languished for long periods during this time and became the subject of several committees, which resulted in specification and tolerance changes on each occasion.

Based on available evidence, the IAEA team has concluded that Iraq's efforts to import these aluminium tubes were not likely to have been related to the manufacture of centrifuges and, moreover, that it was highly unlikely that Iraq could have achieved the considerable re-design needed to use them in a revived centrifuge programme. However, this issue will continue to be scrutinized and investigated.

Magnets

With respect to reports about Iraq's efforts to import high-strength permanent magnets - or to achieve the capability for producing such magnets - for use in a centrifuge enrichment programme, I should note that, since 1998, Iraq has purchased high-strength magnets for various uses. Iraq has declared inventories of magnets of twelve different designs. The IAEA has verified that previously acquired magnets have been used for missile guidance systems, industrial machinery, electricity meters and field telephones. Through visits to research and production sites, reviews of engineering drawings and analyses of sample magnets, IAEA experts familiar with the use of such magnets in centrifuge enrichment have verified that none of the magnets that Iraq has declared could be used directly for a centrifuge magnetic bearing.

In June 2001, Iraq signed a contract for a new magnet production line, for delivery and installation in 2003. The delivery has not yet occurred, and Iraqi documentation and interviews of Iraqi personnel indicate that this contract will not be executed. However, the contract has been evaluated by the IAEA centrifuge enrichment experts. They have concluded the replacement of foreign procurement with domestic magnet production seems reasonable from an economic point of view. In addition, the training and experience acquired by Iraq in the pre-1991 period makes it likely that Iraq possesses the expertise to manufacture high-strength permanent magnets suitable for use in enrichment centrifuges. The IAEA will continue therefore to monitor and inspect equipment and materials that could be used to make magnets for enrichment centrifuges.

Flow forming capabilities

Iraq has used its relatively low-accuracy flow forming capability for the production of rocket parts in steel. Investigations in the field indicate that Iraq has recently started to flow form its own tubes in aluminium as well.

Based upon Iraqi documentation, experts' observations of Iraq's industrial capabilities and the IAEA's knowledge of Iraq's industrial assets - including the availability of raw materials - our assessment to date is that Iraq still possesses an abundance of high-strength aluminium materials procured during the 1980s, and has the expertise needed to produce pre-forms of high quality, but that it currently has low-quality flow forming equipment. In addition, Iraq's lack of experience and expertise in this field makes it highly unlikely that it is currently able to produce aluminium cylinders consistently to the tolerances required for centrifuge enrichment.

Nevertheless, the IAEA will monitor all potentially capable machines and facilities using 24-hour camera surveillance, supported by a regime of unannounced inspections. The IAEA will also continue to assess the level of centrifuge-related expertise remaining in Iraq.

Uranium Acquisition

The IAEA has made progress in its investigation into reports that Iraq sought to buy uranium from Niger in recent years. The investigation was centred on documents provided by a number of States that pointed to an agreement between Niger and Iraq for the sale of uranium between 1999 and 2001.

The IAEA has discussed these reports with the Governments of Iraq and Niger, both of which have denied that any such activity took place. For its part, Iraq has provided the IAEA with a comprehensive explanation of its relations with Niger, and has described a visit by an Iraqi official to a number of African countries, including Niger, in February 1999, which Iraq thought might have given rise to the reports. The IAEA was also able to review correspondence coming from various bodies of the Government of Niger, and to compare the form, format, contents and signatures of that correspondence with those of the alleged procurement-related documentation. Based on thorough analysis, the IAEA has concluded, with the concurrence of outside experts, that these documents - which formed the basis for the reports of recent uranium transactions between Iraq and Niger - are in fact not authentic. We have therefore concluded that these specific allegations are unfounded. However, we will continue to follow up any additional evidence, if it emerges, relevant to efforts by Iraq to illicitly import nuclear materials.

Procurement Patterns

Many concerns regarding Iraq's possible intention to resume its nuclear programme have arisen from Iraqi procurement efforts reported by a number of States. In addition, many of Iraq's efforts to procure commodities and products, including magnets and aluminium tubes, have been conducted in contravention of sanction controls specified under Security Council resolution 661 and other relevant resolutions.

The issue of procurement efforts remains under thorough investigation, and further verification will be forthcoming. An IAEA team of technical experts, customs investigators and computer forensic specialists is currently conducting a series of investigations, through inspections at trading companies and commercial organizations, aimed at understanding Iraq's patterns of procurement.

Conclusion

In conclusion, I am able to report today that, in the area of nuclear weapons - the most lethal weapons of mass destruction - inspections in Iraq are moving forward. Since the resumption of inspections a little over three months ago - and particularly during the three weeks since my last oral report to the Council - the IAEA has made important progress in identifying what nuclear-related capabilities remain in Iraq, and in its assessment of whether Iraq has made any efforts to revive its past nuclear programme during the intervening four years since inspections were brought to a halt. At this stage, the following can be stated:

- There is no indication of resumed nuclear activities in those buildings that were identified through the use of satellite imagery as being reconstructed or newly erected since 1998, nor any indication of nuclear-related prohibited activities at any inspected sites.

- There is no indication that Iraq has attempted to import uranium since 1990.

- There is no indication that Iraq has attempted to import aluminium tubes for use in centrifuge enrichment. Moreover, even had Iraq pursued such a plan, it would have encountered practical difficulties in manufacturing centrifuges out of the aluminium tubes in question.

- Although we are still reviewing issues related to magnets and magnet production, there is no indication to date that Iraq imported magnets for use in a centrifuge enrichment programme.

As I stated above, the IAEA will continue further to scrutinize and investigate all of the above issues.

After three months of intrusive inspections, we have to date found no evidence or plausible indication of the revival of a nuclear weapons programme in Iraq. We intend to continue our inspection activities, making use of all the additional rights granted to us by resolution 1441 and all additional tools that might be available to us, including reconnaissance platforms and all relevant technologies. We also hope to continue to receive from States actionable information relevant to our mandate. I should note that, in the past three weeks, possibly as a result of ever-increasing pressure by the international community, Iraq has been forthcoming in its co-operation, particularly with regard to the conduct of private interviews and in making available evidence that could contribute to the resolution of matters of IAEA concern. I do hope that Iraq will continue to expand the scope and accelerate the pace of its co-operation.

The detailed knowledge of Iraq's capabilities that IAEA experts have accumulated since 1991 - combined with the extended rights provided by resolution 1441, the active commitment by all States to help us fulfil our mandate, and the recently increased level of Iraqi co-operation - should enable us in the near future to provide the Security Council with an objective and thorough assessment of Iraq's nuclear-related capabilities. However credible this assessment may be, we will endeavour - in view of the inherent uncertainties associated with any verification process, and, particularly in light of Iraq's past record of co-operation - to evaluate Iraq's capabilities on a continuous basis as part of our long-term monitoring and verification programme, in order to provide the international community with ongoing and real time assurances.

IRAQ: FOREIGN SECRETARY'S SPEECH TO THE SECURITY COUNCIL:

7 MARCH

Mr President

I'd like to begin by congratulating you on your assumption of the Presidency by wishing you well at a very important moment; and also to echo and underline the thanks which you so generously gave to Vice Chancellor Joschka Fischer and Ambassador Gunter Pleuger for the excellent way in which they chaired the Security Council during the month of February. I would also like to thank Dr El Baradei and Dr Blix for their reports, and to place on record my Government's appreciation for their work and the work, in very difficult circumstances, of all the staff of the IAEA and of UNMOVIC.

Mr President,

I've listened with very great care to what my colleagues speaking before me have said. We are all agreed that Iraq must be fully disarmed of weapons of mass destruction and that Iraq's failure to co-operate immediately, unconditionally and actively with the Inspectors has to be dealt with. As we negotiated 1441 the evidence was there for all of us to see, that Iraq had been and remained in material breach and we all, fifteen members, voted to give the Iraqi regime a final opportunity to comply with its obligations. The first question therefore for this Council is, has Iraq taken this final opportunity to disarm? And I've been very struck, listening with care to all the speeches and of course people have different points of view. But nobody, not one Minister before this Council in my hearing, has said that Iraq is now fully, actively and immediately in compliance with 1441. They have not so far taken this final opportunity. If anybody in this chamber or outside has any doubt about that conclusion, I do commend to members this so called "clusters" report, the outstanding issues, concerning Iraq's proscribed weapons programme, which as a member of the Commission behind UNMOVIC I've already had the privilege of reading. I have read, Dr Blix knows, all 167 pages of that report in every particular. It's a very painstaking piece of work. I thank Dr Blix for publishing it. But it's also a chilling read about the failure of Iraq to comply with successive resolutions of this Council over each day of the past 12 years. There's not been active co-operation in the matters that matter. UNMOVIC, because of that, have not been able to resolve the substantive issues outstanding from 1998. As we all know, a point to which I will return shortly, Iraq refused to admit Inspectors for three years after resolution 1284 was passed, only agreeing to them under the threat of enforcement action and in an attempt to frustrate 1441. Iraq has dragged its feet on as many elements of procedural and substantive co-operation as possible.

Mr President,

Could I draw attention to just one aspect which is often overlooked. Dr Blix referred to the fact that Iraq has recently informed us that, following the adoption of a Presidential decree prohibiting individuals and mixed companies from engaging in work related to weapons of mass destruction, further legislation on this subject is to be enacted. No-one should be taken in by this as a concession. Iraq was ordered, I have the instruction here from this Council, on 2 October 1991 to enact legislation, which in conformity with international law would do precisely what they are now saying they intend to do. What is more, what they have so far done does not cover the operations of the state, only private individuals and mixed companies. So 12 years on, 12 years, after the world saw that Iraq had developed, under the world's noses, weapons of mass destruction and delivery systems, nuclear systems, biological systems, chemical systems, Iraq is still refusing to pass a law saying that such activity by members of state government authorities is illegal. This is not something on which they needed a search, it is not something of which they needed the assistance of Inspectors or ground penetrating radar, it's something they could, and should have, done back in October 1991. And notwithstanding all the pressure they are still refusing to do.

And then we come onto the issue of interviews. Dr Blix and Dr El Baradei have reported. Iraq has done everything possible to prevent unrestricted, unrecorded interviews. There have now been twelve private interviews between UNMOVIC and the IAEA, against an UNSCOM list of 3,500 people previously associated with weapons of mass destruction programmes. We know for a fact that all of these twelve and all prospective interviewees have been threatened and intimidated by the Iraqi regime beforehand and told that their exchanges were being recorded. They weren't being recorded by bugs and tape-recorders the interviewees were told to take into the meetings. They were going to be recorded in any event by bugs placed in the walls of the recording halls, I understand that scientists most likely to have the most incriminating evidence have been locked away by the Iraqi Security Services. There have been no interviews in the safe havens outside Iraq, not one, and the restrictions placed on the interviews is itself the most incriminating evidence that Saddam has something to hide. The Al Samoud episode further confirms Iraq's familiar tactics. Iraq under-declared the number of missile engines it illegally imported. It declared 231 engines but imported 380. Iraq also falsely declared that the missile had a maximum range of 150kms when it was designed to fly, this is not an accident, it was designed to fly considerably in excess of that. And we know that Iraq's agreement to the destruction process, necessary as it is, is a calculation that it can satisfy the Council with a partial response in one only of the 29 categories of unresolved disarmament questions.

Now I have to say Mr President, and with all respect to good colleagues, that it defies experience that to continue inspections with no firm end-date, as I believe has been suggested in the French, German and Russian memorandum, will achieve complete disarmament, unless, as the memorandum acknowledges, Iraq's full and active co-operation is immediately forthcoming. The memorandum is not even a formula for containment, given Iraq's proven ability to exploit the existing sanctions regime to continue to develop weapons of mass destruction. We knew nothing about the missile engines, we knew nothing about the rest of this imported under our noses in breach of the sanctions regime until we passed 1441. And to find a peaceful solution to the current crisis the Council must not retreat from the demands that it set out clearly in 1441. What we need is an irreversible and strategic decision by Iraq to disarm, a strategic decision by Iraq to yield to the Inspectors all of its weapons of mass destruction and all relevant information which it could and should have provided at anytime in the last 12 years. A strategic decision like that taken by South Africa when it decided freely to abandon its secret nuclear programme.

Mr President,

I greatly welcome the progress which the Inspectors have today reported. My earnest wish and that of my government has all along been to achieve disarmament of Iraq's weapons of mass destruction, if humanly possible, by peaceful means. But to achieve that we have to recognise that the progress that has been reported represents only the tip of a very large iceberg of huge, unfinished business required of Iraq. And just as I welcome the progress that we have heard about, I say to the Council that there are very serious lessons for us from what has been reported. Let us consider what has changed. Why has there been this sudden bout of activity when there was no progress at all for weeks before that, when for months and for years before that Saddam Hussein was rearming under our noses? Now it isn't our policy that has changed, not international law that has changed. There has been from the beginning the clearest instructions for Saddam to disarm, no, what has changed is one thing and one thing only — the pressure on the regime. Dr Blix said in his opening remarks 'what's changed may well be due to strong outside pressure", that's absolutely right. In his remarks, Dominique de Villepin described a lot of diplomatic pressure by the Non-Aligned movement by the European Union, by the Arab League and by many others. I greatly welcome all of that diplomatic pressure. Dominique went on to say that the United States and United Kingdom forces lend support to that pressure. With respect to you my good friend, I think it's the other way around, I really do. What has happened, in Dr Blix's carefully chosen words "the strong outside pressure", let us be blunt about this, is the presence of over 200,000 United States and United Kingdom young men and young women willing to put their lives on the line for the sake of this body, the United Nations. Dominique also said the choice before us was disarmament by peace or disarmament by war. Dominique that is a false choice. I wish that it was that easy because we wouldn't be having to have this discussion, we could all put up our hands up for disarmament by peace and all go home. The paradox we face is that the only way we are going to achieve disarmament by peace of a rogue regime, that all of us know has been in defiance of this Council for the past 12 years, the only way we can achieve their disarmament of their weapons of mass destruction, which this Council has said poses a threat to international peace and security, is by backing our diplomacy with a credible threat of force. I wish we lived in a different world where this was not necessary, but sadly we live in this world and the choice, Dominque, is not ours as to how this disarmament takes place, the choice is Saddam Hussein's. It's his choice. Would that it were ours because it would be so easy, but sadly it is not.

There is only one sensible conclusion that we can draw — we have to increase the pressure on Saddam Hussein, we have to put this man to the test. He's shown this week he doesn't need more time to comply. He can act with astonishing speed when he needs to. What's more he knows exactly what has to be done. He knows this because he's the originator or all this, of the information. The Iraqis do not need a Dr Hans Blix and all his staff to produce 167 pages of forensic questions. They have the answer book already. Look how fast they acted to produce 13,000 pages of a declaration albeit much of that was irrelevant.

Mr President,

It takes time to fabricate further falsehoods, but the truth takes only seconds to tell. And I just want to make this clear on this issue of automaticity, which again my good friend Dominique raised. There has never been anything automatic about the threat of force or the use of force. It has always been conditional. It would be utterly irresponsible and in defiance of our solemn duties to this Council, if we were in the business of using force automatically. The truth is that it's not being used automatically, should not be used automatically, it will not be used automatically, and nothing to which my Government has ever put its name ever suggests that that would be the case. What we seek is compliance by Saddam Hussein with 1441.

We are not suggesting that in a matter of days Dr Blix and Dr El-Baradei would be able to complete all their work, they'd be able to verify the disarmament. No-one's suggesting that. But what we are suggesting is that it is perfectly possible, perfectly achievable and necessary for Saddam Hussein and the Iraqi regime to bring themselves into compliance. So that instead of all, either by our words or by our silence, as we have today, admitting that Saddam is not in full compliance, that he has not taken the further opportunity and the final opportunity, we can say the reverse and we can celebrate the achievement of the fine ideals of the United Nations and of one of the central points of the work programme of the UN — that we back if necessary our diplomacy by the credible threat of force.

We remain, as founding members of this United Nations and as Permanent Members of this Security Council, committed to exploring every reasonable option for a peaceful outcome and every prospect of a Council consensus. And in the light of that, and in the light of what I have said, I should tell the Council that I'm asking on behalf of the co-sponsors of our draft resolution — the Kingdom of Spain, the Government of the United States and the Government of the United Kingdom — I'm asking the Secretariat to circulate an amendment which we are tabling which will specify a further period beyond the adoption of a resolution for Iraq to take the final opportunity to disarm and to bring themselves into compliance. But, Mr President, the Council must send Iraq the clear message that we will resolve the crisis on the United Nations terms, the terms which the Council established four months ago when we unanimously adopted Resolution 1441. Thank you very much indeed.

Distr: General
28 February 2003

Original: English

Note by the Secretary-General

The Secretary-General has the honour to transmit to the Security Council the twelfth quarterly report of the Executive Chairman of the United Nations Monitoring, Verification and Inspection Commission (UNMOVIC), which is submitted in accordance with paragraph 12 of Security Council resolution 1284 (1999) of 17 December 1999 (see annex).

03-26060 (E)   270203 270203
0326060

Annex

Twelfth quarterly report of the Executive Chairman of the United Nations Monitoring, Verification and Inspection Commission in accordance with paragraph 12 of Security Council resolution 1284 (1999)

Introduction

1. The present report, which is the twelfth[a] submitted in accordance with paragraph 12 of Security Council resolution 1284 (1999), covers the activities of the United Nations Monitoring, Verification and Inspection Commission (UNMOVIC) during the period from 1 December 2002 to 28 February 2003.

2. The period under review has been one of intense activity for the Commission. In Iraq, inspections and monitoring were resumed on 27 November 2002, requiring a rapid build-up of inspection and support staff and the resolution of operational and logistics issues. In New York the analysis of Iraq's declarations and unresolved disarmament issues went hand in hand with intense planning of inspections and administrative activities.

Briefings and consultations by the Executive Chairman

3. In the period under review, the Executive Chairman of UNMOVIC briefed the Security Council informally on 19 December 2002 and 9 January 2003 on the declaration presented by Iraq on 7 December in response to paragraph 3 of Security Council resolution 1441 (2002), and on the progress of inspections in Iraq and other UNMOVIC activities. In accordance with paragraph 5 of the same resolution, he updated the Council on 27 January on the resumption of inspection activities. He also provided on 14 February, at an open session of the Council, a briefing on UNMOVIC activities.

4. The Executive Chairman and the Director General of the International Atomic Energy Agency (IAEA) visited Baghdad from 19 to 20 January and from 8 to 9 February for talks with representatives of the Government of Iraq. During these visits, they met with Vice-President Taha Yassin Ramadan. In addition, the Executive Chairman met in London with the Prime Minister of the United Kingdom and in Paris with the President of France. In Athens, he met with the Foreign Minister of Greece, which currently holds the European Union Presidency. He also visited Brussels and met with senior officials of the European Commission and the European Union. In New York, he had meetings with Prime Ministers, high-level officials of Member States, as well as with Foreign Ministers, and he also briefed visiting parliamentarians and government officials.

5. The Secretary-General and his senior staff were kept informed, on a continuing basis, of the activities of the Commission.

Declaration submitted by Iraq on 7 December 2002

6.   Responding to the requirement in paragraph 3 of Security Council resolution 1441 (2002) to provide a "currently accurate, full and complete declaration of all aspects of its programmes to develop chemical, biological, and nuclear weapons, ballistic missiles, and other delivery systems", on 7 December, Iraq submitted a declaration to UNMOVIC and the IAEA and, through its President, to the Security Council. The declaration, including supporting documents, comprised more than 12,000 pages.

7.   On 19 December and again on 9 January, the Executive Chairman, in his informal briefings to the Council, presented an assessment of the information contained in the declaration. UNMOVIC experts have found little new significant information in the part of the declaration relating to proscribed weapons programmes, nor much new supporting documentation or other evidence. New material, on the other hand, was provided concerning non-weapons-related activities during the period from the end of 1998 to the present, especially in the biological field and on missile development.

8.   The part that covers biological weapons is, in UNMOVIC's assessment, essentially a reorganized version of a previous declaration provided by Iraq to the United Nations Special Commission (UNSCOM) in September 1997. In the chemical weapons area, the basis of the current declaration was a declaration submitted by Iraq in 1996 with subsequent updates and explanations. In the missile field, the declaration follows the same format, and has largely the same content as Iraq's 1996 missile declaration and updates.

9.   However, some sections contained new information. In the chemical weapons field, Iraq further explained its account of the material balance of precursors for chemical warfare agents, although it did not settle unresolved issues on this subject.

10.   In the missile area, there is a good deal of information regarding Iraq's activities in the past few years. A series of new projects have been declared that are at various stages of development.

11.   As there is little new substantive information in the weapons part of Iraq's declaration, or new supporting documentation, the issues that were identified as unresolved in the Amorim report (S/1999/356) and in UNSCOM's report (S/1999/94) remain. In most cases, the issues remain unresolved because there is a lack of supporting evidence. Such supporting evidence, in the form of documentation, testimony by individuals who took part in the activities, or physical evidence, would be required.

Inspections and inspection capabilities in Iraq

12.   Since the arrival of the first inspectors in Iraq on 27 November 2002, UNMOVIC has conducted more than 550 inspections covering approximately 350 sites. Of these 44 sites were new sites. All inspections were performed without notice, and access was in virtually all cases provided promptly. In no case have the inspectors seen convincing evidence that the Iraqi side knew in advance of their impending arrival.

13.   The inspections have taken place throughout Iraq at industrial sites, ammunition depots, research centres, universities, presidential sites, mobile laboratories, private houses, missile production facilities, military camps and agricultural sites. At all sites, which had been inspected before 1998, re-baselining activities were performed. This included the identification of the function and contents of each building, new or old, at a site. It also included verification of previously tagged equipment, application of seals and tags, evaluation of locations for the future installation of cameras and other monitors, as well as taking samples and discussions with the site personnel regarding past and present activities. At certain sites, ground-penetrating radar was used to look for underground structures or buried equipment. Similar activities were performed at new sites. Inspections are effectively helping to bridge the gap in knowledge that arose due to the absence of inspections between December 1998 and November 2002.

14.   More than 200 chemical and more than 100 biological samples have been collected at different sites. Three quarters of these have been screened using UNMOVIC's own analytical laboratory capabilities at the Baghdad Ongoing Monitoring, Verification and Inspection Centre (BOMVIC). The results to date have been consistent with Iraq's declarations.

15.   UNMOVIC has identified and started the destruction of approximately 50 litres of mustard declared by Iraq that had been placed under UNSCOM supervision and seal at the Muthanna site in 1998. This process will continue. A laboratory quantity (1 litre) of thiodiglycol, a mustard precursor, which had been found at another site, has also been destroyed.

16.   Towards the end of February 2003, a juncture when rotation of inspectors is taking place, the number of UNMOVIC personnel in Iraq reached a total of 202 staff from 60 countries. This includes 84 inspectors. In addition, BOMVIC has a team of United Nations translators and interpreters and a logistics and administrative staff. A unit of 10 United Nations security officers ensures the security of BOMVIC offices 24 hours a day. Medical and communication staff has been provided by the Government of New Zealand as a contribution to UNMOVIC operations. The manpower required to refurbish BOMVIC office space at the Canal Hotel was provided by the Government of Switzerland.

17.   UNMOVIC air operations are carried out by 1 airplane and 8 helicopters, with a total of 57 air staff. These operations are covered by contracts with four different companies. The L-100 plane, which flies between Larnaca and Baghdad, is under a contract with a South African company. Contracts with Canadian, Russian and United Kingdom companies cover the helicopter assets.

18.   With the exception of the crew of the aircraft and the helicopters and the staff provided by the Governments of New Zealand and Switzerland, all UNMOVIC employees of BOMVIC are United Nations staff recruited under the staff rules of the Organization.

19.   A field office was opened in Mosul, in the north of Iraq, the first week in January, with the cooperation of Iraqi authorities. This operation base is temporarily located in a hotel with full communications capabilities. There are currently 28 staff at this location. Planning for the setting-up of prefabricated offices at Mosul airport is currently under way. There is a United Nations security team at the field office, and arrangements have been made to ensure medical assistance to the staff.

20.   UNMOVIC is in the process of planning for a second field office in Basrah, in the south of Iraq, in March. The Iraqi authorities are providing cooperation to this effect.

21.   During the period from 1 December 2002 to 28 February 2003, inspectors have been provided with high technology, state-of-the-art equipment. This includes some 35,000 tamper-proof tags and seals for tagging equipment, 10 enhanced chemical agent monitors (ECAMS), 10 toxic industrial materials detectors (TIMs), 10 chemical monitors (APCC), nuclear, biological and chemical protection (NBC) suits, respirators, dosimeters with reader, a complete chemical laboratory with requisite laboratory supplies and equipment, ground-penetrating radars, 3 portable gas chromatograph-mass spectrometers, 12 ultrasonic pulse echo detectors to screen the inside of warheads, equipment for sampling warheads (MONIKA), 3 alloy analysers, and biological detection and screening equipment to include PCR, ELISA, immunoassay and rapid screening technologies. Additionally, UNMOVIC has used its network of accredited laboratories to analyse a sample of missile propellant. Cameras and other surveillance systems are currently in Cyprus awaiting shipment to Baghdad.

22.   The Commission's Larnaca field office has been expanded. It continues to provide essential logistics and other support.

High-level meetings in Baghdad

23.   On 19 and 20 January and on 8 and 9 February, the Executive Chairman, together with the Director General of the IAEA, visited Baghdad to discuss relevant inspection and cooperation issues. He was accompanied in these missions by a number of UNMOVIC senior staff and experts.

24.   The first meetings in January between the Iraqi side and UNMOVIC and the IAEA were devoted to stocktaking of the inspections which had taken place so far and to resolving certain operational issues. This included the questions of the clarification of the 7 December declaration, provision of documents, the conduct of interviews, air operations, as well as access and Iraqi assistance to the logistic build-up. A joint statement was issued upon conclusion of the talks. While it recorded a number of matters which had been solved, some remained unresolved, such as flights by U-2 surveillance planes, the conduct of interviews, the enactment of national legislation.

25.   At the meeting on 8 and 9 February, the Iraqi side addressed some of the important outstanding disarmament issues. A number of papers were handed over to UNMOVIC, regarding unresolved issues in all three disarmament fields. Expert discussions were held to clarify the contents of these papers. However, they did not contain new evidence, nor did they resolve any of the open issues.

26.   Other matters discussed included the possibility of verifying, through technical and analytical methods, the quantities of biological agents and chemical precursors, which had been declared unilaterally destroyed; the establishment of Iraqi Commissions to search for proscribed items and relevant documents, the necessity of private interviews, and the enactment of national legislation in accordance with the monitoring plan approved by the Security Council in resolution 715 (1991).

5

Interviews

27.   In accordance with paragraph 5 of Security Council resolution 1441 (2002), UN-MOVIC has the right to conduct, at its sole discretion, interviews with Iraqi officials and other persons with or without the presence of observers from the Iraqi Government, both inside and outside of Iraq. In the review period, UNMOVIC requested 28 individuals to present themselves for interviews in Baghdad (without the presence of observers). At first, none of them agreed. At the meeting on 19-20 January, the Iraqi side committed itself to encourage persons to accept interviews in private. Immediately prior to the next round of discussions, Iraq informed UNMOVIC that three candidates, who had previously declined to be interviewed under UNMOVIC's terms, had changed their minds. UNMOVIC is currently examining the practical modalities for conducting interviews outside the territory of Iraq.

Missile programmes declared by Iraq

28.   In its 7 December declaration and again in its semi-annual monitoring declaration, Iraq declared the development and production of two types of surface-to-surface missiles, which, according to the data presented, were capable of surpassing the range limit imposed on Iraq by Security Council resolution 687 (1991) and had indeed done so in a number of tests. Iraq also declared the acquisition of a large number of surface-to-air missile engines for use, after appropriate modification, in the production of these missiles. This import violates the arms embargo established by the Council in paragraph 24 of resolution 687 (1991).

29.   UNMOVIC staff have evaluated and assessed these missile projects – the Al Samoud 2 and the Al Fatah. It has also sought the assessment of a panel of international experts on the matter. To that end, a meeting took place on 10-11 February at United Nations Headquarters with experts from China, France, Germany, the United Kingdom of Great Britain and Northern Ireland, Ukraine and the United States of America. The Russian expert nominated was unable to attend.

30.   As a result of these assessments, it was concluded that all variants of the Al Samoud 2 missile were inherently capable of ranges of more than 150 kilometres and were therefore proscribed weapons systems.

31.   The panel found that clarification of the Al Fatah missile data supplied by Iraq was required before the capability of the missile system could be assessed. UNMOVIC will request such clarification.

32.   UNMOVIC inspection teams proceeded to tag the Al Samoud 2 missiles, as well as related missile components, such as engines.

33.   The experts also reviewed the capabilities of casting chambers at the Al Mamoun facility. These had previously been destroyed under UNSCOM supervision since they were intended for use in the production of the proscribed Badr-2000 missile, but had subsequently been refurbished by Iraq. The experts concluded that these reconstituted chambers could still be used to produce motors for missiles capable of ranges significantly greater than 150 kilometres. Accordingly, these chambers remain proscribed.

6

34.   On 21 February, UNMOVIC, in accordance with relevant resolutions, directed Iraq to destroy the proscribed missile system and the reconstituted casting chambers. The destruction process is to commence by 1 March.

Aerial operations

35.   Subsequent to the high-level discussions on 8 and 9 February, on 10 February, the Government of Iraq formally accepted UNMOVIC's use of aerial surveillance platforms and undertook to take the necessary measures to ensure their safety.

36.   The first such flight was conducted by a high-altitude U-2 surveillance aircraft on 17 February. This aircraft has conducted further flights. The missions are flown by the United States on behalf of UNMOVIC. A Mirage IV medium-altitude surveillance aircraft, flown on behalf of UNMOVIC by the Government of France, undertook its first mission on 26 February. The two aircraft can provide a number of different types of imagery and both are able to provide digital imagery to UNMOVIC in New York within a few hours of the missions taking place. UNMOVIC is currently discussing the use of a Russian AN-30 surveillance aircraft and German unmanned aerial vehicles (UAV) to supplement its aerial surveillance platforms. UNMOVIC already has eight helicopters stationed in Iraq, as well as access to satellite imagery.

37.   The increased capability for aerial surveillance through these new platforms provides UNMOVIC and the IAEA with additional tools to strengthen their operations and to verify Iraq's compliance with its obligations.

Other developments

38.   In December, UNMOVIC asked Iraq to provide, under the fourth subparagraph of paragraph 7 of resolution 1441 (2002), the names of all personnel currently or formerly associated with some aspects of Iraq's programme of weapons of mass destruction and ballistic missiles. The Iraqi response was received at the end of December. However, it was deemed to be inadequate, as it did not even include all those who had been previously listed in Iraq's full, final and complete declaration. Iraq has since then supplemented its list of participants in the missile programme, and has declared itself to be ready to do the same in the other disciplines. This matter is still being followed up.

39.   On 14 January, UNMOVIC received from the National Monitoring Directorate Iraq's semi-annual monitoring declaration for the period from July 2002 to January 2003.

40.   On 16 January, UNMOVIC chemical experts inspecting the Al Ukhaidhir military stores, discovered a number of empty 122-mm chemical munitions. The munitions have been tagged pending their destruction.

41.   Following this discovery, Iraq appointed a commission of inquiry to undertake an investigation and comprehensive search for similar cases at all locations. One find of four more empty 122-mm chemical munitions was reported by that commission at Al Taji munitions stores. Subsequently, UNMOVIC inspectors found two more such munitions at the same site. These six munitions will also be destroyed.

42.   Later in January, Iraq expanded the mandate of the commission to search for any remaining proscribed items on Iraqi territory. A second commission was appointed with the task of searching for any documents relevant to the proscribed items and programmes. It is headed by the former Minister of Oil, General Amer Rashid, and has extensive powers of search in industry, administration and private houses.

43.   On 21 and 25 February, Iraq informed UNMOVIC that two complete R-400 aerial bombs (one of which had liquid contents), plus remnants of what it states were 118 R-400 bombs, had been excavated at Azzizziyah, the declared unilateral destruction site of BW-filled aerial bombs, along with some related components and remnants of other destroyed munitions. UNMOVIC inspectors are currently investigating these finds.

44.   In the course of February, the Iraqi side transmitted to UNMOVIC lists of persons involved in the unilateral destruction during the summer of 1991 in the chemical, biological and missile fields.

45.   After repeated requests by UNMOVIC and the IAEA for national implementing legislation, a presidential decree was issued in Baghdad on 14 February, containing prohibitions for persons and companies in the private and mixed sectors against the production or import of biological, chemical and nuclear weapons. UNMOVIC is requesting clarification of the decree and enquiring whether further legislative actions will follow.

Staffing

46.   As at the end of February 2003, UNMOVIC core staff in the Professional grades at Headquarters comprised 75 persons (of 30 nationalities). Thirteen members of the staff are women.

Training

47.   UNMOVIC has continued to attach high priority to the training of staff and potential staff.

48.   UNMOVIC conducted its seventh basic training course in Vienna from 20 January to 7 February for 59 selected experts from 22 countries. This brings the total number of persons trained by UNMOVIC to 380, including 49 staff members from Headquarters. They comprise 55 nationalities. Further training courses are envisaged.

49.   The Commission is grateful to those Member States that have supported the training activities.

Non-inspection sources of information

50.   With the commencement of inspections in Iraq on 27 November, the pace of work of the Office for Outside Information increased substantially. Countries that had supplied intelligence-related information to UNMOVIC in the previous two years were again contacted in an effort to obtain new up-to-date intelligence to assist in the inspection

8

programme. Also, additional countries were contacted in an effort to expand the base of knowledge currently available. To date, approximately a dozen countries have provided information of potential relevance to UNMOVIC's mandate. Much of that information has been utilized in conducting inspections in Iraq.

51.   The Open Sources Officer has continued efforts to research and make available to UNMOVIC information relating to Iraq's industrial infrastructure that could be used in the production of prohibited weapons. In addition, there is a large volume of public information available suggesting procurement of items by Iraq that could have a dual-use capability.

Communications

52.   The inspectors were provided with the capabilities for clear and secure voice transmission from and within the mission area utilizing state-of-the-art equipment. The network is completely independent of the Iraqi public network. The telecommunications network, both voice and data, has a built-in redundancy and allows for future expansion. This redundancy is achieved by routing connections via two different satellite carriers.

53.   The inspectors have INMARSAT devices and Thuraya satellite phones. Thurayas are used to establish communication from the field. The INMARSAT is being used for the field operations and also as a back-up in the regional offices. Each inspector was provided with a VHF radio and the VHF coverage extends about 80 kilometres around Baghdad. Long-range high-frequency stations were installed in the BOMVIC, the regional office in Mosul, the Office in Larnaca and the Al Rasheed air base.

Goods Review List

54.   On 5 December, in resolution 1447 (2002), the Security Council renewed the Oil-for-Food programme for a further 180 days. The resolution also required that a review of the Goods Review List (GRL) and its procedures be completed by 3 January 2003. Discussions took place during December and the agreed changes were endorsed in resolution 1454 (2002) on 30 December. The changes dealt with additions to the GRL to include, for example, Global Positioning System (GPS) jammers and all-terrain tyres and amendments to the entries on trucks and trailers/low loaders. As a result of the amendments, UNMOVIC performed a reassessment exercise that involved the review of 200 contracts to check if they still contained items on the GRL in the light of the revised lists.

55.   Resolution 1454 (2002) also revised the GRL procedures. The Office of the Iraq Programme (OIP) is required to establish consumption levels for certain specific materials by 1 March. For contracts containing items below these consumption levels, approval is vested in OIP. If the consumption level is exceeded, further exports of these goods will require approval by the sanctions Committee established pursuant to Security Council resolution 661 (1990). Examples of goods subject to this new procedure include atropine, selected pesticides, growth media and certain types of antibiotics.

56.   The GRL procedures were also expanded for UNMOVIC and the IAEA. Both organizations are now required to keep records of certain types of materials and equipment, which could be considered for incorporation into the GRL at 90-day review points.

College of Commissioners

57.   On 19 December, following the resignation, in the autumn of 2002, of Ms. Malmi Marjatta Rautio (Finland), the Secretary-General, in consultation with the members of the Security Council and the Executive Chairman, appointed Ms. Olga Pellicer (Mexico) as a member of the College of Commissioners.

58.   Special sessions of the College of Commissioners were held at United Nations Headquarters on 23 January and 12 February. The Executive Chairman gave the Commissioners a report on the work of UNMOVIC since the previous sessions of the College, and on the discussions held in Baghdad on 19-20 January and on 8-9 February, respectively, as well as on recent developments with respect to the Security Council's deliberations on Iraq.

59.   The College held its twelfth regular plenary session at United Nations Headquarters on 24 and 25 February. In addition to the members of the College, observers from the IAEA and the Organisation for the Prohibition of Chemical Weapons attended.

60.   The Chairman reported on developments during the period under review.

61.   The College commended the Chairman for his recent reports and briefings to the Security Council. The College also discussed a draft paper prepared by UNMOVIC outlining clusters of unresolved disarmament issues. The College welcomed the draft paper and commended it for its approach, in particular, its indication of actions Iraq could take to help to resolve particular issues, which could be successful only if Iraq provided immediate, unconditional and active cooperation. The draft paper would serve as an important source for the selection of the key remaining disarmament tasks called for in resolution 1284 (1999) and would be updated on a continuous basis as new information became available, including especially for the period 1998 to the present.

62.   It was agreed that Commissioners be afforded time until 3 March for submitting any further comments they wished taken into account in the finalization of the paper.

63.   It was decided to hold the next quarterly session on 28 and 29 May.

64.   In accordance with paragraph 5 of resolution 1284 (1999), the Commissioners were consulted on the contents of the present report.

Observations

65.   After three months of inspections, it may be legitimate to ask about results. First, has UNMOVIC come up to its full potential yet? Second, has Iraq cooperated, as required, and has disarmament been achieved?

66. The paragraphs above provide a description of the more important elements in UNMOVIC's work to establish and develop an effective inspection regime to verify that Iraq is free from, or being freed from, all weapons of mass destruction and other proscribed items – disarmament.

• UNMOVIC has, in most areas, more resources and more advanced tools at its disposal than did UNSCOM and, in several respects, UNMOVIC has developed a capacity that goes beyond what was contemplated in its initial planning, e.g., in the number of personnel, number of teams in the field, number of sites visited. Yet, it could certainly further expand and strengthen its activity, e.g., in some form of controls of vehicles. Member States could also provide further support and assistance, notably in the field of information.

• UNMOVIC is presently finalizing an internal document of some importance, namely, a list of the disarmament issues, which it considers currently unresolved, and of the measures which Iraq could take to resolve them, either by presenting proscribed stocks and items or by providing convincing evidence that such stocks or items no longer exist. The list, which in condensed form traces the history of clusters of weapons issues, has been prepared with a view to allowing UNMOVIC to perform its tasks under resolution 1284 (1999) to "address unresolved disarmament issues" and to identify "key remaining disarmament tasks". It could also serve as a yardstick against which Iraq's disarmament actions under resolution 1441 (2002) may be measured.

67. The paragraphs above further describe the actions taken by Iraq to respond to the obligations laid upon it in the relevant resolutions. Several of these are specific, as the obligation under resolution 1441 (2002) to provide a declaration 30 days after the adoption of the resolution. However, there is further the general obligation, prescribed in that resolution, to cooperate immediately, unconditionally and actively and the similar earlier requirement, in resolution 1284 (1999), for cooperation in all respects. Has Iraq provided such cooperation and has it led to disarmament?

68. In comments on this question, a distinction has been made between cooperation on "process" and cooperation on "substance". UNMOVIC has reported that, in general, Iraq has been helpful on "process", meaning, first of all, that Iraq has from the outset satisfied the demand for prompt access to any site, whether or not it had been previously declared or inspected. There have thus been no sanctuaries in space. Nor have there been any sanctuaries in time, as inspections have taken place on holidays as on weekdays. While such cooperation should be a matter of course, it must be recalled that UNSCOM frequently met with a different Iraqi attitude.

69. Iraq has further been helpful in getting UNMOVIC established on the ground, in developing the necessary infrastructure for communications, transport and accommodation. Help has been given by the Iraqi side when needed for excavation and other operations. Iraqi staff has been provided, sometimes in excessive numbers, as escorts for the inspection teams. There have been minor frictions, e.g., demonstrations against inspectors and Iraqi criticism of some questions put by inspectors in the field.

70. A number of other actions might be discussed under the heading "cooperation on process":

(a)   After some initial difficulties with Iraq relating to escorting flights into the no-fly zones, UNMOVIC helicopters have been able to operate as requested both for transport and inspection purposes;

(b)   After some initial difficulties raised by Iraq, UNMOVIC has been able to send surveillance aircraft over the entire territory of Iraq in a manner similar to that of UNSCOM;

(c)   The Iraqi commission established to search for and present any proscribed items is potentially a mechanism of importance. It should, indeed, do the job that inspectors should not have to do, namely, tracing any remaining stocks or pieces of proscribed items anywhere in Iraq. Although appointed around 20 January, it has so far reported only a few findings: four empty 122-mm chemical munitions and, recently, two BW aerial bombs and some associated components;

(d)   The second Iraqi commission established to search for relevant documents could also be of importance, as lack of documentation or other evidence is the most common reason why quantities of items are deemed unaccounted for. Iraq has recently reported to UNMOVIC that the Commission had found documents concerning Iraq's unilateral destruction of proscribed items. As of the submission of this report, the documents are being examined;

(e)   The list of names of personnel reported to have taken part in the unilateral destruction of biological and chemical weapons and missiles in 1991 will open the possibility for interviews, which, if credible, might shed light on the scope of the unilateral actions. Such interviews will soon be organized. Before this has occurred and an evaluation is made of the results, it is not possible to know whether they will prove to be a successful way to reduce uncertainty about the quantities unilaterally destroyed;

(f)   Iraq has proposed a scientific technical procedure to measure quantities of proscribed liquid items disposed of in 1991. UNMOVIC experts are not very hopeful that these methods will bring meaningful results and will discuss this matter with Iraq in early March in Baghdad;

(g)   It has not yet proved possible to obtain interviews with Iraqi scientists, managers or others believed to have knowledge relevant to the disarmament tasks in circumstances that give satisfactory credibility. The Iraqi side reports that it encourages interviewees to accept such interviews, but the reality is that, so far, no persons not nominated by the Iraqi side have been willing to be interviewed without a tape recorder running or an Iraqi witness present.

71.   Cooperation on substance

(a)   The declaration of 7 December, despite the hopes attached to it and despite its large volume, has not been found to provide new evidence or data that may help to resolve outstanding disarmament issues. As has been mentioned above, it did, however, usefully shed light on the developments in the missile sector and in the sector of non-proscribed biological activities in the period 1998-2002;

(b)   The destruction of some items, e.g., small known quantities of mustard, is taking place under UNMOVIC supervision and further such action will take place, e.g., as regards the empty 122-mm chemical munitions;

(c)   Iraq has identified two aerial R-400 bombs, as well as remnants of what it states to be 118 R-400 bombs, at Azzizziyah;

(d)   The destruction of Al Samoud 2 missiles and related items declared by Iraq but found proscribed under the relevant resolutions has been requested and is due to commence on 1 March. Iraqi cooperation is essential;

(e)   The presidential decree, which was issued on 14 February and which prohibits private Iraqi citizens and mixed companies from engaging in work relating to weapons of mass destruction, standing alone, is not adequate to meet the United Nations requirements. UNMOVIC has enquired whether a comprehensive regulation is being prepared in line with several years of discussions between Iraq and UNSCOM/UNMOVIC.

72.   Under resolution 1284 (1999), Iraq is to provide "cooperation in all respects" to UNMOVIC and the IAEA. While the objective of the cooperation under this resolution, as under resolution 1441 (2002), is evidently the attainment, without delay, of verified disarmament, it is the cooperation that must be immediate, unconditional and active. Without the required cooperation, disarmament and its verification will be problematic. However, even with the requisite cooperation it will inevitably require some time.

73.   During the period of time covered by the present report, Iraq could have made greater efforts to find any remaining proscribed items or provide credible evidence showing the absence of such items. The results in terms of disarmament have been very limited so far. The destruction of missiles, which is an important operation, has not yet begun. Iraq could have made full use of the declaration, which was submitted on 7 December. It is hard to understand why a number of the measures, which are now being taken, could not have been initiated earlier. If they had been taken earlier, they might have borne fruit by now. It is only by the middle of January and thereafter that Iraq has taken a number of steps, which have the potential of resulting either in the presentation for destruction of stocks or items that are proscribed or the presentation of relevant evidence solving long-standing unresolved disarmament issues.

Notes

[a] The Commission's 11 previous reports were issued as documents S/2000/516, S/2000/835, S/2000/1134, S/2001/177, S/2001/515, S/2001/833, S/2001/1126, S/2002/195, S/2002/606, S/2002/981 and S/2002/1303.

13

UNRESOLVED DISARMAMENT ISSUES

IRAQ'S PROSCRIBED WEAPONS PROGRAMMES

6 March 2003

UNMOVIC Working document

6 March 2003

Intentionally Blank

UNMOVIC Working document

6 March 2003

UNRESOLVED DISARMAMENT ISSUES
IRAQ'S PROSCRIBED WEAPONS PROGRAMMES

TABLE OF CONTENTS

Intentionally Blank

INTRODUCTION

Security Council resolution 1284 (1999) requires UNMOVIC to "address unresolved disarmament issues" and to identify "key remaining disarmament tasks." Which are these issues and tasks? The Council must have intended UNMOVIC to turn to issues and tasks existing at the time when the Commission has gone into operation and begins to tackle unresolved issues by inspection and is able to assess which are key among them. As inspections resumed on 27 November 2002, it would mean issues and tasks existing on and after that date. UNMOVIC has spent considerable time and effort since it came into being to compile, review and analyze relevant information in this regard.

The starting point has been two documents, which existed when the resolution was adopted and which listed unresolved issues: one report compiled by UNSCOM focusing on material balance questions and presented to the Security Council on 29 January 1999 (S/1999/94) and the other contained in the report of the Amorim panel of 30 March 1999 (S/1999/356). However, UNMOVIC has looked behind these reports into material in its archive, such as full final and complete declarations submitted by Iraq. UNMOVIC has also supplemented the material in the two reports by other information, which has become available since the reports were written. This new information has included material from the backlog of semiannual declarations transmitted by Iraq in October 2002, from the declaration presented by Iraq on 7 November 2002 in response to resolution 1441 (2002), from suppliers, from documents provided by Iraq since the resumption of inspections, from inspection reports by UNMOVIC, from open sources and from overhead imagery and intelligence reports. All this information forms part of a vast database that includes about a million entries.

UNMOVIC evaluated and assessed this material as it has became available and, as a first step, produced an internal working document covering about 100 unresolved disarmament issues, fully referenced to the database, including entries which need to be confidential.

The principal part of the present document represents the second step in the assessment and analysis of the material studied. The unresolved issues discussed in detail in the first working document were grouped into 29 "clusters" and presented by discipline: missiles, munitions, chemical and biological. Each cluster has four sections. The first two sections provide the background, including Iraqi statements and earlier UNSCOM findings. The third section provides UNMOVIC's assessment. It identifies the questions that are deemed outstanding and unresolved. This may be because of the lack of convincing evidence or, in a few cases, because of evidence that conflicts with Iraq's account. The fourth section contains suggestions what Iraq could do to resolve the issues. This is in line with the precept that Iraq shall declare proscribed activities and items and supply evidence that can be verified by UNMOVIC. It is also in line with operative paragraph 7 of resolution 1284 (1999), which states as regards the "key remaining disarmament tasks" that "what is required of Iraq for the implementation of each task shall be clearly defined and precise." While a precise description of the disarmament issue to be resolved is generally not too difficult, an exhaustive definition of the ways in which it may be solved is often hard. It is believed that the requirement of definition of the tasks laid on Iraq was included to protect Iraq against any "moving of the goalposts" in the sense of additional requirements for evidence being raised when Iraq had fulfilled those first indicated. The fourth sections seek to be as specific as it is possible to be in the description of what Iraq can do.

The fact that the fourth section focuses upon what Iraq can do does not imply that UNMOVIC is to be passive. Indeed, in the examination of the clustered disarmament issues, good notes have been taken of what the Commission can and should do to investigate and to verify. It may turn to suppliers for information, it may consult overhead images, it may analyse samples. In some cases, where satisfactory resolution of unresolved issues turns out to be unavailable, the reinforced system of ongoing system of monitoring verification may also provide compensation and confidence.

Although UNMOVIC has endeavoured to include all relevant material, it has been obliged to omit some sensitive information.

The principal part of this document thus presents clusters of "unresolved disarmament issues", which are to be addressed by the inspection process (and Iraq) and from which "key remaining disarmament tasks" are to be identified and selected for early solution. Some of the material used in the cluster part is from the period after 1998. However, a short separate part of this document is specifically dedicated to disarmament questions related to the period after 1998, when UNSCOM inspections ended. Did Iraq resume any proscribed activities in this period and did it produce or import any proscribed weapons or other proscribed items?

The tackling of the questions from this period will differ from the handling of the questions arising earlier. For the period prior to 1998, Iraq has declared proscribed material and activities and the declarations raised many questions of accountancy and material balances. For the period after 1998, Iraq has declared that no proscribed activities have been pursued and no proscribed items arisen. However, such a declaration needs to be supported by evidence. Governments have raised questions relating to this period and some claim to have evidence of proscribed activities. Questions relating to this period have further been discussed in open sources and they can hardly be neglected. Hence, as noted, ways in which they may be approached are discussed in a short separate part of the present document.

As a short background to Iraq's programmes of weapons of mass destruction and the unresolved issues they currently raise, a few pages has been included following this introduction indicating basic factors that appear to have shaped Iraq's policies on weapons of mass destruction. A more extensive discussion of what we know about the development of the programmes is found in an appendix to the document.

NOTES ON FACTORS THAT HAVE SHAPED IRAQ'S POLICIES ON WEAPONS OF MASS DESTRUCTION

The State of Iraq was created in 1921, following the First World War and after the break-up of the Ottoman Empire. Iraq became a mandate under the League of Nations and was administered by the United Kingdom until gaining its independence in 1932. In 1945, Iraq became one of the original member of the United Nations. The monarchy was overthrown in 1958 and a republic was established.

In 1968, the Arab Baath Socialist party seized power in Iraq and embarked on modernizing the country, including its industrial sector. Saddam Hussein become Chief of the Revolutionary Command Council, as well as head of government, the party and the armed forces. In July 1979, Saddam Hussein became President.

The development of weapons of mass destruction began in the late 1960s or early 1970s and, after slow beginnings, gathered pace during the war with Iran from 1980 to 1988. Chemical weapons and long-range missiles were extensively used during that war. By the time of the Gulf War in January 1991, Iraq had a large arsenal of chemical, biological weapons and ballistic missiles. It was also developing a nuclear weapons capability. With the exception of missiles, no such weapons were used during the Gulf War.

The rationale for WMD

The rationale for Iraq's WMD programmes has been said to be the existence of Israel's arsenal and WMD capabilities. A senior Iraqi government official wrote to President Saddam Hussein in 1988 that

"If our country were to obtain and develop chemical and biological weapons, this would be considered the best weapon of deterrence against the enemy in this field.
The principle of "deterrence" is the best means of defence against the Zionist entity, and in this respect we suggest the following:
  a. To continue to develop the types of the chemical weapons with an attempt to manufacture the most dangerous of these types in large quantities.
  b. To secure long-range means, "Missiles carrying chemical heads" for reciprocal threat.
To prepare special storage areas for chemical weapons in the Southern areas of the region, and these areas must [be] within the range of the effectiveness of the current available missiles, and other means to reach the Zionist active targets in order to secure the surprise 'thunder strike", in using and accomplishing the quick reaction to deter the enemy."

However, if Israel seemed to be a priority, Iran was always included in the list of major political enemies. In connection with WMD, a senior Iraqi general told UNSCOM that

"due to the geographical location of Iraq and the traditional threat from Iran – with different and more material and human resources – that Iraq had always been worried of an attack from Iran".

It was explained to UNSCOM inspectors that WMD was seen as a way of countering this threat.

The start of Iraq's WMD programmes may in fact be traced to the late 1960s or early 1970s. Thus the CW programme was initiated in 1968 or 1969, the first identifiable BW programme in about 1974 and the first SCUD missile contract was signed in 1972.

Factors that shaped Iraq's WMD programmes

Iraq's WMD programmes were driven by geography and politics and in particular its conflicts with other nations. Some of the major events are discussed below.

Iraq-Iran War

In September 1980, Iraq engaged in war with Iran in order to capture the historically contested territory of Shatt-al-Arab. For both countries, the war was long and costly in terms of human life and material resources.

The war had a major influence on Iraq's WMD programmes. The chemical programme underwent a major reorganization in June 1981 when emphasis was placed on bulk production of agent and its weaponization. Bomb casings for mustard and tabun were ordered in 1982 and by 1983, bombs were filled with mustard and ready for use. Five months later, larger bombs filled with mustard and tabun were also ready.

In the mid-1980s, Iraq embarked on a SCUD modification programme to increase the range of these missiles to enable them to reach Tehran. The first successful test firings of a modified SCUD, the 650 km Al Hussein missile, took place in August 1987.

As the war ground on, Iraq considered that it was in a fight for survival. The mass counter-offensives by Iranian troops, "human wave attacks", caused particular concern. One senior government Iraqi official told UNSCOM.

"During the Iran/Iraq war, anyone who came to us with an idea of a weapon, we would study and try to develop. The fact is that during the Iran/Iraq war, it was masses of people attacking Iraq. I have to say that these masses, if they do not die, they would be unhappy. Because they know that by dying, they go to heaven. So it was masses of people attacking Iraq. Any idea that was presented to us to find a solution to this problem on the border of 1200 km was welcomed".

The first media reports of the use of chemical weapons by Iraq against Iranian forces was in 1983. According to a UN investigation team, the first attacks employed mustard gas. In the following years more sophisticated chemicals were also reported, notably, the nerve agent Tabun. Iran also used chemical weapons against Iraq.

In 1987, after a number of military setbacks, Iraq called for a cease-fire. Iran rejected the call and Iraq felt that it was in an increasingly precarious position. Towards the end of 1987, Iraq took a decision to change the direction of its BW programme from research and pilot scale production, to one that envisioned large scale production of BW agent. The construction of a dedicated production plant, Al Hakam, for this purpose was started in April 1988.

Appointment of Lieutenant-General Hussein Kamal to head the Military Industrialisation Commission

The Military Industrialisation Commission (MIC) was the government authority in charge of Iraq's military related industries and was responsible for the production of WMD. At the beginning of 1987, Lieutenant-General Hussein Kamal, the president's son-in-law, was appointed to head MIC.

It has been stated to UNSCOM that Lieutenant-General Hussein Kamal's emphasis was on quantity rather than quality. This led to an increase in the production of a wide range of items and to the initiation of several new programmes. Thus, in the missile field, a programme for the indigenous manufacture of SCUD engines began. The biological weapons programme was accelerated under his mandate with the planning of a biological production plant, Al Hakam, towards the end of 1987. Programmes were also initiated to reverse engineer a variety of conventional munitions to adapt them for CW and BW purposes.

Statement by President Saddam Hussein, April 1990

On 2 April 1990, President Saddam Hussein declared:

"I say that if Israel dares to hit even one piece of steel on any industrial site, we will make the fire eat half of Israel. (…) Let them hear, here and now, that we do possess binary chemical weapons which only the United States and Soviet Union have".

The statement by the president stimulated a number of WMD developments. Thus, according to Iraqi statements, a project to develop a new bomb (R-400) for the delivery of CW agents was initiated in April 1990, and hastily organized field tests of BW agents involving live firings of 122 mm rockets were conducted in the following month.

Invasion of Kuwait

Iraq's invasion of Kuwait on 2 August 1990 also accelerated and changed the direction of its WMD programmes. The emphasis was now on production and weaponization for the coming Gulf War. Projects that had direct relevance to the war effort had priority and longer term developments were put on hold.

Decisions on what munitions would be deployed during the war were also made. For example, in the BW field, it was decided that the R-400 bomb, which had been developed for CW purposes, would also be deployed as a BW bomb, and that BW agent would also be deployed in Al Hussein warheads. At the time of these decisions neither of the munitions had been tested with BW agent. According to one senior Iraqi general, the BW programme at this time headed down a *"hasty, unplanned and badly conceived course"*. However, it was inevitable that the coming war would have had a profound effect on the direction and nature of Iraq's WMD programmes.

Iraq's WMD programmes during the Gulf War

According to Iraqi authorities, instructions were given to all MIC establishments that they were to be evacuated of *"all dangerous materials and materials and essential assets"* by 15 January 1991. The Gulf War started two days later. It would appear that most WMD programmes were halted during the war, although Iraq has acknowledged that the conversion of aircraft fuel drop tanks in to spray tanks for BW agents such as anthrax, did continue throughout the war.

Many of the facilities and storage sites associated with Iraq's WMD programmes were destroyed during the war. Thus, for example, many thousands of chemical bombs and rockets were destroyed, as were the main production plants at Al Muthanna and Al Fallujah. Similarly, the main missile engineering facilities were also destroyed. However, some WMD factories escaped destruction during the war including some nuclear facilities and most of the BW facilities. Furthermore, some equipment at plants that were subject to bombing survived because it had previously been evacuated to safe locations. For example, some of the CW bomb making equipment was stored at a sugar factory at Mosul during the war.

Iraq's policy on WMD after the Gulf War

On 3 April 1991, the UN Security Council adopted Resolution 687 (1991), which established the UN Special Commission on Iraq (UNSCOM), and required Iraq to *"unconditionally accept the destruction, removal, or rendering harmless, under international supervision"* its weapons of mass destruction, and ballistic missiles over 150 km range, and all associated facilities, equipment and materials. The first IAEA and UNSCOM inspections took place in May and June 1991.

Early in the inspection process, there were a number of incidents that gave rise to concern over the prospects of the disarmament demanded by Resolution 687 (1991). For example, in June 1991, access by IAEA and UNSCOM inspectors was blocked at two sites and proscribed equipment removed (although later recovered by the IAEA). Following these incidents, the Executive Chairman of UNSCOM and the Director-General of the IAEA visited Baghdad at the end of June 1991, to secure assurances of Iraqi compliance with the resolution.

Iraqi officials later revealed that it had retained some of its weapons for about two months after the adoption of Resolution 687 (1991), because, they argued, Iraq's very existence was threatened at that time. But, in early July 1991, according to Iraqi statements to UNSCOM, Lieutenant-General Hussein Kamal issued instructions for the destruction of weapons and related items. Iraq declared that bombs and warheads filled with CW and BW agents, bulk chemical and biological agents, precursor chemicals, ballistic missiles and missile launchers and other equipment, were subsequently unilaterally destroyed in the summer of 1991 following Lieutenant-General Hussein Kamal's instruction. Iraq has declared that its policy of unilateral destruction was to remove items that would otherwise *"complicate matters and prolong the process with UNSCOM"*. Iraq has further stated it was not its intention to mislead UNSCOM.

In statements to UNSCOM, Iraq has acknowledged that, in the biological field, its approach to ending the programme was different to that in chemical, missiles and nuclear. It has been stated that, although Iraq's BW weapons and agents were unilaterally destroyed in the summer of 1991, a decision was taken to conceal other aspects of its BW programme from UNSCOM. Thus its main BW production facility was converted to a civilian plant to disguise its true nature. By early 1995, however, UNSCOM had gathered overwhelming evidence of an Iraqi BW programme and, on 1 July 1995 the Iraqi side acknowledged that it had had such a programme and had produced BW agents on a large scale, but claimed that it had not produced any BW weapons.

In the years following the adoption of Security Council resolution 687 (1991), UNSCOM and the IAEA supervised the destruction of those elements of Iraq's proscribed weapon programmes that were presented by Iraq or that could otherwise be identified. Intensive investigations of WMD and missile programmes were also conducted in an attempt to verify Iraq's declarations. These investigations were made more difficult by the lack of documentation, most of which, according to Iraq, had been destroyed. One of the major problems experienced by UNSCOM, was quantifying what may have been unilaterally destroyed by Iraq in the summer of 1991, particularly in respect of quantities of biological and chemical agents, precursor chemicals and missile fuel, and in determining when such items may have been destroyed.

In early August 1995, Lieutenant-General Hussein Kamal defected to Jordan. Following the defection, Iraq stated that Lieutenant-General Hussein Kamal had been responsible for the decision to hide aspects of its WMD programmes, including the decision to cover up the BW programme. Shortly after the defection, Iraq handed over to UNSCOM boxes of documents that had been stored at Lieutenant-General Hussein Kamal's chicken farm, known as Haidar Farm. The documents were records relating to Iraq's WMD programmes and comprised research papers, plans, photographs, videotapes and other material. Although not a complete record, they provide a considerable insight into the programmes and their achievements.

Lieutenant-General Hussein Kamal's defection also precipitated new disclosures by Iraq concerning its WMD programmes, particularly in the biological field. Subsequently, in 1996 and 1997, Iraq provided new biological, chemical and missile declarations describing its proscribed programmes. UNSCOM continued its attempts to verify these new declarations, until the end of inspections in December 1998. Its conclusion, at that time, was that there remained many significant outstanding issues, and these were described in a report to the Security Council, S/1999/94 of 29 January 1999, and in the report of the Amorim Panel of 30 March 1999 (S/1999/356).

Intentionally Blank

DEVELOPMENTS FROM DECEMBER 1998 TO PRESENT

UNMOVIC, established under Resolution 1284 (1999), began inspections on 27 November 2002, and has since then obtained a good knowledge of the industrial and scientific landscape of Iraq, as well as of its missile capability and relevant munitions. On 7 December 2002, Iraq provided a declaration required by Resolution 1441 (2002). This declaration covers Iraq's proscribed weapons programmes as well as other chemical and biological programmes and missile developments to December 2002. In October 2002, Iraq also provided UNMOVIC with a backlog of four years of declarations relating to sites subject to monitoring. On 15 January 2003, a further update of semi-annual site declarations was provided. These declarations, together with inspections and other information, form the basis for UNMOVIC's assessment of Iraqi activities from December 1998 to present.

Difficulties of assessment of possible proscribed activity

For a period of almost four years, from the end of 1998 until November 2002, there were no UN weapon inspectors in Iraq. Iraq has maintained that no proscribed activities took place during this interval.

In 1991, Iraq declared its chemical and missile weapons programmes, and made available a number of proscribed facilities and items for UNSCOM to inspect, verify and deal with. These declarations provided a basis on which to question Iraq and to probe its explanations for consistency, etc. Often, this led to the uncovering of more proscribed activities and material. However, with respect to biological and nuclear weapons programmes, Iraq initially declared in 1991 that it did not have such programmes. Consequently, UNSCOM and the IAEA had to take a different approach in order to verify whether this was indeed the case. Inspections in these fields were based on, for example, intelligence reports, supplier information, selective searches for documents and material, and interviews. Iraq was driven to declare its biological and nuclear programmes, although much remains to be explained and verified in the biological area.

For the period 1998 to present, UNMOVIC now faces the same situation in all three disciplines that UNSCOM and the IAEA faced in 1991 regarding biological and nuclear weapons issues. There are no leads, such as stocks of proscribed items, or WMD production facilities for UNMOVIC to inspect. Instead, UNMOVIC must verify the absence of any new activities or proscribed items, new or retained. The onus is clearly on Iraq to provide the requisite information or devise other ways in which UNMOVIC can gain confidence that Iraq's declarations are correct and comprehensive. At the same time, UNMOVIC will avail itself of intelligence reports, supplier information, selective searches for documents and material, aerial imagery from satellites and different aircraft platforms, interviews, remote monitoring with video and other sensors, etc. to gain information that could be used to evaluate various aspects of Iraq's declarations.

Four years without inspection is a significant period. Given the history of Iraq's proscribed weapons programmes (see Appendix), Iraq potentially could have made considerable advancements in that time, particularly in the biological and chemical fields. For example, within a period of about three years, Iraq built most of its chemical weapons plant at Al Muthanna and went into large-scale production of a variety of CW agents and munitions. And it took just two years to build its BW production plant at Al Hakam and produce over 27,000 litres of BW agent. Plants of such a size would of course be easy to detect, but they could also be disguised as dual purpose plants now producing some civilian product. In fact, that is exactly how Iraq presented its BW production facilities to UNSCOM inspectors from 1991 to 1995. Smaller plants and underground or mobile facilities would be harder to detect.

UNMOVIC has received many reports suggesting that Iraq has been engaged in a range of proscribed activities during the absence of inspectors. The information has been of a variety of types, from general assertions to detailed and precise intelligence. Some of it has been presented publicly, much of it has not. It has included overhead imagery, reports from defectors and other sources such as communications intercepts.

Intelligence Information and its interpretation: some examples

As mentioned above, UNMOVIC has received intelligence report from a number of governments. Below are a few examples with some indications of the use UNMOVIC has made of the information, although, for obvious operational reasons, not all of the details are disclosed.

Mobile BW agent production facilities

Several governments have provided UNMOVIC with information relating to truck-mounted BW agent production facilities. The reports, which are reasonably consistent, refer to a series of usually three large articulated trucks that together comprise a complete, but small, biological factory. The reports indicate that one truck would carry fermenters, another the mixing and preparation tanks and the third, equipment to process and store the product. Several such mobile factories are said to exist and BW agent was reported to have been produced in them from 1998 to 2002, with some reports suggesting that production continues.

UNMOVIC has not had direct access to the originators of these reports, some of whom are persons claiming to have been directly involved in the design and manufacture of mobile facilities in Iraq. In theory, such facilities are possible and, indeed, Iraq has acknowledged that in the late 1980s such facilities were seriously considered. Senior Iraqi officials informed UNSCOM that the concept was ultimately rejected because it was considered to be impractical.

The investigation of mobile facilities is inherently difficult. Most of the transport of goods around Iraq is by truck and there are many thousands of vehicles in Iraq that potentially could be used. In any case, if such factories existed, they would not necessarily be on the roads of Iraq after the start of inspections in November 2002. Furthermore, such factories would be easy to dismantle and the components used for innocent purposes. Nevertheless, UNMOVIC has studied ways by which mobile facilities could be investigated and has conducted some initial inspections in this connection. This is an area where Iraq's active assistance and cooperation will be required, both in the development by UNMOVIC of a system of road/rail traffic monitoring and in its implementation. Such a system could be based, for example, on strategically placed vehicle checkpoints that could be moved as required. These checkpoints could be supported by aerial platforms such as helicopters and drones to monitor traffic activity surrounding the checkpoints and track vehicles identified for more scrutiny. Freight trains could be searched at random, not only at loading platforms, but also between stations at, for example, railway crossings. The more comprehensive the system, the better Iraq will be able to address the concerns consistently and repeatedly voiced that it has such facilities and does move proscribed materials by road and rail to evade detection.

Underground Facilities
UNMOVIC has also received many reports of underground facilities involved in a range of proscribed activities from research to the production of CW and BW agents. Such facilities have been reported to be at locations throughout Iraq, from the mountains in the north, to buildings in Baghdad, including a Baghdad hospital.

In some cases, where the location could be positively identified, inspectors have investigated the site using the tools available to them, including ground penetrating radar. However, in many cases, the locations have not been specific and, in such circumstances, further intelligence has been sought.

The result, so far, is that no underground facility of special interest has been found. Although they may be easier to find than mobile facilities, they are still a difficult target and it is always possible that inspectors have missed a hidden entrance. Like mobile facilities, any dedicated underground CW or BW facility could also have been dismantled prior to inspection. UNMOVIC does not dismiss the possibility that such facilities exist and will continue to investigate reports as appropriate. Given the vast number of potential underground "sites" capable of hosting CW or BW production or storage facilities in Iraq, inspections in this area will have to be dynamic and rely on specific intelligence information.

Unmanned Aerial Vehicles
Unmanned Aerial Vehicles (UAVs) that fly autonomously to pre-programmed targets, and Remotely Piloted Vehicles (RPVs), that are controlled from the ground or another aircraft, are of particular interest to UNMOVIC because of their potential to deliver a weapon to a remote target. Even though some UAVs are small and can only carry a few tens of kilogrammes as payload, this could be significant if that payload is a BW agent such as anthrax. Indeed, Iraq has declared that in 1988 it considered RPVs as a delivery vehicle to spray BW agents, but said that it rejected the idea as the aircraft possessed at that time were too small. Subsequently in 1990, Iraq developed a remotely piloted MIG possibly to be equipped with a spray tank for the delivery of a BW agent, (see the clustered issue on Spray devices and Remotely Piloted Vehicles). UAVs/RPVs with a BW or CW payload are, of course, proscribed, as is any UAV/RPV with a range greater than 150 kilometres.

UNMOVIC has received intelligence reports of the development, during the past four years, of UAVs and RPVs that exceed the 150 kilometres limit. In fact, one report describes a UAV with a range of 500 kilometres.

Iraq has not declared the development of any UAV. However, it has declared that it developed during the past few years, two new RPVs with a range of 100 kilometres (see below). The stated design goal for one of the RPV's, designated by Iraq as "RPV-20", was to create a drone with an endurance of one hour that had an autonomous system for guidance and control with GPS navigation. Recent inspections have also revealed the existence of a drone with a wingspan of 7.45 metres that has not been declared by Iraq. Officials at the inspection site stated that the drone had been test flown. Further investigation is required to establish the actual specifications and capabilities of these RPV's and whether Iraq has UAV/RPVs that exceed the 150 kilometers limit.

Movement of proscribed material

There have been many reports claiming that there have been movements of proscribed materials around Iraq, with some such moves reported to have occurred immediately before the resumption of inspections. Such items have variously been stated to be documents, missiles and chemical and biological weapons. As before, the evidence for this has been of variable credibility and in some cases is subject to different interpretations.

Proscribed items may well have been moved around Iraq before inspectors arrived, and possibly continued after their return. However, based on inspections and the information UNMOVIC has seen so far, it is not possible for UNMOVIC to reach any conclusions on the matter. This is another area where Iraq's active assistance and cooperation will be required in UNMOVIC developing and implementing a system of road/rail traffic monitoring to help dispel concerns that movements of proscribed materials are taking place.

Non-Proscribed Developments 1998 to present

While possible proscribed activities over the past four years are difficult for UNMOVIC to detect, UNMOVIC is reasonably knowledgeable of the non-proscribed scientific and technical developments that occurred during this period. Iraq listed such activities in its declaration of 7 December 2002 and in its semi-annual declarations. Most of the locations and activities so declared have now been inspected by UNMOVIC.

Chemical and biological

In the chemical and biological fields, Iraq's civilian scientific and technical capabilities have only slowly increased in the past four years. Iraq has demonstrated the ability to manufacture both chemical and biological equipment, such as simple process equipment and fermenters.

In the chemical area, Iraq has repaired some equipment destroyed under UNSCOM supervision, and has installed such equipment in plants producing chlorine and phenols. Iraq has also refurbished some chemical facilities, and others have undergone a modest expansion. No significant new plants have been constructed.

In the biological field, there has been a new emphasis on higher education in biotechnology and a new genetic engineering facility has been established. Overall, in biological industries, there has been a modest expansion, reflected in an increase in staffing of 10 to 20 %. One new biological fermentation plant has been built for the production of alcohol.

In general, there is little evidence of change in the chemical and biological disciplines beyond that noted above. No proscribed activities, or the result of such activities from the period of 1998-2002 have, so far, been detected through inspections. . There are a number of chemical and biological facilities or production units that could be used for both proscribed and non-proscribed purposes. In order to verify and monitor the status of such facilities, information such as original documents concerning budgets, the employment of certain individuals, planning, imports and log books of key items of equipment should be provided to UNMOVIC.

Missile technology
There has been a surge of activity in the missile technology field in Iraq in the past four years. While UNMOVIC is still evaluating the full extent of this activity, some developments are noted below.

Foremost amongst recent developments are two ballistic missile systems: the Al Samoud 2 (liquid propellant) and the Al Fatah (solid propellant). Both missiles have been tested to a range of greater than that permitted under resolution 687 (1991) with the Al Samoud 2 tested to a maximum range of 183 kilometres and the Al Fatah to 161 kilometres. UNMOVIC convened a panel of international missile experts in February 2003, to consider these missile systems. The experts concluded that the Al Samoud 2, as deployed, is capable of a range greater than 150 kilometres and UNMOVIC has therefore informed Iraq that the missile is proscribed and must be destroyed. Iraq started the destruction of these missiles on 1 March 2003 and is likely to finish by the end of the month. As of February 2003, UNMOVIC's final assessment of the Al Fatah had not been made, pending the collection and analysis of further technical information.

Other missile systems are in various stages of development. A surface-to-air, solid propellant, missile system named the Al Abour is one example. The launcher for this missile is still under development, and will be capable of holding four missiles simultaneously, to be launched vertically.

Although these missile systems have been indigenously developed, they rely heavily on imported technology. The Al Samoud 2, for example, uses engines from an anti-aircraft missile. Iraq has declared that approximately 380 such engines have been imported for this purpose. Engines from cannibalized anti-aircraft missiles already in-country have also been used. All such engines found to be associated with the Al Samoud 2 programme will be destroyed under UNMOVIC supervision.

Iraq further declared the development of a liquid propulsion engine, the Kandoosh, using a combination of liquid oxygen/ethanol. Other new projects include a spin motor for the Al Fatah (previously known as the Ababil 100, solid propellant), GPS guided HY-2 and AM 39 Exocet missiles and replacement of the guidance section for several surface-to-air missiles. Iraq also declared two new remote piloted vehicle (RPV) known as Musaryara 20 and 30 with a declared range of 100 kilometres. Iraq stated, in its December 2002 declaration, that the activities related to the development of the L-29 jet training RPV (the Al Baia'a) were discontinued due to lack of imported equipment. These declarations need to be verified.

Other missile systems with ranges in excess of 150 kilometres may possibly be under development or planned. Indications of this come from solid propellant casting chambers Iraq has acquired through indigenous production or from the repair of old chambers. The size of these chambers would enable the manufacture of a missile system with a range much greater than 150 kilometres. In February 2003, after advice from the panel of experts previously mentioned, UNMOVIC determined that these chambers were proscribed. It supervised the destruction of the chambers in March 2003. As a result, Iraq's capability to produce large solid fuel rocket motors has been diminished.

Iraq has also upgraded its solid propellant test stand at Al Mutasim, enabling it to test higher thrust missiles. At Al Rafah, a liquid propellant missile test stand is under construction, which has been assessed to be capable of testing liquid propellant engines with thrusts greater than that of the SA-2 engine. Furthermore, Iraq has declared that it has resumed research on UDMH, a highly energetic fuel that could be used for proscribed or non-proscribed missile systems.

Iraq's semi-annual declarations

In all three disciplines above, Iraq is required to provide details of sites subject to monitoring, their activities, materials used, products, personnel and other information in its semi-annual declarations. This provides the basis for monitoring. During inspection of these sites information is collected and compared with that declared. Confirmation of the information declared provides confidence that the site has not been involved in any proscribed activity. It is therefore important to the process that Iraq provides accurate and detailed information in its semi-annual declarations.

Although there have been some inconsistencies and discrepancies in Iraq's semi-annual declarations, the largest failing is the lack of information on suppliers. UNMOVIC has noted in the biological area about 40 cases where insufficient information is provided on the supplier, and in the chemical area, about 70. In the missile area however there are almost 500 examples of imports where the supplier has been inadequately identified. On many occasions the imports are simply referred to as coming from the "local market" or from "Iraq" when it is clear that the items actually originated from overseas. In such cases, the actual supplier and country of origin have not been identified. Items have included gyroscopes, chemicals and laboratory equipment. There is evidence to indicate that many of components for Iraq's declared RPVs and missiles originated from overseas and the supplier has been inadequately identified.

Lists of Names Supplied by Iraq

So far, Iraq has submitted lists of names on four separate occasions. Most of these lists have concerned Iraq's past programs and explicitly state that they end in 1991. An exception to this was a submission of 685 names associated with the current Iraqi missile programmes. There are doubts as to the completeness of Iraq's lists of names even for the previous programmes. For instance, Iraq lists less than 132 "experts, specialists, and technicians," to use Iraq's term, as having worked in the entire chemical weapons programme. UNMOVIC databases, on the other hand, indicate that over 325 individuals were engaged in chemical weapons related research or had responsible positions associated with agent production at the Muthanna State Establishment alone. It would be useful to have the employment history these persons and know what they are doing today.

Interviews with the persons indicated above could be an effective method to help resolve outstanding issues relating to Iraq's past weapons of mass destruction programmes as well as existing doubts about what has occurred during the absence of inspectors from 1998 to 2002. It would seem to be in Iraq's interest to not only encourage, but insist that individuals agree to be interviewed in private.

Actions that Iraq could take

Iraq will need to provide more information to support its declaration and other statements concerning activities during the past four years in engender confidence that no proscribed activities occurred in a period when no inspectors were present.

Based on the above considerations, UNMOVIC has developed some ideas of the type of information that could assist. UNMOVIC suggestions of required Iraqi actions include:

- Fully declare the names of individuals who have been associated with Iraq's proscribed programmes.

- Provide the employment records, from 1998 to present, of the above individuals.

- Facilitate the granting of interviews in private to UNMOVIC by individuals identified by UNMOVIC as being relevant to the resolution of disarmament issues in Iraq.

- Provide complete supplier information for items Iraq has declared purchased from the "local market". Most such items have been clearly identified through inspections as foreign made and have not been processed through the UN export/import mechanism. The information to be provided should include the full name and address of the foreign supplier(s) and all intermediary persons, banks, companies, government institutions, etc., both Iraqi and foreign, involved.

- Provide full cooperation in the establishment by UNMOVIC of a system of road/rail traffic monitoring in Iraq and facilitate its implementation.

- Explain, with credible evidence, the purposes for which the various RPV/UAV platforms were created and provide the full names, Iraqi and foreign, of all organizations, institutions etc., and the associated persons involved.

- Provide details on imports for the RPV/UAV programme, such as the supply of engines, GPS guidance systems, airframes, etc. and include the full name and address of the foreign supplier(s) and all intermediary persons, banks, companies, government institutions, etc., both Iraqi and foreign, involved.

Analysis and verification of this information and examination of it for consistency, both internally and with other information, may assist UNMOVIC to determine patterns of activity and whether Iraq is intending to develop RPV/UAVs that would be capable of carrying chemical or biological agent. While this may not result in full certainty that proscribed activities did not take place, in combination with extensive inspections and monitoring, it will help raise the level of confidence that there are no significant gaps in the information Iraq has provided UNMOVIC.

CLUSTERS OF UNRESOLVED DISARMAMENT ISSUES

CONTENTS

Intentionally Blank

I. MISSILE CLUSTERS

a. Scud type missiles

Introduction

In 1974, Iraq started taking delivery of the foreign made Scud-B, a surface-to-surface combat missile with a range up to 300 kilometres, and associated equipment (launchers, ground support equipment). At the beginning of 1987, Iraq started modifying Scud-B missiles to extend their range. After several tests, on 3 August 1987, a test missile achieved a range of approximately 615 kilometres. This modified missile was subsequently designated as Al Hussein. After this success, Iraq decided to reverse-engineer the Scud-B missile. At the beginning of 1988, the director of the Military Industrialization Commission (MIC) tasked a facility designated as Project 1728 to indigenously develop and produce Scud-type engines.

Background

In August 1991, Iraq declared the import of a total of 819 Scud-B combat missiles with a matching number of conventional warheads. It also declared matching quantities for the import of main fuel (818 tonnes) and oxidizer (2895 tonnes) for those missiles. Iraq further declared that it had imported 11 Scud-B missile transporter-erector-launchers (TEL), and had declared the indigenous production of four additional launchers (known as Al Nida) from imported trucks and 50-tonne trailers. These missiles, launchers and propellants constituted the core elements of Iraq's missile force before the Gulf War. UNSCOM was satisfied that 817 out of 819 imported Scud-B missiles had been accounted for. This finding was endorsed by UNSCOM Commissioners in November 1997. However, UNSCOM could not account for approximately 25 imported warheads.

Iraq had declared the unilateral destruction of significant quantities of Scud-B propellants. However, this was not supported by documentation. Iraq did not provide two inventory diaries, known to UNSCOM and requested by it, that had covered the time of the destruction of the proscribed missile propellants. Iraq has maintained its position that it did not have these diaries when UNMOVIC repeated the request in January 2003. In June 1998, Iraq indicated that, due to the stated limited storage lifetime of the main fuel (7 years) and of the oxidizer (10 years), they would no longer have been usable.

UNSCOM could not confirm the existence of other suppliers of Scud-B combat missiles to Iraq.

Prior to the Gulf war (1988-1990), Iraq had also made extensive efforts to develop its capability to indigenously produce Scud-type missiles. In this respect, Iraq declared that it had been able to indigenously produce a total of 80 combustion chamber/nozzle assemblies, of which 54 to 57 had been rejected due to poor production quality. Iraq had declared the unilateral destruction of the combustion chamber/nozzle assemblies. However, the methods used for this destruction prevented UNSCOM from achieving a full accounting of the 80 assemblies.

Iraq also stated in 1997 that, in April 1990, it had indigenously produced seven "training" engines, which had been delivered to an operational missile unit for training purposes. Iraq stated that these engines had been unilaterally destroyed, along with the imported missiles in July 1991. UNSCOM did not find any remnants of such engines and, therefore, could not verify this declaration. These assertions were repeated in a document provided to UNMOVIC on 8 February 2003.

In February 1998, Iraq declared that, prior to the Gulf war, it had indigenously produced 121 Scud-type warheads. This was discussed during a Technical Evaluation Meeting in 1998 and, although Iraq orally provided information concerning the production of these warheads, it did not support the information with any documentation. UNSCOM could not find remnants for approximately 25 of the declared indigenously produced warheads. UNSCOM was not able to obtain a full picture of Iraq's warhead production.

In February 1996, Iraq admitted that, before the Gulf War, it had started to construct facilities to produce Scud-B propellants and that construction had continued after the adoption of resolution 687 (1991). However, Iraq stated that the facilities never became operational and were eventually converted to civilian use and submitted for monitoring by UNSCOM until December 1998.

Iraq imported key engine components that it could not indigenously produce. For example, Iraq declared that, between mid-1989 and mid-1990, it had received from a foreign supplier 35 turbo-pumps out of an initial order of 305. According to Iraq, a total of 14 turbo-pumps had been used in testing activities and the remainder had been unilaterally destroyed in July 1991. The extensive methods used for the unilateral destruction prevented UNSCOM from making a full accounting for the declared turbo-pumps. UNSCOM also obtained documentary proof that two turbo-pumps did not arrive in Iraq until six months after the date Iraq declared it had used them in static tests.

Iraq stated that, due to the lack of certain equipment, components and know-how, Project 1728 had not been able to produce a complete engine. However, in 1998, UNSCOM concluded that, by late 1990, Iraq had had the capability to indigenously manufacture, from indigenously produced and foreign parts, a limited number of Scud-type engines and missiles. It should nevertheless be noted that, in 1998, Iraq was experiencing some difficulties in indigenously producing/assembling an Al Samoud engine, a smaller liquid propulsion engine based on the same technology as that of the Scud-B.

Before the Gulf War, Iraq had the capability to indigenously manufacture warheads, airframes, and certain engine components but had to rely on imports for some key engine components as well as guidance and control (G&C) components. Iraq had attempted to indigenously produce Scud-B type propellants and was able to assemble an indigenous launcher.

UNSCOM found that Iraq had continued to engage in activities after they had become proscribed by the adoption of resolution 687 (1991). For example, Iraq had established working groups as late as November 1993 to work on Scud-B guidance and control systems. Iraq stated that the working groups were able to produce only preliminary production drawings and that they had been disbanded two weeks after having started work.

Following Lieutenant-General Hussein Kamal's defection, the Iraqi authorities handed over to UNSCOM a small number of Scud-B guidance and control equipment and various other parts that had been imported for its pre-Gulf War missile activities.

Iraq stated in early 1996 that, in 1995, a foreign middleman had offered Iraq five disassembled second-hand TELs of a size much larger than the Scud-B TELs. According to Iraq, since it had had no interest in the offer, the proposal had been rejected and the parts had never been delivered.

In 1995, Iraq declared that it had not informed UNSCOM of the work it had carried out at the Al Sadiq factory in 1992/1993 for some 18 months as the work had only been related to non-proscribed missile production. UNSCOM questioned this rationale given that Iraq had declared similar work at another facility.

On 3 March 2003, Iraq provided two documents concerning the material balance for combat warheads and the local production of liquid fuel engines. Earlier, on 25 February 2003, Iraq also offered to provide UNMOVIC with metal fragments, which it had informed UNSCOM were from indigenously produced engines. At that time, it had refused to provide the items to UNSCOM as it had objected to UNSCOM seeking an analysis of the items at laboratories outside of Iraq.

In the material balance for combat warheads document, Iraq indicated its readiness to discuss the details of the unilateral destruction of the warheads in 1991, and offered to conduct a recount. It also suggested that joint excavations be conducted at the unilateral destruction site and at the site where destruction had been carried out under UNSCOM supervision. Iraq also provided the names of eight persons who it states had carried out the transport and destruction of warheads in 1991. UNMOVIC is still reviewing the information and other details provided in the document. It is still not clear whether the activities suggested could help resolve any part of the outstanding issues in this area.

As for the document on local production of liquid fuel engines, it states *inter alia* that Iraq did not reach the stage of producing a combat-level engine until 17 January 1991. The document also provides a list of 46 persons, in addition to the five senior staff that had been named in its 1996 FFCD, who it states were the main scientific and engineering staff in Project 1728. An analysis of the information provided is underway.

Assessment
Although UNSCOM reported that all but two of the 819 declared imported Scud-B combat missiles had been "effectively" accounted for, the stated consumption of some missiles could not be independently verified. This was the case for 14 Scud-B missiles as targets in a missile interception project. While such use is supported by some documentation contained in the so-called Scud files, it is questionable whether Iraq would have really used, what were at that time, valuable operational assets in the pursuit of such a project. Furthermore, available data could only corroborate a very small number of declared missile launches at that time. It cannot be

excluded that Iraq retained a certain numbers of the missiles. The additional information Iraq provided on 8 February 2003 on the missile interception project does not resolve the outstanding questions.

Iraq's thorough methods of unilateral destruction prevented an assessment of its achievements in the indigenous production of Scud-B engines. Furthermore, the methods used prevented a clear accounting of the "training" engines and some specific key components of the indigenously produced liquid propellant engine. The lack of evidence to support Iraq's declarations on its destruction of these indigenously produced "training" engines, as well as on the key engine components, such as turbo-pumps, raises the question whether they were all destroyed as declared. Iraq could, in fact, have produced a small number of Scud-type liquid propellant engines from both imported turbo-pumps and locally produced engine components.

Moreover, the lack of documentation to support the destruction of a significant amount of Scud-B liquid propellant, and the fact that approximately 50 warheads were not accounted for among the remnants of unilateral destruction, suggest that these items may have been retained for a proscribed missile force. After investigating Iraq's statement that, due to the limited storage lifetime, the propellants would now be useless, UNMOVIC has assessed that the propellants would in fact still be usable and would therefore need to be verified as destroyed.

Questions also arise with respect to activities related to proscribed guidance and control systems that Iraq had conducted from 1992 to 1995. It is difficult to accept Iraq's statement that they were for non-proscribed missiles. Of particular concern are the guidance and control working groups that Iraq says had been established for a very short period of time in November 1993. The concern is that Iraq may have been conducting reverse engineering of proscribed guidance and control systems as part of its missile activities even after the adoption of resolutions 687 (1991) and 715 (1991). Furthermore, it cannot be excluded that Iraq has retained such guidance and control equipment.

Another indication of possible proscribed activity is the offer that Iraq said it received from a middleman for five disassembled TELs. Some parts were already shipped to an adjacent country. Although Iraq said that it had rejected the offer, no evidence has been provided in support. These parts might have allowed the assembly of one or two TELs, which would have been another piece for a reconstituted Scud-type missile force. In this connection, Iraq has, so far, been unable to locate a 50-tonne trailer that it declared it had imported for the indigenous production of the Al Nida mobile launcher and which it claims had been stolen. Iraq also did not provide UNSCOM with the parts of an imported Scud TEL, which it states it had disassembled.

The 2002 CAFCD and its supporting documents, the most recent semi annual declarations, and the material submitted to UNMOVIC on 8 February 2003 provide no significant new information relevant to the aforementioned issues.

The following action is required to address the foregoing issues:

To clear up the uncertainty as to whether Iraq has engines and key engine components that could be used for the production of proscribed missiles, Iraq should submit the remnants of the seven engines, which it claimed were "training" engines, to UNMOVIC to allow for their analysis and verification. The examination and analysis of these remnants could help determine the origin of the material used in the manufacture of the engines as well as their nature. Iraq should also submit to UNMOVIC the melted remnants of the destroyed key components for analysis. This could assist in the verification of Iraq's declaration of the destruction of the turbo-pumps.

Iraq should also provide documentation such as production records and quality control documents to support the information it had submitted during the Technical Evaluation Meeting in 1998. This information could allow UNMOVIC to establish the number of indigenously produced warheads.

In order to address the broader question of the existence of a possible Scud-type missile force, Iraq should provide specific documentation in support of its declarations. An example would be the two reports written by the missile force commander on 30 January 1991 and in May 1991 that, on the basis of Iraq's own declarations and outside information, are known to exist. The first report could help clarify the state of the combat missile force at the end of the Gulf War. The second report could allow clarification of the status of the missile force just after the adoption of resolution 687 (1991). Iraq should also provide technical documentation concerning the interception missile project in order to support its declaration on the use of Scud-B missiles as targets in the project. The provision of the two diaries that relate to the unilateral destruction of the proscribed missile propellants should also be provided. Iraq's most recent response to UNMOVIC's request on these matters provides no further clarification.

As for the activities related to guidance and control systems, such as gyroscope reverse engineering and procurement of various guidance and control components, Iraq should also provide UNMOVIC with all the Scud-B guidance and control drawings and hardware and documentation that it may still have.

Iraq's intent in conducting proscribed missile activities or procurement after the adoption and its acceptance of resolutions 687 (1991) and 715 (1991) needs to be clarified. In addition, the scope of these activities cannot be fully established until convincing evidence and answers are provided by Iraq.

Guidance and control activities, including research and development, will need specific attention due to their particular dual-use nature.

Actions that Iraq could take to help resolve the issue
- Present any retained proscribed missiles and associated equipment, including the 50-tonne trailer declared to have been stolen and the parts from a disassembled imported Scud TEL.

- Present the remnants of the seven engines, which it claimed were "training" engines, for analysis and verification. As proposed by Iraq on 8 February 2003, the fragments found by Iraq on 4 August 1997 should also be presented for analysis.

- Present the melted remnants of the destroyed key components, including the turbo-pumps for analysis.

- Present documentation or other evidence to support the information it had submitted during the TEM in 1998 on the number of indigenously produced warheads.

- Present other specific documentation, such as the two reports written by the missile force commander on 30 January 1991 and in May 1991; technical documentation, such as videotapes and tracking data, concerning the interception missile project; and the two diaries that relate to the unilateral destruction of the proscribed missile propellants.

- Present any remaining Scud-B guidance and control drawings, documentation and hardware.

- Explain and present credible evidence on why it had conducted proscribed missile activities and procurement after the adoption and acceptance by Iraq of resolutions 687 (1991) and 715 (1991).

b. SA-2 Missile Technology

Introduction
The SA-2 (also known as Volga) is a medium range two-stage surface-to-air missile with a solid propellant booster and a liquid propellant engine for the upper stage. Iraq first acquired SA-2 missile systems from a foreign supplier in the early 1970s. The SA-2 was designed to intercept aircraft, cruise missiles and other aerial targets at medium altitudes. Iraq's military industry carried out several projects that involved the modification or reverse engineering of SA-2 missiles to achieve longer ranges - up to or beyond 150 kilometres - in a surface-to-surface mode.

Background
In July 1991, Iraq declared that, from June 1988 to July 1989, two missile projects, Fahad 300 and Fahad 500, had been working on the modification of the SA-2 missiles into surface-to-surface missiles with ranges of 300 and 500 kilometres respectively. Iraq stated that the Fahad 300 was tested but the project was abandoned due to the missile's lack of accuracy. Work did not proceed with the Fahad 500 project. UNSCOM supervised the destruction of nine Fahad 300 missiles in 1991. UNSCOM could neither verify Iraq's declarations regarding missiles consumed in testing, nor the number of SA-2 missiles modified. It is therefore not possible to exclude that some of these converted missiles may still remain in Iraq.

Between 1991 and 1993, Iraq also worked on a project to develop a surface-to-surface missile originally called "G-1" and concealed this activity from UNSCOM until after the defection of Lieutenant-General Hussein Kamal in 1995. Subsequently, in its 1996 FFCD, Iraq described a previously undeclared project within a wider missile programme. Experiments were conducted using certain major parts from the SA-2 missile. Iraq declared that the missile was not intended to reach proscribed ranges and that it did not exceed such ranges when fitted with a 450 kg warhead and a reduced fuel load. UNSCOM was unable to verify the declared range achieved by this missile. However, it assessed that the system was inherently capable of reaching proscribed ranges.

The "G-1" project was also linked with the so-called "Al Rafidain" project, which sought to reverse engineer and indigenously produce an SA-2 missile. In addition to the different role of the missiles, Iraq declared that they differed in the volume and number of fuel tanks. After the "G-1" project was said to have been cancelled in 1993, work continued within the Ababil programme to produce another design for a ground-to-ground missile based on SA-2 technology, which later was renamed as Al Samoud.

According to Iraq, from the beginning of 1992 until October 1993, the team of engineers that had worked previously on the reverse engineering of the "Scud" missile was tasked to work at Al Sadiq engineering facility on the indigenous manufacture of liquid propellant engines based on the SA-2 design. In January 1994, Al Sadiq facility merged with Al-Karama Establishment. The production of various parts was distributed among several establishments of the Military Industrialization Commission (MIC). With a view to producing five engines, several components were manufactured. However, Iraq declared, no complete engines were produced. In order to conceal this activity from UNSCOM, drawing designator numbers were changed to refer to helicopter parts. Iraq later declared, in its 1996 FFCD, that Al Sadiq was charged with the production of liquid propellant engines for the "Ababil 100" project.

In the context of its nuclear inspections, an IAEA inspection team was taken to Al Sadiq by Iraq in November 1993. All the equipment remaining there at that time was recorded. On the IAEA's recommendation, UNSCOM subsequently inspected the facility and found no evidence of any production having occurred at the facility after November 1993. Dual-use equipment from Al Sadiq facility was gradually transferred to declared sites. However, the work that had been undertaken at Al Sadiq prior to the IAEA inspection was not declared to UNSCOM until 1995. Some of the components produced were declared to have been destroyed unilaterally. Little documentary evidence exists to support Iraq's declarations regarding the nature of missile engine production activities at this facility.

After discovery of Iraq's efforts to develop ballistic missile systems based on the modification of the SA-2, UNSCOM became concerned about the potential use of the technology incorporated in this system and decided to include the SA-2 in its monitoring activities in 1996.

After resumption of the inspection regime based on resolution 1441 (2002), Iraq declared that the design configuration for the Al Samoud was modified to increase the diameter of the airframe from 500 millimetres to 760 millimetres. The modified missile was referred to as Al Samoud 2. Iraq conducted 23 flight tests of the Al Samoud 2, 13 of which reached ranges greater than 150 kilometres, the maximum being 183 kilometres. Iraq declared the production of 76 Al Samoud 2 missiles, 118 warheads and 9 Al Samoud launchers. During an inspection, an Iraqi engineer stated that the 500 millimetres configuration was no longer being produced and explained that the larger missile provided a better length/diameter ratio, which increased the stability of the missile.

During the period 2000-2002, nine static tests were carried out using another fuel, AZ-11, that contained up to 11% of Unsymmetrical Dimethyl Hydrazine (UDMH), in an effort to achieve increased performance. Iraq stated that these tests had failed and the project cancelled.

An Iraqi engineer stated that Iraq was now indigenously producing the Volga engine turbopump starter, the oxidizer and fuel shut-off valves, the oxidizer and fuel start valves and the regulator valve (partially).

Also related to the Al Samoud question is a number of Volga engines imported outside of the export/import mechanism and in contravention of paragraph 24 of resolution 687 (1991) over the past few years. In its 2002 CAFCD, Iraq has declared that it had imported 131 Volga engines; however, during an inspection, UNMOVIC found 231 Volga engines that were stored at a missile facility responsible for the production of the Al Samoud/Al Samoud 2. Iraq provided copies of the contracts, which accounted for 234 engines, and which clearly show that the equipment was smuggled into Iraq, via a neighboring country. Iraq further informed an inspection team of the arrival of 149 Volga engines at Al Samoud Factory, which would raise the total imported engines to about 380.

At the same time, Iraq declared that it had dismantled a certain number of Volga missiles, some of which were used in the production of the Al Samoud/Al Samoud 2.

During an inspection, an Iraqi engineer stated that a total of 567 Volga engines were obtained both from an outside source and through the scavenging of Volga missile sustainer engines for conversion into engines for the Al Samoud/Al Samoud 2.

Iraq has also declared the development of a telemetry station for the Al Samoud 2, which, as of February 2003, has not been verified by UNMOVIC.

Assessment

Iraq has not declared any existing liquid propellant ballistic missile development except for the Al Samoud 2, nor has it declared any new information about "G-1", Fahad 300/500, "Rafidain" project and the work at Al Sadiq engineering facility. It is therefore not possible for UNMOVIC to fully understand and to verify Iraq's declarations on its earlier missile development projects based on the SA-2 missile. Of particular concern is the limited amount of documentary evidence concerning the activities at Al Sadiq. Questions arise as to why this work was not declared to UNSCOM, like similar work on missile development conducted at other facilities. It is also not possible to fully understand the relationships between the different SA-2 based projects. However, based on the knowledge UNMOVIC presently has on these projects, they can be considered as initial steps towards the development of an indigenous liquid propellant engine capability.

Iraq's statement that it abandoned the Fahad 300/500 projects appears to be credible, first, because of the missile's lack of accuracy and thus low value as a military weapon and, second, because of the apparently successful development of the later Al Samoud missile. However, little documentary evidence has been presented to confirm the claimed destruction of all remaining Fahad missiles. Accordingly, it cannot be excluded that some Fahad 300 missiles still remain in Iraq. Moreover, Iraq would have had little difficulty in converting additional SA-2 missiles into Fahad 300s if it so desired.

As to the "G-1" Project, it is not possible to verify Iraq's declarations on the work it conducted under the project. As assessed by UNSCOM, the missile, in the configuration declared by Iraq, was capable of reaching a proscribed range. By Iraq's own admission, the smaller indigenously produced fuel tanks, which were intended to limit the range, were never installed in the missile. If the smaller tanks had been used, a reduction in the mass of the warhead would still have enabled the missile to reach a proscribed range.

Among the projects relevant to SA-2 missile technology mentioned above, the most significant missile development appears to be the Al Samoud 2. The modification on the missile, which was declared to have started in June 2001, was made despite a 1994 letter from the Executive Chairman of UNSCOM directing Iraq to limit the diameter of the liquid propulsion missile to less than 600 millimetres. Furthermore, a November 1997 letter from the Executive Chairman of

UNSCOM to Iraq prohibited the use of engines from Volga/SA-2 surface-to-air missiles for the use in ballistic missiles.

An international panel of experts convened by UNMOVIC in February 2003 found Al Samoud 2 to be capable of reaching more than 150 km. UNMOVIC has therefore concluded that the missile is proscribed pursuant to resolutions 687 (1991) and 715 (1991). Of particular note is the fact that, while Iraq stated that it was still developing the Al Samoud 2, a number of them have already been delivered to the armed forces (some 63 missiles as of February 2003).

A more adequate and coherent description of various SA-2 related projects, including their organizational structures is required. With respect to Al Sadiq, Iraq should provide all the information concerning the work carried out at that facility during the period 1991–1993, such as production documentation and quality assurance records.

Actions that Iraq could take to help resolve the issue
- Present any remaining Fahad missiles.

- Present Al Samoud 2 missiles and related major parts, including those that were imported.

- Present all Al Samoud 2 drawings, research and production documentation.

- Present a more adequate and coherent description with credible evidence of the various SA-2 related projects, including their organizational structures.

- Present a more adequate and coherent description with credible evidence of the work carried out at Al Sadiq in the period 1991–1993, including production documentation and quality assurance records.

- Present verifiable information on inventory and consumption of SA-2 missiles, including on imported missiles and on missiles that have been fired against aircraft and those that have been dismantled.

- Explain how the parts it dismantled from SA-2 missiles were used in its Al Samoud 2 programme.

c. Research and development (R&D) on ballistic missiles capable of proscribed ranges

Introduction

Before the Gulf War, Iraq was engaged in developing a medium-range ballistic missile (MRBM) with a range of between 1,000 to 3,000 kilometres, as well as what it referred to as a "Space Launch Vehicle" (SLV). This work included flight simulation analyses, the development of concepts and related technologies for missile staging, separation and clustering mechanisms for missiles and a missile engine that used Unsymmetrical Dimethyl Hydrazine (UDMH) fuel, which is more powerful than that used in the Scud-B missile. Iraq had also acquired foreign technical support in developing MRBMs and SLVs.

After the Gulf War, by Iraq's own admission and from information obtained by UNSCOM, Iraq had conducted proscribed R&D after 1991 on clustering missile engines and on multistage missiles, some of which were based on work that had been conducted before the Gulf War.

Background

Iraq was engaged in various ballistic missile programmes from the mid-1980's onwards.

One programme was the Scud-based three-stage missile referred to by Iraq as "Al Abid SLV." The first test launch of Al Abid SLV, which used five Scud engines strapped together as the first stage, was conducted on 5 December 1989. In seeking to further develop Al Abid, Iraq stated in January 1997 that it had sought assistance from a foreign expert in designing a turbo-pump capable of simultaneously feeding four clustered Scud-type engines for the first stage of the SLV and that the expert had completed 85 percent of the turbo-pump design during June and July 1990. At the same time, Iraq declared that Project 1728, which was involved with the manufacture of Scud-type liquid propellant engines, had been instructed to design, or acquire the design, for a new 30-tonne thrust liquid propellant engine using UDMH as fuel. The same foreign expert who designed the turbo-pump was engaged for this purpose during the period May to July 1990. He completed 95 percent of the preliminary design of the engine. UNSCOM's analysis of the known design characteristics confirmed that the engine was designed for the second stage of Al Abid SLV.

With respect to UDMH fuel, Iraq declared in its 1996 missile FFCD and repeated in the 2002 CAFCD that, in 1989, it had signed a contract for the import of 10 tonnes of this fuel for use in ballistic missiles that it might develop. In January 1990, Iraq conducted a static test of a Scud engine using the imported UDMH fuel. According to Iraq, the test was unsuccessful and the remaining UDMH fuel was kept in storage. The UDMH fuel was stated by Iraq to have been unilaterally destroyed by explosion in 1992 as no real use for it could be found in the civilian sector.

While UNSCOM had independently acquired knowledge and information about Iraq's activities concerning the turbo-pump, the 30-tonne thrust engine and the static test of a Scud engine using UDMH fuel, Iraq's acknowledgement of these activities took place only in September 1995, i.e. after the defection of Lieutenant-General Hussein Kamal.

In 1994, UNSCOM found evidence suggesting that Iraq had also been developing and testing warhead separation mechanisms for the Scud-based Al Hussein/Al Abbas missiles in 1989/1990. After the defection of Lieutenant-General Hussein Kamal, Iraq acknowledged that at the same time it had conducted these tests, it had also contacted a number of foreign companies for the supply of approximately 100 sets of a supersonic parachute system that could be used to reduce the speed of a separated warhead. Iraq provided more than one explanation for the purpose of the parachute system, e.g. that it was needed to help solve missile instability problems and that it was intended to be part of a system for taking pictures of outer space. According to Iraq, it received only one parachute system, which was delivered in October 1989. Iraq further stated that the parachute system had not been used and had been kept in storage until late 1995, when it was given to UNSCOM. UNSCOM could not verify whether only one parachute system had been delivered to Iraq.

In December 1995, Iraqi engineers informed UNSCOM that, in 1993, Lieutenant-General Hussein Kamal had also ordered them to design a turbo-pump capable of simultaneously feeding four clustered Al Samoud engines. They stated that the objective was to provide a set of drawings so as to enable the production of the turbo-pump when required. They further stated that, in 1993, Lieutenant-General Hussein Kamal had also ordered the design of a 7-tonne liquid propellant engine, but that no calculations or designs had been made and that the project had never been seriously pursued.

In January 1997, UNSCOM discovered computer diskettes containing computer files with a missile flight simulation programme. The files contained evidence that, in July 1992, a flight simulation of a three-stage missile based on Scud-type missiles had been carried out. The simulated missile was of a different configuration than that of Al Abid SLV. UNSCOM concluded that the diskettes had been part of a larger collection of computer diskettes the existence of which had not been disclosed by Iraq. UNSCOM also discovered that, from the end of 1994 to February 1995, Iraq had calculated the trajectories for six different scenarios of multistage SLVs using SA-2 engine parameters. The calculations showed that the ranges of the simulated SLVs could have been much greater than 150 kilometres.

After resumption of the inspection regime based on resolution 1441 (2002), UNMOVIC inspected a new larger liquid propellant test stand being constructed in Al Rafah. Iraq has explained that this new test stand was for both horizontal and vertical testing of the Al Samoud engine.

In its January 2003 semi-annual declaration, Iraq stated that it had resumed R&D on the preparation of UDMH at the Ibn Sina General Company and Al Basil State Company.

Assessment
Concerning the R&D activities before December 1998 it is assessed that the SA-2 based SLVs Iraq studied during 1994-1995 were not viable. All of the different scenarios calculated by Iraq used nine SA-2 engines strapped together for the first stage, which is not technically or militarily feasible. The Scud-based three-stage SLV that Iraq had simulated in 1992 was based on a more

technically rational design than the SA-2 based SLVs. Iraq did not, however, seem to have sufficient knowledge of the guidance and control (G&C) component of cluster and multistage missiles, nor did it have any known engine test facilities capable of testing second and upper stage missile engines in a vacuum, or in an assumed vacuum. In this context, Iraq could not have been able to produce missile systems only on the basis of such theoretical designs and computer simulations.

What is of concern is the apparent intent behind such activities and, in particular, the conscious decision to act in contravention of resolution 687 (1991) and to conceal these activities from UNSCOM. The results of the R&D arising from these activities could provide a suitable foundation from which Iraq could design less ambitious and less complex proscribed missile systems that would be within its technical and resource capabilities. Iraq needs to explain the precise nature of its activities concerning clustering, staging and separation mechanisms, particularly after the adoption of resolution 687 (1991).

Iraq needs to provide documents that would substantiate its declared destruction of the UDMH fuel. In addition, Iraq needs to declare all of the input/output data it generated during the computer simulations of the Scud-based SLVs.

Iraq also needs to declare all of the input/output data it generated during the computer simulations of the Scud-based SLVs. Iraq needs to declare all drawings of the 7-tonne thrust engine and the turbo-pump it developed to simultaneously feed four clustered SA-2 engines. Iraq also needs to provide UNMOVIC with credible evidence that it abandoned R&D of the turbo-pump and the engine. In addition, Iraq needs to submit for destruction under UNMOVIC's supervision all materials related to its work on the SA-2 based SLVs.

As Iraq has recently declared that it had resumed R&D of UDMH fuel, it needs to clarify the purpose for such activity. Concerning the new larger test stand in Al Rafah, Iraq needs to clarify the purpose of the stand, including the reason why it has developed a horizontal test stand.

Actions that Iraq could take to help resolve the issue
- Present all materials related to its work on the SA-2 based SLVs.

- Explain with credible evidence the precise nature of its activities concerning clustering, staging and separation mechanisms, particularly after the adoption of resolution 687 (1991).

- Present documents or other evidence substantiating its declared destruction of the UDMH fuel.

- Present all of the input/output data generated during the computer simulations of the Scud-based SLVs.

- Present all drawings of the 7-tonne thrust engine and the turbo-pump developed to simultaneously feed four clustered SA-2 engines.

- Present verifiable evidence that it abandoned R&D on the turbo-pump and the engine.

- Explain with credible evidence why it had resumed R&D on UDMH.

- Explain with credible evidence why it has developed a horizontal test stand at the Al Rafah site.

d. FROG (Luna) Special Warheads

Introduction

The 9K52 Luna rocket, also known as Free Rocket Over the Ground ("FROG"), is an unguided, spin-stabilized, short-range, battlefield support artillery rocket with a range between 70 to 90 kilometres, depending on its configuration. The FROG was originally conceived to be fitted with a 450-kilogramme high explosive (HE), nuclear or chemical warhead. An improved version of the FROG can also carry a cargo warhead for delivering bomblets or mines. During the Cold War it was one of the most common rockets in the Short-Range Nuclear Force (SRNF) at the division level in the Warsaw Pact. Iraq had only received the conventional warhead version.

Background

The FROG rocket system is not proscribed under resolution 687 (1991). However, it was subject to monitoring under paragraph 43 of the OMV plan.

In its 1996 FFCD, Iraq stated that, in May 1988, a project designated "*Luna S*" was initiated to convert the FROG rocket warhead into a cluster warhead constructed of aluminum and certain components of the Ababil 50 rocket. According to Iraq, Al Muthanna State Establishment rejected the proposal to use an aluminum shell as a container for CW agents and the project was abandoned in July 1988. Iraq stated that only sketches had been produced and that no prototypes had been built.

Documents found at the Haidar Farm in 1995 were sent to a supporting Government for analysis in April 1996. In June 1997, the supporting Government provided a written assessment that the documentation contained all the necessary files and specifications to build a non-conventional warhead, probably a chemical warhead for the FROG rocket. The assessment also stated that some documents had been dated in March 1989 and in August 1990, which contradicted Iraq's statement that all work relating to non-conventional warheads for such rockets had been abandoned in 1988.

Assessment

Iraq had the capability to develop indigenously and produce non-conventional warheads for weapons system such as the Scud missile. It can, therefore, be assumed that Iraq also had the same capability for a short-range missile like the FROG. In addition, documentary evidence suggests that Iraq had worked on developing this capability at least until August 1990.

While there is no evidence that Iraq continued such work after 1990, given the inconsistencies and inaccuracies in Iraq's missile declarations, the possibility cannot be ruled out. Iraq should provide further evidence to support its assertion that it had abandoned its work on producing a non-conventional warhead for the FROG and to explain the documents, which contradict this assertion.

Actions that Iraq could take to help resolve the issue

-   Present credible evidence to support its assertion that it had abandoned its work on producing a non-conventional warhead for the FROG and explain the documents, which contradict this assertion.

Intentionally Blank

e. Development of solid propellant missile systems before and after the Gulf War

Introduction

Iraq had contracted in 1984 with another country for an advanced short-range ballistic missile designated as Badr 2000. The missile was to have two stages with a solid composite propellant rocket motor for the first stage and a liquid propellant engine for the second stage. The missile would be capable of delivering a payload of approximately 320 kilogrammes at a maximum range of 750 kilometres. The missile was based on technology far more advanced than that used in the Scud-type missiles and would have provided a very accurate means of delivery for both conventional and non-conventional warheads.

Background

In 1991, Iraq declared that, in early 1984, a foreign country had offered the Badr-2000 missile system to Iraq. Iraq stated that, in the beginning, it had had the impression that the project was at an advanced stage of development and that production of the entire missile system had been under way in third countries. However, during the discussions prior to signing a contract, it became clear that the proposed missile system was only at the research and development stage. Nevertheless, in 1984, Iraq decided to sign an initial contract for 85 missiles and the provision of equipment to manufacture the missile's solid propellant rocket motor. In 1987, since the supplier could not fulfill its contractual obligations due to difficulties in obtaining key equipment, another contract was signed with the same supplier for a reduced number (17) of missiles, including the transfer of production know-how. Iraq stated that, due to long delays in implementing the contract and financial difficulties, it decided to withdraw from the project. In addition, the success of the Scud-based Al-Hussein missile convinced Iraq to terminate the contract at the beginning of 1989.

In April and May 1992, UNSCOM verified that the three declared Badr-2000 facilities (Yawm Al Azim, Dhu Al Fiqar and Taj Al Ma'arik plants) had been damaged during the Gulf War. In April/May 1992, further destruction of equipment and buildings at those facilities took place under or without UNSCOM supervision. Iraq subsequently built facilities at these locations for the production of non-proscribed missiles, such as the short-range Ababil 100 which is now referred to as Al Fatah.

In 1995, UNSCOM confirmed with the Government in question that it had cooperated with Iraq in the development of a surface-to-surface missile and that such cooperation had been halted in 1989. However, UNSCOM could neither verify the specifics of the contracts with the Government, nor clarify what was exactly delivered to Iraq. Of particular concern were the parts, items and technology transfer linked with the contract that had been signed in 1987 and said to have been aborted in 1989.

Nevertheless, through its verification and assessments, UNSCOM came to the conclusion that Iraq had neither received operational Badr-2000 missiles nor all of the equipment required for their military deployment.

After resumption of the inspection regime based on resolution 1441 (2002), Iraq declared that large quantities of illegal imports of chemicals, such as ammonium perchlorate (APC) and aluminum powder in connection with solid propellant missiles such as the Al Fatah, Al Uboor and some other missile systems. Those compounds are major ingredients for the production of solid propellant. Iraq also declared the indigenous production of APC and aluminum powder.

Iraq has declared an indigenously produced propellant casting chamber with a diameter that would be useful for the manufacture of composite propellant missiles with a range considerably in excess of what is permitted under resolution 687 (1991). During the inspection of Taj Al Ma'arik plants, a.k.a. Al Mamoun factory, two additional casting chambers with an even larger diameter than the one mentioned above were discovered. Iraq declared that two of the casting chambers were provided by a foreign country and that, originally, these chambers were imported for the Badr-2000 programme project. Although UNSCOM had deemed them proscribed and supervised their destruction, Iraq had managed to reconstitute them. Iraq explained that the depth of the reconstituted chambers had been shortened from the original 8 meters to 6 meters, which was sufficient to produce the rocket motor for Al Ubour. UNMOVIC has not verified the sources and purpose of these chambers yet.

During an inspection of Al Mu'tasim factory, the team noticed that Iraq had reinforced and therefore upgraded the capability (possibly up to 100 tonnes) of a static test stand for solid propellant rocket motors.

Concerning Al Fatah solid propellant missile, Iraq declared that 96 Al Fatah missiles and 11 launchers had been produced, or were currently under production. Of these, 32 missiles were declared as deployed. Iraq declared that 33 tests of Al Fatah (unguided version) had been conducted, eight of which exceeded 150 kilometres in range, the longest being 161 kilometres.

The Al Ubour solid propellant, air-to-air missile, had a rocket motor of the same type as the Al Fatah, however, the grain composition was different. Two Al Ubour motor cases have so far been produced. Iraq declared that no flight tests of Al Ubour had yet been performed, although one static test has been conducted. Iraqi engineer explained to an inspection team that the launcher for the Al Ubour missile was capable of holding four missiles simultaneously, to be launched vertically.

Assessment

In attempting to acquire not only operational missiles but also the associated know-how and the means of production of a two-stage missile with a solid rocket motor and a liquid propulsion engine, Iraq had apparently sought to establish a sound technological basis for an industrial infrastructure capable of producing an advanced short-range ballistic missile (SRBM - up to 1000 kilometres range).

UNMOVIC understands the purpose of the Badr-2000 programme and is confident that it has never reached the production stage and that no operational delivery means had been obtained by Iraq.

However, in the absence of detailed information from the supplier, particularly concerning the 1987 contract, it cannot be excluded that some Badr-2000 related technological or production equipment was obtained and possibly still remains in Iraq. The provision by Iraq of the delivery schedule that was attached to the contract signed in 1987 would greatly assist UNMOVIC in the verification process.

Since the resumption of the inspection process, UNMOVIC has noted a vigorous development of both Al Fatah and Al Ubour missiles. This is supported by the refurbishment and the preservation of two large casting chambers in Al Mamoun, the upgrade of capability of a test stand in Al Mu'tasim, the illegal import and the attempt to indigenously produce chemicals used for solid propellant. The international panel of experts convened by UNMOVIC in February 2003 concluded that more information was required on the specifications of Al Fatah. The panel also concluded that the two large reconstructed casting chambers could be used to produce rocket motors for missiles capable of ranges greater than 150 kilometres.

Actions that Iraq could take to help resolve the issue

-    Declare all the sources of its import of equipment, raw materials and technology that were acquired for the solid propulsion missile programme, since 1998.

-    Declare the design drawings of Al Ubour missile, including launcher and the associated radar system in order for UNMOVIC to verify that this missile is actually surface-to-air missile.

-    Explain with credible evidence the reason for upgrading a test stand in Al Mu'tasim.

-    Present the delivery schedule that was attached to the contract signed in 1987, and declare all the equipment, material and technology it had acquired for the Badr-2000.

Intentionally Blank

II. MUNITIONS AND OTHER DELIVERY MEANS, CLUSTERS

a. Scud-type Biological and Chemical Warheads

Introduction

Iraq produced warheads for Scud-type missiles. These warheads were designed for the delivery of chemical and biological agents, and are referred to throughout this paper as "special warhead."

The special warhead was designed to accommodate a canister made of either aluminum or stainless steel and capable of holding approximately 150 litres of agent. UNSCOM found in almost all cases that Iraq's biological warheads had stainless steel canisters and chemical warheads had aluminum canisters. The payload of the special warhead was less than that of the original high explosive warhead. To compensate for the lesser weight and consequent change in the centre of gravity of the missile, lead ballast was added to the nose cone of the special warhead.

To produce these special warheads, Iraq both modified original Scud warheads and indigenously manufactured warheads using some imported components, for example structural rings, which it purchased from a foreign supplier.

Background

In 1991, Iraq declared that it had possessed 30 Scud-type chemical warheads. UNSCOM confirmed that these warheads had been used for chemical agent. Iraq destroyed 29 of these warheads under UNSCOM supervision. One warhead was removed from Iraq by UNSCOM for analysis.

In 1992, Iraq declared an additional 45 Scud-type chemical warheads, which it stated had been unilaterally destroyed in the summer of 1991. Later, Iraq declared that some of these had actually been biological warheads. By 1998, UNSCOM managed to verify the destruction of 43 to 45 of these warheads from remnants, but not before Iraq's declarations had changed many times. In addition, Iraq admitted to UNSCOM that it had added warhead nose cones to a declared warhead destruction site inspected by UNSCOM in an attempt to convince UNSCOM that all declared warheads could be accounted for. Some aspects of the filling and destruction processes remained unverified.

Immediately after the defection in August 1995 of Lieutenant-General Hussein Kamal, Director of the Military Industrialization Corporation (MIC), General Ra'ad, Director General of Project 144 (Iraq's former prime missile facility), stated *"initially there was an order for 75 containers, later another 25 were ordered. The order was fulfilled and sent to Al-Muthanna"*. [Muthanna was only filling special warheads with agents and later in the same statement Ra'ad describes how the warheads were filled at Al Muthanna]. However, on 29 and 30 September 1995, Lieutenant-General Amer Al Sa'adi, then Acting Director of MIC, stated that the total number of special warheads was 75 (25 biological and 50 chemical). Later, during a high level meeting in April 1997, Lieutenant-General Amer Al Sa'adi stated that it had been wrongly reported to UNSCOM that there had been 75 chemical plus 25 biological warheads produced.

The numbers resulting from Iraq's latest statements on the subject were 50 chemical warheads and 25 biological warheads.

Iraq purchased Scud missiles with conventional (high explosive) warheads. Iraq used several missiles in testing that did not require the use of a warhead. UNSCOM did not find any indigenously produced warheads that had been filled with high explosive, but did find some that had been filled with agent. The foregoing suggests that all of Iraq's indigenously produced warheads had been intended for special purposes.

In 2003, Iraq declared that it was able to produce Scud-type warheads, including the U-ring from raw material. However, because the material specification of the raw material was not appropriate and because it took a long time to manufacture, Iraq stated that it chose to import the U-rings, which it did in 2 groups. One group of U-rings was ready-to-use and one group required final machining. Iraq also declared that the structural rings for the Scud airframe were imported in the same 2 groups and that the group requiring final machining was interchangeable between the airframe and the warhead. Hence, for UNMOVIC to thoroughly account for warhead U-rings that were imported in the condition requiring final machining, an accounting would have to be made of all such airframe and warhead rings. During recent inspections it was noted that several thousand of these rings were in Iraq's possession in 1998 and that approximately half were used in the Al Samoud 2 programme during the absence of inspections. Therefore, an accurate and verifiable accounting of the rings imported in the condition requiring final machining is no longer possible.

After convening a Technical Evaluation Meeting, UNSCOM assessed that Iraq's declaration that 15 biological warheads had been destroyed simultaneously at a location in Nibai known as P3 conflicted with physical evidence collected at the site. This finding indicated that not all these warheads had been destroyed at the same time as declared by Iraq. This suggests that some special warheads were retained for a period and, if so, it would be logical to assume that some missiles and associated propellant might also have been retained.

UNSCOM's investigations showed that Iraq had not provided the true locations where, prior to the declared unilateral destruction, the above-mentioned 15 biological warheads had been hidden. In December 1998, Iraq pointed to new locations where it stated the special warheads had been hidden before being moved to the site where they were unilaterally destroyed. UNSCOM inspected these new locations but did not have time to complete the discussions with Iraq on this matter. The location of the warheads prior to destruction is significant since the time of their departure from the hide site should agree with the time of their arrival at the destruction site. Previous declarations of this kind have been verified or refuted using high-altitude imagery.

It was observed by UNSCOM that only chemical warheads were found during the period before Iraq's admission in 1995 that it had had an offensive biological weapons programme. This may suggest that Iraq destroyed the biological warheads only after it had declared the weaponization of biological agents, which would raise concerns over the possible retention of missiles as well during that period. In July 1998, Minister Amer Rashid promised UNSCOM that he would investigate how this could have occurred but failed to produce any findings before UNSCOM's departure in December 1998.

In April 1998, UNSCOM took samples from the excavated remnants of the special warheads. Chemical analysis revealed traces of degradation products related to nerve agents. Of the warheads sampled, Iraq had consistently maintained that those were filled with alcohol. (This is further discussed in the VX cluster).

Assessment

Although UNSCOM verified the destruction of 73 to 75 of the 75 special warheads that Iraq declared, a number of discrepancies and questions remain, which raise doubts about the accounting of the special warheads, including the total number produced: statements by some senior Iraqi officials that Iraq had possessed 75 chemical and 25 biological Scud-type warheads; the finding that, at a minimum, 16 to 30 structural rings remain unaccounted for; Iraq's numerous changes to its declarations on these matters; Iraq's admitted action taken to mislead UNSCOM on the location and number of special warheads; the physical evidence which conflicts with Iraq's account of its destruction of biological warheads; and the fact that no remnants of biological warheads were found by UNSCOM until after Iraq's admission in 1995 that it had had an offensive biological weapons programme.

As a consequence of the accounting questions above, uncertainty remains concerning the types and numbers of chemical and biological agents it filled into the special warheads. The finding of degradation products related to nerve agents, on some warhead remnants suggests that its declaration may not be complete.

Iraq has declared that it only ever produced warheads using rings that were imported in the read-to-use condition and so suggests this as the means of accounting. If the original production records of the indigenously produced warheads were provided to UNMOVIC and were found to support this declaration, such an accounting method could be acceptable.

Some doubts exist regarding Iraq's assertion that it could not do the final machining required for the semi-finished structural rings. This has been reinforced by General Sa'adi's statement, in July 2002 to UNMOVIC, that the manufacture of such rings was easy. In 2003, Iraq explained that prototype warheads rings had been indigenously produced prior to the Gulf War. Although they were produced from the incorrect grade of material, they were found acceptable. However, Iraq did not pursue production due to the lack of appropriate material and the fact that it was a time consuming process.

To help resolve these issues, Iraq should provide documents to support its assertion that it had only produced 75 special warheads and provide an explanation for the evidence UNSCOM found which contradicts Iraq's assertion that it had simultaneously destroyed 15 biological warheads at Nibai. Such documents could include: all the meeting minutes from an Iraqi High Level Committee that, according to Iraq, had been formed, on 30 June 1991, to address the issue of retaining proscribed materials and weapons, official written records ordering the destruction of warheads and the diary of Brigadier Ismail dealing with missile-related activities in 1990 and 1991 in its entirety.

Iraq should follow up the investigation that Minister Rashid had promised UNSCOM as to why no biological warheads were found until after 1995.

This issue is linked to the wider issue of whether Iraq had retained Scud-type missiles, propellant and a launching capability after the declared destruction dates.

Actions that Iraq could take to help resolve the issue
- Present any remaining Scud-type special warheads to UNMOVIC.

- Present further evidence to support its declarations concerning the number of special warheads that it had produced, such as a complete production-planning chart and supporting documents.

- Provide a credible explanation for why no biological warheads were found until after 1995 and present documentary evidence in support.

- Verify its declaration of the locations of the biological warheads immediately prior to their transport to Nibai P3, where it said they had been destroyed.

- Present further explanation supplemented with verifiable evidence is required of Iraq concerning its declaration that it had unilaterally destroyed, at the same time and location, 15 biological warheads at Nibai, P3.

b. R-400 and R-400A Bombs

Introduction

Prior to 1988, Iraq designed and produced all of its aerial munitions designated for CW use for high altitude delivery. In 1990, however, the R-400 type bombs were indigenously produced especially for low altitude CBW delivery. The bomb has a 90 litre capacity with a steel body, longitudinal burster tube, nose fuse and tail fin assembly with a retarding parachute mechanism. The R-400 type bombs were intended for external carriage on fighter or attack aircraft.

Background

According to Iraq's 1996 CW FFCD and 2002 CAFCD, the Military Industrial Commission (MIC) and the Air Force selected an imported conventional 400 kilogram aerial bomb, which Iraq referred to as the BRIP-400, as a model for the CBW bomb. The Iraqi Air Force was familiar with the BRIP-400, which it had in stock and had tested with airburst and impact fuses.

The CW bomb designed and produced by Iraq consisted of the imported tail section of the BRIP-400 attached to a locally manufactured body, base plate and nose section which included a burster tube. Iraq eventually designated this new bomb as R-400. Iraq declared that MIC had ordered Al Nasr State Establishment (NSE) to produce 1,000 bodies and nose and base sections for CW purposes. The Air Force supplied the tail assemblies and fuses from its stocks. According to Iraq's CW declarations, the prototypes of the R-400 aerial bombs were produced in April 1990. The R-400 bomb was the first, and according to Iraq's declarations the only, special aerial bomb that met the new Air Force requirements for the deployment of special munitions from low altitudes that allowed the aircraft to operate in areas protected by a modern air defence system.

Iraq stated that, in August 1990, NSE was ordered to produce an additional 200 R-400 bodies for BW use: each body was to have an internal epoxy coating and a black stripe painted on the outer casing to differentiate it from the previous CW-related order. These bombs were designated as R-400A. Iraq stated, however, that because of the lengthy process required for application of the internal coating, 25 R-400 bombs designated for aflatoxin fill had no internal coating and no black stripe.

During the period 1992-1998, Iraq changed its declarations on the quantity of bombs it had produced several times. For example, in 1992, Iraq declared in its FFCD that it had produced a total of 1200 R-400 bombs. With the admission of the offensive BW programme in 1995, this number was subsequently changed to a total of 1,550. Given the lack of specific information from Iraq, UNSCOM could not calculate the total number of R-400 bombs that Iraq had produced for its BW/CW programmes.

With respect to its CW programme, Iraq declared in its 1996 CW FFCD and also in its 2002 CAFCD that, in total, 1,024 bombs had been filled with an alcohol at the Muthanna State Establishment (MSE). Iraq stated that it had planned to use the alcohol in the bombs as a component of binary Sarin, with the other major component added just prior to use. However, documentary evidence showed that another 165 unfilled bombs and 35 possibly unitary

Sarin/Cyclosarin bombs had been produced but remained outside the scope of the initial order. Iraq stated that the R-400 bombs were transferred to various air bases during the period July to August 1990.

For its BW programme, Iraq stated in 1995 that, during December 1990, 200 tail assemblies were sent to Al Hakam to be integrated with the body. According to Iraq, it had filled 157 BW bombs and the completed bombs were marked at Al Hakam with the Arabic letters equivalent to A (for botulinum toxin), B (anthrax) and C (aflatoxin) to designate agent content. Iraq declared that, in January 1991, R-400A BW bombs were equally divided and sent to Airstrip 37 and Al Azzizziyah firing range and stored there until July 1991.

Iraq stated that coalition bombing destroyed some of its CW R-400 bombs. The remaining R-400 and its BW R-400A bombs were said to have been either unilaterally destroyed in 1991 by burning and explosion or destroyed under UNSCOM supervision. In addition, Iraq declared that rejected and surplus bombs were melted down at NSE. In total, at least 300 to 350 R-400 and R-400A bombs remained unaccounted for by UNSCOM. Lieutenant General Sa'adi, counselor to the Presidency, informed UNSCOM that documentation on the inventory (a list of bombs with agent fill and serial numbers) of R-400 and R-400A bombs had also been destroyed.

UNSCOM found that the accounting for some of the unilaterally destroyed bombs was not possible given the hazardous conditions created by the method of destruction. In addition, Iraq has produced no documentation that could have substantiated its statements that the surplus and rejected R-400 bombs had been melted at NSE. The one document submitted as evidence of the meltdown did not specifically refer to R-400s. In addition, photographic evidence shows that biological R-400A bombs had been located at Al Walid Air base in October 1991, which is not consistent with Iraq's FFCD and CAFCD.

Through sampling of excavated bombs at Al Azzizziyah in 1997, UNSCOM found botulinum toxin in an R-400 bomb. Iraq had never declared that it had filled R-400 bombs with this agent. Sampling of R-400 chemical bombs did confirm the presence of the alcohol component for binary Sarin/Cyclosarin.

Assessment
During the period 1992-1998, Iraq changed its declaration on the quantity of bombs it had produced from 1,200 to 1,550. Over the same period, Iraq changed its declaration as to the types of CBW agent fill, leaving UNMOVIC with little confidence in either the numbers produced or types of agent filled. It is not clear from Iraqi statements and documentation how many R-400 bombs had been ordered for CW purposes and the fill between unitary weapons and binary components. Although Iraq has stated that it ordered the production of 200 R-400A bombs, this may not have been the only order.

In addition, photographic evidence shows that R-400A bombs had been located at Al Walid Airbase in October 1991. This contradicts the declaration by Iraq that R-400A bombs had only been deployed to Al Azzizziyah and Airfield 37 and that all such bombs had been destroyed in July or August 1991.

UNMOVIC does not have a complete understanding of the coding system for the R-400 bombs. Iraq's explanation that this was in some way random or based on materials available is not credible. The classification and marking of the R-400s, which indicated the agent fill, should have been fundamental to their deployment and use.

By its design and technical parameters, the R-400 bombs could be quite suitable as a delivery means for some chemical warfare agents, but less so for the proper aerosolization of biological agents. With an impact fuse, the R-400 could have been effective for delivering a Sarin weapon; fitted with an air burst fuse it could have been suitable for delivering persistent agents, such as VX and Mustard. With respect to biological agents, the relatively large volume of liquid agent together with the small burster tube and thick bomb walls means that much of the agent would not be dispersed as respirable particles but as relatively large droplets. However, any use of biological weapons by Iraq, regardless of their technical efficiencies, could have a significant political and psychological impact.

Al Azzizziyah firing range was declared as the destruction area for all of the filled biological R-400 bombs and was excavated under the supervision of UNSCOM in 1997. UNSCOM identified three intact bombs and fragments of about another 20 R-400 bombs. Excavation was stopped because of the risk of unexploded ordnance in the area. In February 2003, Iraq notified UNMOVIC that it had recommenced excavation of R-400 bomb fragments at Al Azzizziyah firing range. As at 03 March 2003, Iraq had recovered eight complete bombs, 94 base plates and over 250 bomb fragments from a number of excavation sites at the range. Analysis of samples taken from the intact bombs as well as from the bomb fragments cannot confirm the content of the bombs although further analysis continues. Some fragments had a black stripe and there was evidence on some fragments of an epoxy coating, both indicative of biological agent-filled bomb.

It should be noted that, given the uncertainties surrounding R-400 production and the fact that the base plates from R-400A bombs are indistinguishable from R-400 bombs (and may be exactly the same as the BRIP-400) it is unlikely that the results from the excavation will enable this issue to be resolved.

As it has proved impossible to verify the production and destruction details of R-400 bombs, UNMOVIC cannot discount the possibility that some CW and BW filled R-400 bombs remain in Iraq.

It is known that Iraq already possesses the technical knowledge and infrastructure for producing R-400 type bombs, and could easily construct bomb bodies from existing resources. Any moulds that may have been destroyed could have been reconstituted, photographic analysis of the tail assemblies supports the conclusion that Iraq used only one type of tail assembly and parachute system for the new bomb and Iraq probably has a number of tail assemblies from existing stocks of conventional bombs available for use.

Actions that Iraq could take to help resolve the issue

- Present any remaining R-400 bombs and relevant moulds.

- Provide more supporting documentation on production, inventory, delivery, etc. relating to the R-400 and R-400A bombs it manufactured.

- Provide further documentation explaining the coding system it had used with the R-400 type bombs, including the coding assigned to specific CBW agents.

- Provide credible evidence that the R-400 bomb production line stopped after September 1990.

c. Major Aerial Bombs

Introduction

Bombs dropped from aircraft can be used to disseminate large quantities of chemical or biological agents. They are typically compatible with either impact or airburst fuzing (proximity or time delay) and can be configured as either bulk (single mass of agent) or cluster (multiple sub-munitions) munitions. Although bombs are an efficient means to disseminate most chemical agents, bulk bombs are an inefficient means to disseminate biological agents. Bombs are also compatible with the production of certain chemical agents in-flight via the reaction of binary components, i.e., binary bombs.

Chemical and biological bombs are typically configured to disseminate their agent fill via explosive aerosolization. Alternatively, chemical bombs can rely on a frangible body and the forces of impact to scatter their agent fill. Lastly, bombs can be configured to rapidly release their contents during flight.

Background

Iraq produced or procured a number of bomb types capable of being filled with chemical or biological agents. These included the various imported and domestically produced napalm bombs, bombs intended for use with white phosphorus or similar smoke producing compounds and other conventional bombs that can be configured in a way that permits the insertion of a burster tube. Representative examples include the LD-250, BR-250, AALD-500, BR-500, R-400, Qaa Qaa-500 and the SDN-750. These are all fundamentally similar in that they all incorporate steel bodies, longitudinal bursters, and tail fins. They differ in size, dimensions and exact shape. Some of these bombs were imported and some were domestically assembled. All of the bombs (in this class) were meant for external carriage on fighter/attack aircraft.

Iraq also produced the DB series of aluminum bombs, including the DB-0, DB-1 and DB-2. There is some uncertainty regarding the configuration of the DB-0 and DB-1 bombs. Although designed for use with an incendiary material such as napalm, these bombs were either tested or intended (DB-2) for use with toxic agents.

Aerial chemical bombs constituted a major part of Iraq's arsenal of chemical munitions with approximately two-thirds of all weaponized agent being loaded into six types of bombs. Between 1983 and 1990, Iraq produced or procured over 30,000 aerial bombs for use with chemical or biological agents.

Iraq provided some documentary evidence to support its declarations (the 1996 FFCD and the 2002 CAFCD) concerning the procurement, production, filling and consumption of these bombs. However, these declarations are, in part, contradicted by an Air Force document detailing consumption of chemical bombs during the Iran-Iraq war.

UNSCOM accounted for, and supervised the destruction by Iraq of, more than 2,000 filled and some 10,000 empty bombs. UNSCOM also supervised the destruction by Iraq of some 100 pieces of equipment and machinery constituting the aerial bomb production plant, including rolling and welding machines, mechanical presses, moulds, etc. However, due to the absence of credible evidence, UNSCOM was not able to fully verify Iraq's declared unilateral destruction of some 2,000 empty bombs and some 450 mustard bombs destroyed as declared by Iraq in a fire accident.

Assessment

Due to the lack of complete and verifiable information regarding import, production and consumption, UNMOVIC cannot verify Iraq's declarations regarding aerial bombs.

The "Air Force document" recently received by UNMOVIC introduces additional uncertainty in accounting as it indicates that 6,526 fewer aerial CW bombs (of gauges 250, 500 and DB-2 types) had been "consumed" during the Iraq Iran War. Iraq has explained that the "Air Force" document, which had been complied by one of its officers in 1995, was incomplete. According to Iraq, data on consumption of CW filled munitions positioned at three airbases was not included as the airbases had been occupied in 1991 and the records destroyed. This explanation is being reviewed by UNMOVIC.

Iraq's declarations of its biological test results with bombs were inconsistent with its declared programme actions that followed these tests.

Iraq's use of a variety of aerial bombs for BW and CW purposes is important because it demonstrates the following abilities: conversion of indigenously produced conventional bombs for chemical use (e.g. Qaa Qaa-500), procurement of foreign munitions intended for use with smoke compounds and instead loading them with either chemical or biological agents (e.g. BR-250, LD-250, AALD-500 and BR-500), adapting foreign munition designs for use with prohibited agents (DB-0, DB-1, DB-2 and R-400 series).

By 1998, known stocks of bombs specifically associated with chemical or biological agents had been destroyed along with the moulds and equipment used to manufacture these munitions. However, Iraq's indigenous chemical and biological bombs were largely unsophisticated designs and were not particularly difficult to fabricate. Additionally, the personnel needed to design and fabricate these munitions remained available. Therefore, while Iraq's inventory of aerial chemical and biological bombs was presumably eliminated, its ability to reconstitute that inventory remains largely intact.

Actions that Iraq could take to help resolve the issue

- Provide any remaining quantities of aerial bombs configured for CW or BW purposes or provide verifiable evidence of their destruction.

- Provide credible evidence, documentary or other concerning import, production and consumption of aerial bombs configured for CW and BW purposes.

- Explain in greater detail and with supporting credible evidence the rationale, outcome and major decisions taken regarding the testing and use of aerial bombs in the BW programme.

- Provide the name and present location of the officer who produced the "Air Force document".

Intentionally Blank

d. Major Rockets and Artillery Projectiles

Introduction

Artillery and multiple rocket launcher systems (MRLS) can be used to deliver large quantities of chemical or biological agents to targets within a few tens of kilometers of the firing point. Artillery projectiles and rocket warheads can be configured to contain bulk liquid agent, binary chemical agent components or sub-munitions that contain an agent. Additionally, projectiles and warheads can be configured to disseminate their agent load as an aerosol or to eject sub-munitions. Projectiles differ from warheads in that projectiles are typically of much heavier construction and therefore contain less agent than would a warhead of similar diameter. Projectiles and warheads are both compatible with impact and airburst fuzes. While projectiles and warheads are both suitable for use with a wide range of chemical agents, neither is as well suited for use with biological agents.

Background

Iraq's chemical arsenal included artillery projectiles and rocket warheads for a variety of guns/howitzers and multiple rocket launching systems. 122-mm MRLS systems and 155-mm howitzers were major systems in Iraq's ground forces, and thus, the corresponding warheads and projectiles were selected for filling with chemical agents. Iraq also declared prior work with other projectiles.

Iraq did not provide full documentation to support its declarations concerning the total number of rocket warheads and projectiles produced, procured, filled and consumed. In addition, on several occasions from 1991 to 1997, Iraq's declarations concerning munitions changed significantly. In an attempt to compensate for the insufficiency and ambiguity of the declarations, UNSCOM requested Iraq's principal suppliers to provide information concerning Iraqi munition procurements. Unfortunately, the requested information was not provided, thus UNSCOM was unable to validate Iraq's declarations regarding the disposition of 122-mm rocket warheads and 155-mm artillery projectiles. This issue is further complicated by Iraq's procurement of large quantities of similar munitions for conventional military purposes from the same suppliers.

Artillery projectiles

Although Iraq had the capability to produce 155-mm chemical projectiles, it declared that some 85,000 suitable empty projectiles were imported for subsequent filling. Of the 70,000 projectiles filled with chemical agents, principally Mustard, more than 54,000 were declared as expended between 1984 and 1988 and 13,500 as remaining before the Gulf War.

Iraq primarily filled 155-mm projectiles with high purity Mustard that remained stable during long-term storage. However, Iraq also provided some information and documents on the development and tests of 155-mm binary nerve agent (Sarin and Cycolosarin) projectiles. UNSCOM found several examples of these munitions at the Muthanna State Establishment. Iraq stated that, despite positive test results, no industrial-scale production of binary 155-mm projectiles occurred.

Iraq declared that it had unilaterally converted approximately 15,500 empty 155-mm artillery projectiles, purchased for chemical warfare use, into conventional high explosive munitions in 1992-93. UNSCOM attempted to verify the disposition of these munitions and found approximately 1,800 of these projectiles at the Babylon Ammunition Depot. UNSCOM was satisfied with its findings and did not pursue the matter further.

Iraq has provided a number of explanations regarding the disposition of approximately 550 unaccounted for Mustard filled 155-mm projectiles. UNSCOM, having determined that the Mustard contained in Iraq's 155-mm projectiles was likely to remain stable for a long period, treated this issue as a serious matter. The high purity of Sulphur Mustard contained in artillery shells, after over 12 years of storage, was recently confirmed by UNMOVIC.

Rocket warheads
Iraq declared the procurement or indigenous production of more than 100,000 122-mm chemical warheads from 1985 to 1990, making it the most numerous of Iraq's chemical munitions. At least seven distinct models of warheads were procured or produced. In excess of 36,000 warheads were declared as having been filled with nerve agents. Iraq declared that tens of thousands of 122-mm chemical warheads were either consumed between 1986 and 1988 or were destroyed in 1991 during the Gulf War. Over 14,000 warheads or warhead and rocket motor combinations were handed over to UNSCOM. Additionally, Iraq declared the unilateral destruction of more than 26,000 warheads.

Iraq declared that all 122-mm chemical warheads were filled with nerve agents. Iraqi quality control records excavated by UNSCOM showed that 122-mm warheads were filled in anticipation of immediate use rather than for long-term storage. According to the documents, Iraq had experienced technical difficulties in storing warheads filled with nerve agents, including degradation of the agent within months and several cases of leakage.

UNSCOM did not find any evidence to support Iraq's declarations concerning the unilateral destruction of some 15,000 empty aluminum 122-mm warheads. However, UNSCOM did find evidence that supported some of Iraq's declarations regarding the destruction (both unilateral and as a result of bombing during the Gulf War) of tens of thousands of other 122-mm warheads. Accounting was not possible due to the circumstances of the destruction.

During UNMOVIC inspections in January 2003, 12 empty 122-mm chemical rocket warheads were found in a storehouse at a storage depot 170 km southwest of Baghdad. Iraq later provided four additional from a building in another storage depot. Two more 122-mm rocket warheads were found later at the same depot by an UNMOVIC inspection team. A Commission of Inquiry has been set up by Iraq to investigate why these warheads were stored at these sites or whether any more such warheads or other proscribed munitions are stored at other locations in Iraq. According to a document from the Commission, which was handed over to UNMOVIC in February 2003, the 12 warheads were part of a batch of less than 20 warheads received by Al Muthana in 1989 for training and reverse engineering purposes.

Assessment

122-mm warheads and 155-mm projectiles are a militarily efficient means for the dissemination of a variety of chemical agents. While 155-mm projectiles filled with Mustard could be stored for decades, it is less likely that any remaining warheads filled with nerve agents would still be viable combat munitions. However, any remaining unfilled projectiles or warheads, if properly stored and maintained, could still be used for future chemical warfare applications.

Regarding the missing 550 Mustard filled 155-mm projectiles, UNMOVIC has been unable to resolve the status of these items and remains concerned due to their probable military utility. According to an investigation made by the Iraqi "Depot Inspection Commission", the results of which were reported to UNMOVIC in March 2003, the discrepancy in the accounting for the mustard filled shells could be explained by the fact that Iraq had based its accounting in the 2002 CAFCD on approximations. The new accounting will be reviewed by UNMOVIC.

It is noted that UNSCOM was satisfied with Iraq's declaration that it had converted over 15,000 155-mm projectiles, originally intended for use with chemical agents, to conventional munitions by filling them with high explosives. Because of the original proscribed nature of these items, UNSCOM would have been justified in destroying these munitions.

The 122-mm chemical rocket warheads found by UNMOVIC in January 2003 were stored in a storehouse that Iraq claims were overlooked from 1991, when a batch of some 2000 were deployed there during the Gulf war. Sealed casings containing some of the rocket warheads were dated April 1988 (4/88). The one rocket warhead with a liquid content has been sampled and analysed by UNMOVIC. The liquid was found to be water contaminated by hydrogen sulphide, which seems to be consistent with the fact that coloured water was used for trial purposes to simulate a CW agent. However, the finding of these 16 rocket warheads could be taken as a demonstration for the absence of a complete and accurate inventory for this type of munition in Iraq.

Iraq has been vague as to exactly how many field tests with 122-mm rocket warheads occurred and the number of warheads involved. UNMOVIC shares UNSCOM's view that it seems likely that Iraq would have documented the results of these tests and that it may have conducted more warhead tests than declared. For example, video tapes from the Haidar Farm cache shows Muthanna personnel conducting tests of a cluster bomb that appears to utilize submunitions based, in part, on 122-mm warhead components.

Iraq met its pre-1991 requirements for artillery projectiles and rocket warheads through a combination of importation and indigenous production. It is unlikely that gaps and uncertainties in the accounting for the thousands of unfilled chemical munitions can be solved without the presentation by Iraq of additional evidence concerning the disposition of these items. Additionally, as of 1998, Iraq still had significant stocks of conventional 122-mm warheads and 155-mm projectiles similar to those previously modified for use with chemical agents. Iraq's industries appear fully capable of modifying these conventional munitions for use with chemical agents as well as the indigenous production of most or all of their components.

Actions that Iraq could take to help resolve the issue

- Present any existing quantities of 155 mm Mustard filled artillery shells and 122-mm rocket warheads.

- Present more detailed information and supporting documentation on the import, indigenous manufacture, delivery and inventory of the special rocket warheads, and components thereof, which were produced or acquired for the CBW programmes.

- Present more detailed information and supporting documentation on the various special warhead and canister field-tests, including tests relating to the development of binary systems.

- Present complete documentation from all military organizations, detailing their consumption of special munitions.

- Presen all documents or letters referenced in the document from the Commission of Inquiry.

e. Spray devices and Remotely Piloted Vehicles

Introduction

A spray device can be an efficient and effective means to disperse wet or dry chemical or biological warfare agents (CBW) over a large area. Such a delivery system does not involve the extreme temperatures and pressures associated with explosive dissemination. In general, spraying achieves a higher dissemination efficiency than explosive aerosolisation. Spray dissemination may be either along a line trajectory or from a point source, upwind or directly over the target. Spray devices can be employed with a variety of delivery systems such as fixed wing aircraft (manned and unmanned), helicopters, trucks, boats, special operations personnel and cruise missiles.

Two types of spray devices were acknowledged to have been considered by Iraq: modified auxiliary fuel tanks (tanks used to extend the range of an aircraft, known as "drop-tanks") and modified agricultural sprayers. Drop-tanks can be modified by the addition of spray nozzles to convert them to CBW dispersal devices. Iraq had imported a large number of drop-tanks for a variety of aircraft and some of these tanks were observed during inspections. Iraq also had available domestically manufactured drop-tanks, spray and other devices.

Background

In its 1996 CW FFCD and its 2002 CAFCD, Iraq declared that, in 1988, it had worked on the modification of drop-tanks for CW use. Iraq stated that the work had turned out to be *"inconclusive"* and was abandoned that same year. However, the CW FFCD mentioned that, in 1990, personnel from its chemical weapons production facility, Al Muthanna State Establishment (MSE), took part in a *"task"* to modify Mirage F1 drop-tanks for the dispersion of Biological Warfare (BW) agents. The CW FFCD also cited a letter dated 10 December 1990 from the Director General of MSE to the Deputy Director of the Military Industrialisation Commission (MIC), which referred to *"successful tests of spraying mustard gas by planes which proved to be very effective"* and stated that Mustard agent was stockpiled for that purpose. Iraq declared that it had possessed 295 tonnes of bulk Mustard agent. (UNSCOM supervised the destruction of the Mustard during the period 1992 to 1993).

However, in its 1997 BW FFCD and its 2002 CAFCD, Iraq associated the same tests with its work on a BW drop-tank, explaining that MSE staff had worked on the BW tank in the belief that it was for CW purposes. The BW FFCD and CAFCD also stated that, as part of the Mirage drop-tank project, four Mirage F1 drop-tanks, each having a capacity of 2,200 litres, had been modified by the addition of venturis and valves. The valve controls the flow of agent out of the tank into the venturi where the agent is reduced to a stream of small droplets.

According to Iraq, the project had commenced in November 1990. The first flight test with a prototype tank was conducted in the second week of December, followed by three further tests conducted by 13 January 1991. The tests used a mixture of different materials - potassium permanganate, water, glycerine and non-pathogenic *Bacillus subtilis* spores as a BW simulant. Iraq declared that, although it had planned to modify a total of 12 drop-tanks, due to lack of valves, it was only able to modify three tanks in addition to the prototype tank. Documents provided by Iraq support its statement that, by July 1991, it had possessed at least three modified BW drop-tanks. However, the documents make no reference to the prototype drop-tank. Work on these tanks continued throughout the Gulf War and was completed in March 1991. Iraq stated that it had unilaterally destroyed the three drop-tanks in the summer of 1991 and that the prototype and the associated Mirage F1 aircraft had been destroyed by aerial bombardment during the Gulf War. Iraq stated the tanks were never deployed or used.

UNSCOM inspected and verified the remains of the three modified drop-tanks Iraq stated it had unilaterally destroyed. The venturi dissemination devices were not found among the remains. However, one such device was presented by Iraq to UNSCOM in April 1998. An inspection of the airbase where the prototype drop-tank was said to have been destroyed failed to yield evidence of either the prototype modified drop-tank or the associated Mirage F-1.

In its June 1996 BW FFCD, Iraq declared another project to investigate the modification of a MiG-21 fighter aircraft. This declaration stated that the MiG-21 remotely piloted vehicle (RPV) was to deliver a BW agent in a Mirage F-1 drop tank to an area without losing a pilot. The June 1996 FFCD details a project to modify a Mirage F1 drop tank *"for the dissemination of BW agents from fighter aircraft"*.

Despite this earlier declaration, Iraq declared in its September 1997 BW FFCD and in the CAFCD the modification of a MiG-21 fighter plane into a RPV *"to deliver a munition"* to a target as well as a separate project to modify Mirage F1 drop tanks for the dissemination of BW agent.

In addition to the drop-tanks and the MiG-21 RPV, Iraq declared that research and development on several BW aerosol generators took place from July 1987 to September 1988. The work culminated in a series of field trials using a modified crop dusting helicopter to spray non-pathogenic *Bacillus subtilis* spores. Iraq stated that it had assessed the results of field trials to be inconclusive and that no attempts were made to create a weapons system based on this work. According to Iraq, no further work was conducted on the helicopter device beyond September 1988. In March 1996, Iraq turned over to UNSCOM various items related to the project.

However, an Iraqi report of the field tests stated that the modified crop dusting device was *"useful for spraying fluids containing micro-organisms and their products (bacteria, fungi and their toxins)"*. This is contrary to Iraq's declaration that the results had been inconclusive. Based on interviews and the test report, UNSCOM considered that the tests had actually been successful. Given that components of the system were unaccounted for, UNSCOM questioned whether the development had continued beyond 1988, possibly to deployment.

UNSCOM also reported evidence of another aerosol generator that appeared to be based on the modified crop duster. Its development began in the same timeframe as the development of the helicopter device but continued after that work was said to have been completed. UNSCOM found the objectives of this "parallel" aerosol project unclear and that it was uncertain whether development had continued to deployment. Iraq has denied the existence of any "parallel" development.

In its July 1998 semi-annual missile declaration, Iraq provided information on a project called Al Bai'aa for the conversion of an L-29 aircraft into an RPV, which it stated was intended for air defense training. The declared design goal was to achieve a range of 30 kilometres with a 100 kilogramme payload. However, in its CAFCD, Iraq declared that the Al Bai'aa project stopped in the year 2000.

Assessment

There is a clear contradiction in Iraq's explanation of its development of spray tanks. Iraq has maintained that it started its development work by producing a spray tank for biological agents and has denied that it had developed a similar system for chemical agents. This explanation is contradicted by a letter dated 10 December 1990 from the Director General of MSE to the Deputy Director of the Military Industrialization Commission (MIC), a copy of which was given to UNSCOM by Iraq to support a different matter relating to VX. The letter, however, also contains a reference to the stockpiling of Mustard agent for a successfully tested aircraft spray system. This indicates that also had a well-developed drop-tank for chemical agent. By the date of the letter, 10 December 1990, it is also clear that the CW drop-tank was developed before the BW drop-tank. Therefore, Iraq's further explanation that the reference in the letter to Mustard agent was associated with BW drop-tanks cannot be correct.

The conclusion therefore drawn from the MSE letter is that, by December 1990, Iraq had a design for a separate device capable of spraying Mustard agent. The specifications of this CW delivery device, for example whether it was based on a modified Mirage drop-tank or other spraying device, are unknown to UNMOVIC. It is known that Iraq had tested different types of aerial spray or other devices capable of disseminating Mustard agent.

Given that the group that had successfully developed the CW spraying device was later engaged in the modification of the BW drop-tank, the likelihood of success of that project was greatly increased. The development of tanks for CW and BW uses should not be considered as two separate projects but rather as one continued project.

Iraq's assertion that it was unable to modify 12 drop-tanks for BW purposes because of a shortage of valves is contradicted by a letter dated 25 August 1991 from the Department of Aeronautical Engineering to Al Muthanna. The letter requests the return of unused valves, thus indicating that such components had not been in short supply as claimed by Iraq. It is therefore possible that additional tanks were modified. While Iraq has provided documents showing that, as of July 1991, it had at least three modified BW drop-tanks, they do not address the prototype drop-tank. Since no remnants of the prototype tank have been found, it has not been possible to verify its destruction.

Spraying devices modified for CBW purposes may still exist in Iraq. A large number of drop tanks of various kinds, both imported and locally manufactured, are available and could be modified. Since spraying devices are an efficient means of disseminating CBW agents, and since Iraq declared continued research after January 1991, it is likely to have been a high priority in the CBW program.

Although Iraq's September 1997 BW FFCD referred to the MiG-21 RPV project as intended for the delivery of a munition, in earlier declarations and in discussion, Iraq stated that the project was for the delivery of BW agent from a modified Mirage drop tank. The use of a Mirage drop tank on a MiG aircraft, although possible, would pose considerable aviation engineering problems.

Given its payload and range, the MiG-21 RPV could have been intended for the delivery of either CW or BW agents. In addition, the spray system would have most likely have been based on a MiG-21 fuel tank as opposed to the fuel tank of a Mirage F-1. Given that Iraq had already successfully conducted spraying of Mustard from planes, it is possible that it was a MiG system that had been used in the tests and that the RPV project was an extension of this programme. Further information is required to determine the extent and the objectives of the project and whether it was terminated in April 1991 as declared by Iraq.

Work on another aircraft, the L-29 jet trainer, to convert it to a RPV started in November 1995 and continued until at least 2000. The L-29, although smaller and less capable than the MiG, could still be used to deliver CBW agent in quantities that would pose a significant threat to neighbouring countries. Iraq has declared that the work on the L-29 has stopped but that work continues on smaller RPVs. Iraq has also declared in its BW CAFCD a number of smaller RPVs that are capable of carrying a payload of up to 20 kilogrammes to a range of less than 30 kilometres. This payload could represent a significant biological payload if dry agent is used. Of concern is the more general question of Iraq's intentions with respect to RPVs as CBW delivery systems and the relationship to the spray tank development. Iraq has also declared in its Missile CAFCD two other RPVs, both capable of a 100 kilometre range with a designed payload of 30 kilogrammes.

With respect to aerosol generators, the modified crop duster Iraq developed had potential as a BW dissemination device. There are many agricultural aircraft spray systems in Iraq. These units are identical to the devices that were modified for BW dissemination. In addition, components imported for these or other spray devices were available in Iraq in 2003. Modified aircraft fuel tanks were found at Khan Bani Sa'ad Airfield in December 2002. These tanks were stated to have been part of an indigenously manufactured agricultural spray system that was stated to have been produced by the Air Force. The expertise gained in the development of the generators and the evidence of "parallel" work on a similar device that was not declared, is of some concern.

Iraq should provide additional information regarding its efforts to develop spraying devices and delivery systems for CBW agents. This should include an account of the development of the successfully tested CW spray device, the numbers produced, technical details of the system such as flow rates, dissemination efficiencies, and the number and designs of venturis, nozzles and valves. If any modified spray devices remain they should be destroyed if they are found to have been intended for CBW purposes. In addition, Iraq should provide information on the management and organizational structure of the MiG-21 project, its place in the CBW programmes and the concepts of use of the weapon.

Actions that Iraq could take to help resolve the issue

- Present any existing spray (drop) tanks or other spray devises modified for CBW purposes.

- Provide documents or other evidence that explain what type(s) of spray-devices it had developed or had planned to develop, and for which agents, for the MiG-21 RPV and any other RPV.

- Account for all of the L-29 aircraft, provide all records of unmanned flight tests and explain the presence of an L-29 at Tallil Air Force base in 1997.

- Account for all of the smaller RPV and UAV aircraft and provide all of the flight-testing records up to the present (March 2003).

- Provide all of the procurement details relating to RPV components including records from 1998 to 2003.

- Provide details on the control mechanisms for the smaller RPVs, the location of the transmitters and the frequencies used.

- Provide documents that explain the letter of 10 December 1990 from the Director General of the MSE to the Deputy Director of MIC. The letter indicates that, contrary to Iraq's declarations to UNSCOM by December 1990 it had successfully developed a CW spray-tank.

- Provide further explanation and documentation on their work on spray (drop) tanks for CW purpose.

- Explain the letter dated 25 August 1991, which appears to contradict Iraq's declaration to UNSCOM that, due to a shortage of valves, it could not produce more spray tanks.

Intentionally Blank

f. Other Chemical and Biological munitions

Introduction

Chemical and biological warfare (CBW) agents can be filled into a variety of munitions including cluster bombs, fragmentation weapons, spray tanks, missile warheads, bombs, rockets, mortar projectiles and artillery shells.

It is possible to modify a range of conventional munitions to make them suitable for a chemical or biological agent fill. The modification usually involves replacing the high explosive with the chemical or biological agent and an explosive-filled burster tube with an appropriate fuse. In addition, the munition must be leak proof and made of material that does not adversely react with the chemical or biological agent. Some munitions, because of their design or size, are more suited for chemical or biological agents; for example, fragmentation weapons or flechettes (a munition similar in size and shape to a dart) are well suited for a BW agents like *Clostridium perfringens* while rocket propelled grenades are suited to a Sarin fill.

Background

In its 1996 chemical FFCD and its CAFCD, Iraq acknowledged an interest in chemical agent filled cluster bombs. It also declared that it had conducted two tests of the CB-250 cluster bomb in 1987. Iraq stated that, because of the negative results (attributed to incorrect fusing), further tests were abandoned. In August 1996, a high-ranking Iraqi official interviewed by UNSCOM stated that cluster bombs were part of the BW programme. Later the same day, in the presence of his superior officers, he retracted the statement. In October 1996, a senior Iraqi official admitted to UNSCOM that the head of the Technical Research Centre, the organization responsible for directing Iraq's production of BW agent, had directed him to visit the Al Noaman cluster bomb factory, to evaluate the use of cluster bombs for BW purposes. In its 1997 BW FFCD (and repeated in the CAFCD), Iraq did not acknowledge any interest in cluster bombs for BW purposes and an UNSCOM biological inspection team, which visited the Al Noaman factory in 1997, reported that no evidence had been found linking the factory to biological weapons. However, in February 2003, an UNMOVIC inspection team found a component of a 122mm CBW cluster submunition in a warehouse at the Al Noaman Factory. Iraq stated that this was a leftover from the past declared chemical simulant test program that was abandoned.

With regard to fragmentation weapons, a senior Iraqi official had acknowledged experimental laboratory work on the sub-dermal introduction of *Clostridium perfringens* resulting in gas gangrene. Iraq has denied that this research was exploited for weapons development, such as for use in fragmentation weapons or flechettes. According to Iraq, it also considered the possible use of land mines for BW. However, one Iraqi scientist noted that the antipersonnel land mines at Al-Qa'a Qa'a had been considered unsuitable for filling with liquid BW agent. UNSCOM had no evidence of Iraq filling chemical or biological agents in land mines.

Iraq declared that it did some basic research using tear gas in rocket-propelled grenades (RPG) and in explosive canisters. However, UNSCOM found no evidence that Iraq actually developed RPGs filled with chemical agent.

Assessment

During the 1980's, Iraq showed considerable interest in developing cluster munitions filled with "special agents". Cluster munitions are well suited to dispersing CBW agent. Iraq's interest in cluster munitions for chemical agent in particular, may have been linked to its need to counter "human wave" tactics Iran had used in its conflict with Iraq. The ceasefire in the Iraq/Iran war, in August 1988, rather than the lack of technical success, may have lessened the urgency to develop chemical and biological cluster munitions.

The involvement of the Muthanna State Establishment (MSE) Iraq's main CW production facility, with the Al Noaman factory in the development and testing of special (chemical or biological) sub-munitions, confirm Iraq's interest in cluster bombs. Video evidence from the Haidar Farm suggests that Iraq was modifying existing munitions to be compatible with the locally made cluster bombs. In particular, Iraq used elements from the 122-mm special warheads to produce sub-munitions for the cluster bomb. From early 1987 to mid-1988, Muthanna continued with the development and testing of various components of 122-mm warheads including an all-way fuse and an aluminium casing. Iraq tested the fuse and dispersion pattern by dropping the 122-mm canisters from an aircraft and a crane. A component of such a sub-munition was found at the Al Noaman Factory in February 2003.

UNSCOM discovered in some of the Haidar Farm documents mention of an agreement between MSE and the same foreign company that supplied the Al Noaman cluster bomb factory to Iraq. It is unclear whether the project, codenamed Project 101, was related to the development or production of cluster bombs suited to CBW agents. When questioned on this Project during a February 2003 inspection, the Al Noaman Factory manager, NMD representatives and representatives from the past CW program all denied any knowledge of such a project.

Iraq should provide all documentation relating to Project 101 so as to determine the nature and extent of the link to Iraq's CBW programme.

During an interview with UNSCOM in August 1996, a high-ranking Iraqi official with extensive knowledge of the BW programme stated that not more than two conventional cluster bombs had been modified for BW purposes. UNMOVIC notes that the official had unequivocally repeated his statement linking cluster bombs to the BW programme. The retraction of this statement the same day in the presence of his superior officers was never adequately explained to UNSCOM. Other evidence of Iraqi interest in developing cluster munitions for BW agents exists, such as the visit to the cluster bomb factory by a senior Iraqi official in the BW programme.

The foregoing suggests that Iraq's interest in cluster munitions, and the developments it did make, may have progressed well beyond what it had declared.

Iraq produced 340 litres of concentrated *Clostridium perfringens*, the causative agent of gas gangrene, in 1990. *Clostridium perfringens* is most effective as a BW agent when it comes in contact with open wounds. It would, therefore, be expected that Iraq would have tested (or had the intention to test) the agent with fragmentation devices or flechettes.

Actions that Iraq could take to help resolve the issue

-       Present any CBW cluster munitions that it may find.

-       Provide additional information regarding CBW related cluster munitions, especially concerning the work done by "project 101" and the project's relationship to the Al Noaman cluster bomb factory and the BW programme.

-       Provide a credible explanation and documentation for the cluster bomb sub-munition component, its intended use and agent fill.

Intentionally Blank

III. CHEMICAL CLUSTERS

a. Tabun

Introduction

Tabun (GA) has the chemical name O-ethyl N,N-dimethylphosphoramidocyanidate. Tabun was the first chemical warfare nerve agent produced and weaponized. It can have a lethal effect if inhaled or deposited on the skin. It is a colourless to brownish liquid giving off a colourless vapour that has a faintly fruity smell (none when pure).

In 1984, a team of specialists appointed by the UN Secretary-General investigated claims by Iran that Iraq had used chemical weapons in their conflict. The specialists determined that both Tabun and Mustard, a blister agent, had been used. The Security Council strongly condemned in general terms the use of chemical agents through several statements by the President of the Security Council (see, e.g. UN documents S/17932, S/18305) and Security Council resolution 612 of 9 May 1988.

Background

In its 1996 FFCD, and in the 2002 CAFCD, Iraq declared that it had produced 210 tonnes of Tabun. 140 tonnes had been weaponized, of which a certain quantity had been consumed during the period 1984 to 1986. Iraq further declared that it had unilaterally destroyed 30 tonnes. Iraq has stated that the quality of the agent produced had been poor and that it could not be stored for a long period of time. Iraq explained that this, as well as technical production problems, led it in 1986 to cease making Tabun and concentrate on the production of the nerve agent Sarin.

UNSCOM supervised the destruction of 40 tonnes of Tabun, which it determined had a purity of only 30%. However, UNSCOM could not verify Iraq's declarations concerning its production, weaponization, consumption and unilateral destruction of Tabun.

Iraq declared that it had produced Tabun from sodium cyanide (NaCN), ethanol and N,N-Dimethylphosphoramidic dichloride (D4). With respect to NaCN, 191 tonnes cannot be physically accounted for – Iraq explained that this may have been due to an order not completely filled by the supplier. With respect to ethanol – it is a ubiquitous chemical that Iraq produces indigenously – no material balance was submitted by Iraq or requested by UNSCOM.

Iraq declared that it had used 469 tonnes of phosphorousoxy chloride ($POCl_3$) in the production of the intermediate D4, as a result, 477 tonnes should have remained after the Gulf War. However, Iraq destroyed 576 tonnes under UNSCOM supervision, which is more than should have remained according to Iraq's figures. Iraq also declared the existence of a $POCl_3$ plant, which was mechanically complete, but non-operational as parts of the control system were missing. UNSCOM inspected this plant and determined that it had not been used. Subsequently, Iraq destroyed key components of the plant under UNSCOM supervision.

Iraq declared that it had imported at least 570 tonnes of DMA.HCl and provided letters of credit in support. Iraq declared that it has used 275 tonnes in the production of D4. Twohundred and seventytwo tonnes were destroyed under UNSCOM supervision. UNSCOM reported that it could not fully account for 30 tonnes of DMA.HCl that Iraq declared destroyed through aerial bombardment during the Gulf War although it had seen evidence of destruction.

Assessment

Iraq has not provided adequate evidence to support its declarations of the quantities of Tabun and the precursors for Tabun that it imported, produced and consumed. However, documentary evidence suggests that Tabun was produced using process technology and quality control methodologies that would result in the agent being degraded to a very low quality through the action of a resulting by-product. This matter should however be further clarified with Iraq.

One bottleneck for Tabun production is the availability of precursors. Iraq may have retained up to 191 tonnes of NaCN and up to 140 tonnes of DMA·HCl, but there is no evidence that any $POCl_3$ remains unaccounted for. NaCN and DMA·HCl are relatively stable, if properly stored, and could therefore still be viable today.

All the Tabun precursors (NaCN, $POCl_3$ and DMA·HCl) are covered by List A of the export/import mechanism. Therefore, any legitimate acquisition of these chemicals by Iraq should be notified to the United Nations and become subject to monitoring. As of December 2002, Iraq has declared the use of less than 10 tonnes of NaCN at a number of facilities in non-prohibited activities such as electroplating, metal coating and heat treatment of tools. There are legitimate civilian uses for $POCl_3$ and DMA·HCl, such as pesticides production ($POCl_3$), leather processing or detergents and rocket fuel production (DMA.HCl).

The raw materials to produce DMA.HCl are available to Iraq, and it may have continued its past R&D work and developed the technology to produce DMA.HCl. During recent inspections of a research facility, UNMOVIC became aware of a research program conducted for the synthesis of DMA.HCl. It was explained that the research program was related to rocket fuels. It is possible that $POCl_3$ can be produced if Iraq has retained phosphorous trichloride (PCl_3) – some quantities of PCl_3 are unaccounted for – and reconstituted a plant for the production of $POCl_3$ based on a turnkey plant it had obtained in the late 1980s. There is however no evidence of a plant capable of producing $POCl_3$ in Iraq.

Another bottleneck for Tabun production would be the limited availability of some key equipment needed for processing and storage of corrosive intermediates.

Iraq's assertion that it decided in 1986 to stop production of Tabun and concentrate on the production of Sarin is plausible and appears to be supported by UNSCOM's findings.

Actions that Iraq could take to help resolve the issue
- Present any outstanding quantities of NaCN, or provide credible evidence to support that all quantities delivered have either been consumed or destroyed.

- Explain with credible evidence the process used for production of Tabun and clarify whether any volume of solvent is included as part of the quantity of Tabun declared produced (1996 FFCD and 2002CAFCD).

- Provide credible evidence that all quantities of DMA.HCl delivered and produced have either been consumed or destroyed.

- Provide any additional documentation to support the quantities of chemicals declared destroyed through aerial bombardment. Such documentation may include bills of lading, inventory records, Iraqi reports or memos from the early 1990s that mention the quantities and identity of the chemicals.

Intentionally Blank

b. Sarin and Cyclosarin

Introduction

Sarin (GB) has the chemical name O-isopropyl methylphosphonofluoridate. Cyclosarin (GF) is a closely related chemical and has the chemical name O-cyclohexyl methylphosphonofluoridate. Sarin is a colourless liquid that gives off a colourless vapour and a weakly fruity smell. Cyclosarin is a colourless and odourless liquid when pure.

Sarin and Cyclosarin are lethal nerve agents. The toxicity of nerve agents is mainly due to their interference with the transfer of nerve impulses, which may ultimately lead to death. Sarin is highly volatile (non-persistent) and therefore, in combat use the respiratory system is its main exposure route. Cyclosarin is less volatile (more persistent) than Sarin and significant hazards exist through the respiratory system and skin exposure.

Sarin was developed in Europe in the late 1930s, and later stockpiled and weaponized. A Sarin binary weapons system based upon the mixing of two precursors, methylphosphonyl difluoride (MPF) and isopropanol, has been developed. The practical routes used to produce Sarin and Cyclosarin are identical up to the final step. The final step differs in the type of alcohol (isopropanol or cyclohexanol) that is used to produce the final agent. A mixture of Sarin and Cyclosarin results in a product having properties from both agents.

Background

In its 1996 FFCD, and in the 2002 CAFCD, Iraq declared that it carried out R&D work on several compounds that are closely related to Sarin. However, Iraq declared that only Sarin and Cyclosarin were produced on an industrial-scale and weaponized. Iraq declared that, during the period 1984 to 1990, 795 tonnes of Sarin-type agents (GB, GF and a mixture of GB/GF) were produced. According to Iraq, approximately 732 tonnes of these agents were weaponized in aerial bombs, rocket and missile warheads. Iraq further declared that about 650 tonnes were consumed, during the period 1985 to 1988 and 35 tonnes were destroyed through aerial bombardment during the Gulf War. Iraq destroyed 127 tonnes of Sarin-type agents under UNSCOM supervision, including 76 tonnes in bulk and 51 tonnes from munitions. The figure of weaponized agent was based on an estimate of the average payloads of munitions and the quantity of agents produced represents crude quantities. Therefore, the figures given here of agent produced and their subsequent disposition do not precisely balance.

In addition, Iraq declared that 1024 aerial bombs and 34 missile warheads were filled with alcohols (isopropanol and cyclohexanol) in 1990, as a crude type of binary system for Sarin-type agents. This binary-type system involved filling a munition with alcohol and then manually adding the other precursor (MPF) just prior to the munition being required. Iraq destroyed 337 alcohol-filled aerial bombs and 14 alcohol-filled missile warheads under UNSCOM supervision. UNSCOM was able to verify the unilateral destruction of 527 alcohol-filled aerial bombs and 20 alcohol-filled missile warheads through documentary evidence and observation of remnants. UNSCOM has reported that remnants consistent with 160 aerial bombs that Iraq declared as destroyed during the Gulf War were seen but the circumstances of destruction were not fully verified.

Discrepancies in the accounting of the Sarin-type agents declared as remaining in 1991 include about 4,800 rocket warheads and 12 aerial bombs filled with these agents, which constitutes about 40 tonnes of Sarin-type agents.

Iraq has declared that it carried out experiments on true binary weapons systems using artillery shells and rockets between 1983 and 1990. These binary weapons systems involved the precursors MPF and alcohol being kept separate in the munition. The physical forces associated with the firing of the weapon cause the precursors to mix and react with one another during flight. This work was carried out at Muthana State Establishment (MSE) and the Technical Research Centre (TRC). Iraq further declared that, while in 1989 and 1990 it had obtained some encouraging results, they were not reliable enough to warrant a move to the production stage. Iraq has provided documentary evidence that details the successful testing of a binary munition for Sarin in 1989, in a report of the TRC *"On the progress of research into Binary Chemical Weapons"*, in conjunction with MSE. Further information about Iraq's work on a binary weapon for Sarin was obtained from documents from the Haidar farm, and from interviews carried out with Iraqi personnel.

Iraq declared that it had used two methods to produce all of its Sarin-type agents. From 1984 to 1987, Sarin was produced at a dedicated plant at the Samarra site of MSE by reacting isopropanol with a mixture of two precursors known as methylphosphonyl dichloride (MPC) and MPF. From 1988, Sarin-type agents were produced at a multi-purpose plant at MSE in addition to the dedicated plant, by the reaction of the appropriate alcohol(s) with MPF. The precursors MPC and MPF were ultimately produced from imported precursors. According to documents provided by Iraq, by the end of 1990 the Samarra site was producing Sarin-type agents at the rate of 1 tonne per day.

The production plants declared by Iraq to have been involved in Sarin-type agents production were found by UNSCOM to be damaged by aerial bombardment during the Gulf war. Remaining chemical process equipment from these plants was subsequently destroyed by Iraq under UNSCOM supervision.

Some precursors that can be used for the production of Sarin-type agents, which were declared by Iraq as having been destroyed through aerial bombardment during the Gulf War (MPF, thionyl chloride and cyclohexanol) or lost due to improper storage (phosphorus trichloride), could not be fully verified by UNSCOM. Others (hydrogen fluoride (HF) and cyclohexanol) were returned to Iraq for civilian use, under UNSCOM monitoring.

According to documents discovered by UNSCOM in Iraq, the purity of Sarin-type agents produced by Iraq were on average below 60%, and dropped below Iraq's established quality control acceptance level of 40% by purity some 3 to 12 months after production.

Assessment

Sarin-type agents constituted a significant part of Iraq's CW arsenal - about 20% of all CW agents that Iraq declared it had produced - and thus an extensive amount of experience and know-how was gathered during production.

There is no evidence that any bulk Sarin-type agents remain in Iraq - gaps in accounting of these agents are related to Sarin-type agents weaponized in rocket warheads and aerial bombs. Based on the documentation found by UNSCOM during inspections in Iraq, Sarin-type agents produced by Iraq were largely of low quality and as such, degraded shortly after production. Therefore, with respect to the unaccounted for weaponized Sarin-type agents, it is unlikely that they would still be viable today.

The short lifetime of the Sarin-type agents produced was one reason why, in 1988, Iraq switched to a binary-type system. Using this system, Sarin-type agents would not be produced until shortly before required, thus the quality of the agent at the time of use would be much higher than if it had been produced and stored for a long period. Accounting for all munitions filled with alcohol has been verified by UNSCOM. However, questions remained with regard to the manner of the destruction of 160 aerial bombs that Iraq declared as having been destroyed during the Gulf War. These questions may have implications on the accounting of aerial bombs filled with biological agents.

In the absence of further documentation, it cannot be ascertained whether Iraq developed its true binary weapons system for Sarin into large-scale production of binary artillery shells and rockets. To help resolve this issue, Iraq should identify all facilities (in addition to MSE and TRC) that had been involved in production/modification of artillery shells and rockets as true binary weapons. In addition, Iraq should also provide clarification of all details concerning its design for binary weapons systems.

To produce Sarin-type agents, Iraq must have the key precursor MPC as well as hydrogen fluoride (HF) and alcohols. No MPC has been declared or noted during inspections. The alcohols are widely available and have legitimate civilian uses in Iraq. Some 300 tonnes of HF was declared stored at the Arab Detergent Company (ARADET) in December 2002. This represents a significant increase from the amount declared stored there in 1988.

UNSCOM could not fully verify Iraq's accounting for precursors it had acquired for the production of Sarin-type agents due to the manner in which they were destroyed and stored. Iraq may have retained imported chemicals to produce MPC, which is stable if properly stored. Such imported chemicals, thionyl chloride and phosphorus trichloride (PCl_3) (if redistilled), may be viable after years in storage. Documentary evidence and the properties of PCl_3, support to some extent Iraq's assertion that the chemical was lost during storage. However, it cannot be excluded that Iraq has retained some portion of the 1772 tonnes UNSCOM could not account for. The import of thionyl chloride and PCl_3 became problematic for Iraq, from 1988 onwards, due to export/import restrictions introduced by the Australia Group. Thionyl chloride and PCl_3 were subsequently included in the UN export/import monitoring lists.

To UNMOVIC's knowledge, the only precursors for Sarin-type agent production that Iraq may have been capable of producing indigenously (although no such production had been declared) were cyclohexanol and thionyl chloride, as the starting materials for production of these precursors are available in Iraq. While the specific chemical process equipment required to construct such plants could be obtained by removing them from various facilities in Iraq, to UNMOVIC's knowledge, there is no such plant. Therefore, unless precursors remain from Iraq's CW programme before the Gulf War, or are clandestinely acquired since then, Iraq would not possess all of the chemicals required to produce Sarin-type agents. Iraq would also need to use "corrosion resistant" process equipment for some processes involved in this production sequence. The bottleneck for Sarin-type agent production would then be the limited amount of such process equipment available to Iraq.

Assuming improvements in its quality control and process to produce the agent, it is possible that Iraq today has the capability to produce Sarin-type agents of a storable quality. If not, Iraq might instead produce readily storable precursors such as MPC, which can be used for Sarin production when needed. However, no evidence of precursors has so far been observed by UNMOVIC inspection teams.

Actions that Iraq could take to help resolve the issue

- Present any outstanding quantities of PCl_3, or provide credible evidence that all quantities imported have been consumed, destroyed or spoiled.

- Identify all facilities, in addition to MSE and TRC, involved in production/modification of munitions (artillery shells, rockets, etc.) into true binary weapons.

- Explain with credible evidence, all details regarding the design for binary weapons munitions.

- Provide credible evidence to support the declared quantities of thionylchloride imported, produced and destroyed through armed action, explaining how more was destroyed by UNSCOM than declared available.

- Provide any additional documentation to support the quantities of chemicals declared destroyed through aerial bombardment. Such documentation may include bills of lading, inventory records, Iraqi reports or memos from the early 1990s that mention the quantities and identity of the chemicals.

c. Mustard

Introduction

In military terminology, the common names "Mustard" or "Mustard Gas" refer to a specific family of chemical warfare agents comprising a variety of compounds that are similar in chemical structure. Sulphur Mustard, bis(2-chloroethyl)sulphide, is one member of this family of chemicals. Sulphur Mustard, an oily liquid, has a characteristic garlic smell and yellow to dark-brown colour.

Sulphur Mustard is a systemic poison that affects all human tissues. It is a strong blistering agent when in contact with the skin and lethal when inhaled. Due to its low volatility, it is a persistent CW agent.

Sulphur Mustard was first synthesized and identified in 1854, and later became one of the most important chemical warfare agents. Despite a century of research, there is still no antidote against it. This is one of the reasons why it is still considered to be one of the most important chemical warfare agents.

There are two major synthetic routes for the production of Sulphur Mustard. The first one includes thiodiglycol and a chlorinating agent, and the second involves ethylene and sulphur chloride. Both these synthetic routes lead to the same principal chemical, but with different composition of by-products.

Background

Of the total of 3,950 tonnes of CW agents declared produced during the period 1982 to 1990, 2,850 tonnes were Sulphur Mustard. According to Iraq, 2,443 tonnes of this Mustard were weaponized in artillery projectiles and aerial bombs. In the 1996 FFCD, and in the 2002 CAFCD, Iraq further declared that 2070 tonnes of Mustard were consumed from 1983 to1988 and 100 tonnes were discarded during production. Iraq destroyed 596 tonnes of Mustard under UNSCOM supervision: 295 tonnes in bulk and 301 tonnes from munitions.

The uncertainties in the accounting of Mustard declared as remaining in 1991 include up to 550 artillery projectiles and up to 450 aerial bombs filled with this agent, which would constitute up to about 80 tonnes of Mustard. However, based on a document recently received from Iraq, this quantity could be substantially higher.

Iraq did not provide complete documentation on the production and disposition of Mustard for the entire period of its production, weaponization and consumption, which is what would be required to assess the accuracy of the declared remaining quantities in 1999. Nonetheless, Iraq provided some records on the production and weaponization of CW agents for the years 1987 and 1988. These records support Iraq's declarations on Mustard production and weaponization for these two years. However, the record of the consumption of chemical munitions, including those filled with Mustard, contained in the Air Force document recently handed over to UNMOVIC, does not support Iraq's declarations on the consumption of these munitions during the period 1983 to 1988.

Iraq declared that all its Mustard had been produced from imported thiodiglycol, thionyl chloride and phosphorus trichloride at a dedicated production plant located at the Samarra site of the Muthanna State Establishment. According to the documents provided by Iraq, by the end of 1990, the Samarra site was able to produce Mustard at a rate of 10 tonnes per day. UNSCOM found the declared Mustard production plant had been heavily damaged by aerial bombardment during the Gulf War. Remaining chemical process equipment from its dedicated plant was destroyed by Iraq under UNSCOM supervision. Iraq declared that significant quantities of precursors for Mustard production were either destroyed through aerial bombardment during the Gulf War (thiodiglycol and thionyl chloride) or lost due to improper storage (phosphorus trichloride). UNSCOM was not able to fully verify these declarations.

Iraq studied other alternative routes for the production of Sulphur Mustard from locally available materials. According to the documents received from Iraq, it had considered to produce Mustard using another process that involved the starting materials ethylene, sulphur and chlorine. However, UNSCOM did not find evidence suggesting that this process had actually been used by Iraq on an industrial scale, most likely because the process it had followed was somewhat simpler and an adequate supply of precursors was available.

From multiple sources of evidence, UNSCOM determined that Iraq was able to produce good quality Sulphur Mustard, suitable for long-term storage. According to UNSCOM, while there were no recorded problems in storing bulk agents, Iraq's documents referred to many cases of leakage of aerial bombs filled with Mustard, due to the growing internal pressure inside munitions, caused by degradation of the agent. UNMOVIC analysed the contents of artillery shells that had been stored for at least twelve years. The results revealed that the shells still contained high purity Sulphur Mustard.

Assessment

Production of high quality Mustard was achieved through the acquisition of high quality starting materials, use of high quality chemical process equipment and practical experience gained by Iraqi personnel over several years of continuous Mustard production. Judging by the quantities produced, weaponized and used, Mustard constituted an important part (about 70%) of Iraq's CW arsenal.

There is much evidence, including documents provided by Iraq and information collected by UNSCOM, to suggest that most quantities of Mustard remaining in 1991, as declared by Iraq, were destroyed under UNSCOM supervision. The remaining gaps are related to the accounting for Mustard filled aerial bombs and artillery projectiles. There are 550 Mustard filled shells and up to 450 mustard filled aerial bombs unaccounted for since 1998. The mustard filled shells account for a couple of tonnes of agent while the aerial bombs account for approximately 70 tonnes. According to an investigation made by the Iraqi "Depot Inspection Commission", the results of which were reported to UNMOVIC in March 2003, the discrepancy in the accounting for the mustard filled shells could be explained by the fact that Iraq had based its accounting on approximations.

The "Air Force document" recently received by UNMOVIC introduces additional uncertainty in accounting as it indicates that 6,526 fewer aerial CW bombs had been "consumed" during the Iraq Iran War. This would mean that approximately 1000 tonnes of agent (predominantly Mustard, but also Sarin and Tabun) had not consumed as previously thought. Iraq has explained that the "Air Force" document, which had been complied by one of its officers in 1995, was incomplete. According to Iraq, data on consumption of CW filled munitions positioned at three airbases was not included as the airbases had been occupied in 1991 and the records destroyed. This explanation is being reviewed by UNMOVIC. The Sulphur Mustard contained in artillery shells that had been stored for over 12 years, had been found by UNMOVIC to be still of high purity. It is possible that viable Mustard filled artillery shells and aerial bombs still remain in Iraq.

UNMOVIC cannot verify Iraq's statements that all quantities of Mustard remaining in 1991 were fully declared and destroyed, without explicit documentary evidence on its total production and disposition. Neither can UNMOVIC ascertain the completeness of the accounting for major precursors acquired by Iraq for Mustard production due to uncertainties in their disposition. With the quantities of precursors physically unaccounted for as of 1998 (about 190 tonnes thiodiglycol, 100 tonnes thionylchloride and an undeterminable portion of 1772 tonnes phosphorous trichloride PCl_3) Iraq could have the chemicals to produce limited quantities of high quality Mustard. Imported chemicals such as thionyl chloride and thiodiglycol could still be usable, if properly stored in the original manufacturer's packaging. PCl_3 may also be usable after years in storage, if redistilled.

The acquisition of the foregoing chemicals should have been difficult for Iraq from 1988 onwards due to international export/import control restrictions introduced by the Australia Group. These chemicals were subsequently included in the UN export/import monitoring list. Ethylene oxide and chloroethanol, alternative starting materials for the production of the major precursor thiodiglycol, are also on the export/import monitoring list.

Iraq does not appear to have a dedicated facility capable of producing Mustard and its key precursors. Significant modifications would be required to convert existing chemical production facilities for this purpose. Iraq would have to utilize "corrosion resistant" equipment (for the processing of the chlorinating agent), which it possesses in limited quantities. However, Iraq had some items of dual-use equipment distributed all over the country at legitimate facilities that could be removed and assembled for the construction of a dedicated Mustard production plant.

Iraq is self-sufficient with respect to the availability of starting materials required for production of Mustard (i.e. ethylene, sulphur and chlorine) from its petrochemical complex and sulphur mines. Thus, Mustard would be the easiest agent for Iraq to produce indigenously. While no industrial-scale production was ever known to have taken place using this process, this would be the most likely choice for Iraq. A sulphur chloride plant would have to be constructed, which should not be an obstacle as Iraq had done so in the past to indigenously produce thionyl chloride.

It is unlikely that remaining gaps in the material balance of Mustard produced and weaponized from 1982 to 1990 can be solved without Iraq providing additional evidence to support its declarations. Such evidence may include storage inventories, and production, destruction and consumption records.

Actions that Iraq could take to help resolve the issue

- Present any quantities of Mustard filled 155 mm artillery shells and aerial bombs or provide credible evidence of their destruction.

- Present any remaining quantities of phosphorous trichloride, or provide credible evidence that all quantities imported have been consumed, destroyed or spoiled.

- Present any remaining quantities of thiodiglycol, or provide credible evidence that all quantities imported have been consumed, destroyed or spoiled.

- Present any remaining quantities of chloroethanol, or provide credible evidence that all quantities imported have been consumed or destroyed.

- Present complete documentation from all military organizations, detailing their consumption of CW special munitions.

- Provide credible evidence to support the declared quantities of thinoylchloride imported, produced and destroyed through armed action, explaining how more was destroyed by UNSCOM than declared available.

- Provide the name and present location of the officer who produced the Air Force document.

d. VX

Introduction

The term VX is used to refer to O-ethyl S-[2-(diisopropylamino)ethyl] methylphosphonothiolate, which is one member of a class of chemicals known as V-agents that have similar chemical structures. VX is a colourless and odourless liquid when pure; with impurities, it resembles motor oil in appearance and has a smell reminiscent of rotten fish.

VX is a lethal nerve agent and is one of the most toxic known CW agents. Nerve agents primarily interfere with the transfer of nerve impulses, which may ultimately lead to death. VX is readily absorbed through the skin, which is the main exposure route in combat use. VX is not very volatile and is, therefore, considered a persistent CW agent.

The first chemicals belonging to the V-agent class were synthesized and identified in the period 1952 to 1953. Shortly after, systematic investigation of this class of chemicals began. As a result, VX was developed and weaponized in both unitary and binary configuration. There are several synthetic routes for the production of VX, although those that yield high quality VX are longer and/or more sophisticated than for most other CW agents.

Background

Until 1995, Iraq had only admitted to having produced lab-scale quantities (grammes) of VX. Thus, in its March 1995 FFCD, Iraq declared the production of 0.26 tonnes of VX using readily available pilot-scale equipment at the R&D department of the Samara site of the Muthanna State Establishment (MSE). However, in its declarations, Iraq declared that, in total, 3.9 tonnes of VX had been produced at industrial-scale plants at MSE.

Iraq declared that initial laboratory experiments on V-agents had taken place around 1975-76, but that the first serious research work had only started in 1985. This work focused on VX in particular. By late 1987, a synthetic method had been selected, which will be referred to as "route A". A production trial using this route was carried out at one of the existing multi-purpose plants at MSE. Iraq stated that it had considered the resulting VX to be of unsatisfactory quality.

In February 1988, Iraq carried out intense research on VX to come up with a better method. This included work with stabilizers, which are chemicals used to preserve the quality of the VX produced. In March 1988, Iraq developed another method to produce VX, which will be referred to as "route B". That same month, a production trial was carried out at a second multi-purpose plant at MSE. In the following weeks, a third plant at MSE was specifically modified for the production of VX using route B. During May 1988, three production trials were carried out at this plant. The resulting VX, as well as that produced in March, was analyzed over a period of time and found to degrade rapidly. There is documentary evidence to support Iraq's declarations on all the aforementioned events that occurred between 1985 and the end of May 1988.

Iraq declared that, 2.4 tonnes of VX had been produced in the five production trials that had taken place between late 1987 and the end of May 1988. Iraq declared that it had weaponized 0.4 tonnes of VX in three aerial bombs for the purpose of corrosion and stability tests and noted that an artillery rocket was filled with VX to study corrosion and stability. Iraq further declared that all the VX produced between late 1987 and the end of May 1988, had been destroyed later in 1988 because it had degraded. There is documentary evidence to support that MSE had filled three aerial bombs with VX during 1988. Other documents indicate that the quantities of VX declared to have been produced between late 1987 and the end of May 1988 are approximately correct. UNSCOM sampled locations where Iraq stated it had disposed of VX. The sampling could not determine the quantities of destroyed VX that had been discarded, but it did reveal the presence of degradation products of VX and a degradation product of a chemical known to be a stabilizer for VX.

In April 1988, Iraq conducted research on the stability of the semi-final product (which Iraq refers to as *"dibis"*), obtained using route B. Iraq apparently reasoned that, if this precursor was stable, strategic stocks could be built up and converted to VX when required, thus circumventing the instability problems associated with storage of the final VX product. Data from Iraq's research showed that after eight months of storage, there was practically no decrease in the stability of dibis. Consequently, the research department recommended that dibis be produced in quantity as a strategic source of VX. This is confirmed from documentary evidence and interviews conducted with Iraq. Iraq also declared work on a dibis based binary weapons system.

Other research carried out in 1988 includes work on two more synthetic routes to produce VX. These routes will be referred to as "route C" and "route D". Route D was described by Iraqi researchers as *"the optimum method for obtaining high purity and yield. However, its procedure requires a longer time."* The researchers noted that there is a *"production problem concerning the application of this research"* because it involves *"a process that requires special technology not available in the production sites"*. Route C was referred to as a method of producing VX directly or as a binary weapons system. Work on the application of route C as a binary weapons system continued in 1989. The research got as far as tests *"in cooperation with the section on munitions research to set up a technique that fits the munition specific to the binary system."* Although Iraq declared a small amount of this work in its 1996 FFCD, and provided some more details in subsequent letters and interviews, information of this work has mostly been derived from documents obtained from the Haidar Farm.

Iraq declared that, in April 1990, it had produced a quantity of dibis using route B. It appears that this dibis was later converted into 1.5 tonnes of VX. Iraq declared that the resulting VX degraded rapidly and was destroyed in the summer of 1991. As with VX destroyed in 1988, UNSCOM took samples but was unable to determine the exact quantities of VX that had been declared destroyed by Iraq on either occasion. Iraq has provided practically no evidence to support its VX related activities, for the year of 1990, stating that all such information had been destroyed. To support this latter assertion, Iraq provided UNSCOM with handwritten notes that recorded the issuance of oral instructions, *inter alia*, to destroy any evidence indicating the presence of VX and a key precursor of VX, *"Iraqi choline"*.

In its declarations, Iraq supports its statement that, by the end of 1990, there was no VX remaining from its past CW activities, by providing the following documents: a memorandum listing munitions, final agents and other materials at MSE, as well as at various stores and munitions depots as of 18 December 1990; an inventory of the final and intermediate substances stored at MSE as of 31 December 1990; a memorandum listing munitions that MSE had ready for removal as of 31 December 1990; a memorandum listing munitions and final agents available at MSE as of 5 January 1991. No VX or dibis is mentioned in any of these documents. However, two VX precursors ("Iraqi choline" and "MPS") are present on the inventory of final and intermediate substances stored at MSE, as of 31 December 1990. Iraq also provided a document from the 10th of December 1990 that reviews the *"essential activity"* carried out at MSE in that year. No achievements relating to VX are detailed, but the document mentions work on the production of the *"essential substance MPC from which VX and other agents can be prepared"*. The document also contains a handwritten annotation by Lieutenant-General Hussein Kamal directing MSE to *"concentrate on producing the intermediate substance of the nerve agents as well as on producing VX as a final product"*.

UNSCOM found that the production plant specifically modified at MSE to produce VX had been heavily damaged during the Gulf War. UNSCOM's inspection reports document that Iraq made an attempt to retain the remaining equipment from this plant by providing incorrect declarations with respect to its past use. UNSCOM subsequently determined that this equipment originated from a plant involved in VX production and the equipment was destroyed by Iraq under UNSCOM supervision in late 1997. UNSCOM also found that the two multi-purpose plants used for VX production had been completely destroyed during the Gulf War. However, UNSCOM was unable to verify the status of pilot-scale equipment declared in 1995 as having been used for VX production at the R&D department of MSE because the buildings associated with this department were heavily damaged during the Gulf War.

Iraq declared that significant quantities of precursors for VX production were destroyed through aerial bombardment during the Gulf War (thionyl chloride, phosphorus pentasulphide, diisopropyl amine and chloroethanol), lost due to improper storage (phosphorus trichloride) or destroyed by Iraq in the absence of UNSCOM inspectors (*"Iraqi choline"*). UNSCOM was not able to verify these declarations in full.

UNSCOM hosted a Technical Evaluation Meeting (TEM) attended by a number of international experts in February 1998 to discuss the issue of VX. The TEM concluded *"Iraq was capable of producing significant quantities of VX before January 1991. This may have been as much as 50 to 100 tonnes of VX, albeit of an uncertain quality."* Regarding weaponization, the team concluded it did not have sufficient information to reach any specific conclusion.

Except for the artillery rocket and three aerial bombs filled with VX for corrosion and stability tests, Iraq declared that VX had not been weaponized. However, in April/May 1998, UNSCOM took remnants of missile warheads that had been unilaterally destroyed by Iraq for analysis. The analysis showed traces of VX degradation products, and a chemical known to be a stabilizer for VX. Iraq has repeatedly denied the authenticity of these findings. In a second set of analyses (June 1988) one of the laboratories reported the presence of a degradation product of nerve agents (G- or V-agents) in one sample. (This chemical could also originate from other compounds such as precursors or, according to some experts, a detergent). Two other laboratories found no nerve agent degradation products. Documentation available to UNMOVIC suggests that Iraq, at least, had had far reaching plans to weaponize VX.

Assessment

Iraq's VX programme included extensive efforts in a number of areas such as synthetic routes, stabilizers, and binary munitions. Given Iraq's history of concealment with respect to its VX programme it cannot be excluded that it has retained some capability with regard to VX.

Iraq has pointed to original storage inventory documents as evidence that it had not weaponized VX or produced VX after April 1990. It is noted that, in addition to other indications to the contrary mentioned in this cluster, the inventory and memoranda do not provide an exhaustive list of sites where CW munitions could have been stored. It is also noted that the quantity of VX/dibis Iraq declared it had produced in 1990, and unilaterally destroyed in 1991, is not recorded in any of the storage inventory documents or memoranda provided by Iraq. This should have been recorded in the 31 December 1990 *"Inventory of Final and Intermediate Substances at MSE"*. VX is a final agent and dibis is an intermediate. The inventory records, for example, stocks of Iraqi Choline, which is a precursor required to produce dibis.

The information available to UNMOVIC at present suggests that Iraq did not carry out industrial-scale production of VX in the latter half of 1988 or in 1989. At that time there did not appear to be any military requirement for it. Research on VX did however continue, with one of its objectives being to improve its stability.

During times of war, or imminent war, it would make sense for Iraq to produce VX through route B, which involves only about half as many process steps as route D. VX produced through route B must be used relatively quickly after production (about 1 to 8 weeks), which would probably be satisfactory for wartime requirements. However, if no war were imminent or underway, it would make more sense for Iraq to produce VX that can be stabilised and stored for long periods of time until needed. Of the routes that Iraq is known to have studied at the R&D level, and obtained a fair degree of success, route D would seem to be the route of choice to produce high purity VX.

Iraq had produced high purity VX using route D in laboratory/pilot-scale equipment. Based upon the documents provided by Iraq, it is doubtful that any significant quantities of VX were produced using this route before the Gulf war. In the case of VX produced through route D, if Iraq's quality control and process technology has been improved, then Iraq may be able to stabilise the product (Iraq informed UNSCOM that it had not attempted to stabilise VX produced through route D). VX thus stabilised, may be weaponised and stored, or stored as bulk agent. VX produced through route D, and stabilized, could still be viable today.

As regards binary weapons, it is not certain how far Iraq progressed using route C or dibis without further documentation. Based upon its absence from MSE's report of the essential activity carried out in 1990, it is unlikely that the work progressed very far up until that time.

It would have made no sense for Iraq to conceal a programme that in its estimation was a failure and in which it had no future interest. It is possible the programme was not quite the failure claimed by Iraq or Iraq wished to retain some capability to restart the programme in the future, for example through the retention of key precursors and know-how.

The major remaining issue relating to Iraq's VX production capability is the fact that there are significant discrepancies in the accounting for all the key precursors (phosphorus trichloride, thionyl chloride, phosphorus pentasulphide and "Iraqi Choline") required to produce VX. A few other chemicals are required to produce VX, using any of the routes Iraq focused on in the past, these are however readily available.

The only precursors useful for VX production that Iraq was known to be indigenously capable of producing were absolute ethanol and possibly, thionyl chloride. In the case of thionyl chloride, the starting materials and know-how were available. While the chemical process equipment to construct plants for VX, or its precursors, could have been obtained by removing equipment from various facilities in Iraq, no such plants have been identified by UNMOVIC.

To measure the quantity of VX unilaterally destroyed in 1990, Iraq in February 2003 proposed a procedure to quantify the discarded VX. Iraq also suggested a method to measure the quantity of "Iraqi Choline" unilaterally destroyed by Iraq in 1991. UNMOVIC has held an initial round of discussions with Iraq on this subject and will continue to assess the feasibility of the proposal. There are some concerns, however, that the accounting cannot be done with a reasonable margin of error. Furthermore, even if quantification of the choline could be achieved, it would not resolve the issue of potential retention of precursors for VX production. There are significant unaccounted for quantities of the two choline precursors diisopropylamine (DIPA) and chloroethanol. With respect to VX, UNMOVIC has pointed out that the issue is not whether 1.5 tonnes of VX was dumped at the site but rather if the VX produced in 1990 was of storable quality, i.e. of high purity and stabilized.

Actions that Iraq could take to help resolve the issue
- Present any outstanding quantities of phosphorous trichloride and phosphorous pentasulphide, or provide credible evidence that all quantities imported have been consumed, destroyed or spoiled.

- Present any quantity of the immediate precursors for "Iraqi choline", diisopropylamine (DIPA) and chloroethanol, or provide credible evidence that all quantities imported and produced have been consumed, destroyed or spoiled.

- Present all documents and other evidence relating to work on VX development (including concepts of use, production, R&D, scaling up, stabilization, destruction orders and decision to abandon the VX program).

- In connection with Iraq's assertion that it had been unable to weaponize VX, explain with credible evidence 1) why the VX it declared produced in 1990 and unilaterally destroyed in 1991, was not indicated in the 1990 MSE storage inventory, 2) why a nerve agent degradation product was found on a swipe sample from a warhead by one laboratory.

- Present credible evidence for the finding of a VX stabilizer spread over a large area and depth indicative of quantities far in excess of the few grammes of VX stabilizer Iraq declared it had used.

- Present credible evidence that there were no more than 2 batches of VX produced from the second half of 1988 up to the beginning of the Gulf war.

- Present documentary information on munitions designed to be filled with VX, including binary-types.

- Provide credible evidence to support the declared quantities of thionylchloride imported, produced and destroyed through armed action, explaining how more was destroyed by UNSCOM than declared available.

e. Major Chemical Process Equipment

Introduction

Major chemical process equipment used in Iraq in the production of CW agents include reactors, condensers, heat exchangers, distillation and absorption columns, scrubbers and filling equipment. All commercially available construction materials used in the chemical industry have some level of corrosion resistance. However, the chemical process equipment referred to below is for the most part highly "corrosion resistant". This term refers to equipment where all surfaces that come into direct contact with the chemical being processed are constructed from high nickel alloys, ceramic, glass, ferrosilicons, titanium alloys, tantalum alloys, zirconium alloys, graphite, fluoropolymers or silver.

Production of chemical warfare agents as referred to below, relates to all the steps from raw material or imported chemical to intermediate and final precursors through to final chemical warfare agent. Some of the chemical processes involved in the production of CW agents require process equipment constructed from "corrosion resistant" equipment. While less corrosion resistant equipment could be used for most, if not all, CW agent chemical processes, such equipment would wear out fairly quickly when used for some of the chemical processes involved in the agent production. The civilian chemical industry uses equipment constructed from all types of construction materials, including those that are "corrosion resistant". Hence, chemical process equipment that is suitable for CW agent production is also suitable for civilian chemical production and vice-versa – it is for this reason that such equipment is considered to be dual-use equipment.

Background

Security Council resolution 687 (1991) called for the destruction, removal or rendering harmless, inter alia, of all Iraq's research, development, support and manufacturing facilities related to CW activity. Iraq declared, between 1991 and 1997, primarily in its 1995 and 1996 CW FFCDs, thousands of pieces of chemical process equipment at facilities involved in CW agent production. In the course of on-site inspections, UNSCOM found that almost all Iraq's declared CW agent production facilities had either been completely destroyed or heavily damaged during the Gulf War. Due to the extent of destruction, it was not possible to verify the fate of all declared chemical process equipment. Therefore, UNSCOM appears to have focused on verification of the disposition of only major pieces of chemical process equipment.

UNSCOM documents indicate that it was able to locate about 380 of an approximate total of 450 pieces of major chemical process equipment declared by Iraq. (It is understood UNSCOM considered, that due to its specifications, this equipment was critical for manufacturing of CW agents.) Some 100 pieces of the declared equipment that survived the Gulf War were destroyed by Iraq under UNSCOM supervision between 1992 and 1994. There were about 80 pieces that UNSCOM observed damaged and considered unusable. In addition, there were approximately 200 pieces of dual-use equipment located by UNSCOM, which Iraq claimed had not been procured or used for CW agent production. On the basis of this assertion, UNSCOM initially released the equipment for distribution by Iraq to various civilian facilities where the equipment was placed under monitoring. However, it is understood that, in 1996, UNSCOM determined that these pieces had been procured and used in CW agent production. Consequently, in 1997, Iraq destroyed all these pieces of equipment under UNSCOM supervision. With regard to the approximately 70 pieces of equipment not specifically identified (from the 450 pieces of major chemical process equipment declared by Iraq), UNSCOM has recorded that it observed tens of pieces of equipment buried under debris of buildings destroyed during the Gulf War. It is understood that an exact numerical accounting of these pieces could not be achieved because of the state of destruction. However, UNSCOM found other evidence (such as imagery) supporting Iraq's claims that the equipment indeed was destroyed inside production buildings. There were 29 pieces of equipment, according to Iraq's 2002 CAFCD, excavated from those production buildings, and moved to storages in 1999 and 2000, in order to protect them from stealing.

On the basis of supplier information, UNSCOM also found that, in addition to the above chemical process equipment, Iraq's CW agent production organization procured 18 pieces of major chemical process equipment for use by other organizations not directly involved in Iraq's CW programme. UNSCOM located this equipment and placed it under monitoring after Iraq demonstrated that the equipment had not been intended for CW use.

In 1997, Iraq orally informed UNSCOM of the existence of a further 16 pieces of glass pilot-scale equipment. UNSCOM determined that the equipment had been procured for Iraq's CW agent production and Iraq was requested to provide an explanation. Iraq then declared and provided, for physical verification, an additional 181 pieces of glass pilot-scale equipment. These pieces of glass pilot-scale equipment, which were unused, had been removed from Iraq's CW agent production facility prior to the beginning of UNSCOM inspections. These pieces of newly declared equipment, totaling 187 pieces, were destroyed by Iraq, under UNSCOM supervision, in late 1997. The fact that a number of dual-use equipment procured for CW purposes only became known in 1997 decreased UNSCOM's confidence in Iraq's accounting of chemical process equipment and led UNSCOM to address *"verification of the completeness of declarations provided by Iraq on the material balance of CW production equipment removed from the Muthanna State Establishment prior to the UNSCOM inspections"* as a priority issue.

While UNSCOM had verified most of the major chemical process items declared by Iraq, it noted that Iraqi documentation on financial accounts suggested that more equipment might have been supplied to Iraq than been declared. A document analysed by UNMOVIC from the Haidar Farm, detailing financial transactions of Iraq's CW agent production facility, shows a credit balance of 738,145 Iraqi Dinars (at that time, equivalent to about US$ 2.2 million) with fifteen foreign companies as of 31 December 1988. Some of these foreign companies are known to have supplied Iraq with chemical process equipment. UNSCOM noted that *"...the verification of equipment from the latest contracts, delivered to Iraq in 1988 and 1989, was not possible due to the lack of information from the foreign suppliers"*.

Assessment
It is possible that, since Iraq had a credit balance with some foreign suppliers at the end of 1988, some equipment was delivered sometime before the beginning of the Gulf War. The significance of the aforementioned is to a certain extent diminished by the fact that there are several hundred major pieces of "corrosion resistant" chemical process equipment, procured for civilian purposes

by non-CW agent production facilities and located at these facilities. While used for legitimate non-CW agent related purposes, these pieces of chemical process equipment are of the same type as those used by Iraq for producing CW agents. By using existing production equipment, from various civilian chemical facilities, it is theoretically possible to assemble a CW production plant. The usefulness of such a plant would be dependent on the availability of the CW agent precursors. The production units inspected so far by UNMOVIC cannot produce key precursors or CW agents in their present configuration.

An absence of such "corrosion resistant" chemical process equipment would place limitations on reaction processes involving fluorination (and, therefore, Sarin & Soman production). Such dual-use equipment would also be preferable for reaction processes requiring heat and chlorinating agents (and, therefore, the preferred equipment for most of the Mustard and nerve agents). Iraq has the capability to produce stainless steel and carbon steel chemical process equipment, and the import of the raw materials (stainless steel and carbon steel) is not subject to notification under the UN export/import mechanism. However, Iraq is currently unable to line such equipment with glass or fluoropolymers, and is thus unable to make them "corrosion resistant". Iraq has the capability to indigenously manufacture most pieces of "corrosion resistant" chemical process equipment from metal sheets. The bottleneck would be the fact that it has a limited number of "corrosion resistant" metal sheets. Iraq is unable to produce these sheets itself and therefore has to import them. The import of such sheets is subject to notification under the export/import mechanism. According to its 2002 semi-annual declaration, Iraq did use some of the sheets it had in storage and machined these into equipment. These equipment are now under monitoring.

A key item of chemical process equipment is a chemical reactor, and there are limited numbers of these available in Iraq. According to Iraq's 2002 semi-annual declaration, some reactors have been excavated from the Samarra site of Muthanna State Establishment (MSE) and moved to storage. These reactors are however in various states of disrepair. Other types of equipment, recovered from the Samarra site, could possibly be repaired or salvaged for the "corrosion resistant" alloys they are manufactured from to be subsequently machined into new processing equipment.

In its recent semi annual declaration, and in its 2002 CAFCD, Iraq has declared that it has repaired 3 pieces of production equipment it previously destroyed under UNSCOM supervision. This was further explained in a document handed over to UNMOVIC in February 2003.

Actions that Iraq could take to help resolve the issue
- Provide credible evidence of the outcome of the 738,145 Dinar credit balance with foreign suppliers in 1988.

- Provide an inventory, with credible evidence, for all buried equipment at the Samarra site of MSE.

Intentionally Blank

f. Soman

Introduction

Soman (or GD) is the common name used to refer to the CW agent O-Pinacolyl methylphosphonofluoridate. Soman is a colourless liquid with a fruity odour; with impurities it has an odour of camphor. Soman is essentially a Sarin-type agent and therefore closely related to Sarin (GB) and Cyclosarin (GF), with respect to production technology and precursors. The practical routes used to produce Soman are identical to those for Sarin except for the final step. The final step differs in the type of alcohol that is used to produce the agent (pinacolyl alcohol instead of isopropanol or cyclohexanol).

Soman is a lethal CW nerve agent. The toxicity of nerve agents arises mainly from their interference with the transfer of nerve impulses, which may ultimately lead to death. Atropine administered rapidly after exposure can help in the recovery of individuals exposed to most nerve agents. However, atropine is ineffective against Soman - special treatment not generally available on the battlefield is required.

Background

In the 1996 FFCD, and in the 2002 CAFCD, Iraq declared that, in 1985, it had carried out work on the synthesis of Soman at the R&D level. It further declared that some R&D on the synthesis of the essential precursor pinacolyl alcohol had been carried out between 1987 and 1988. Different degrees of purity and yields had been obtained for the various steps in this multi-step synthesis. A purity and yield of 90% was reported for the final step in the synthesis from the penultimate precursor, pinacolone. The Iraqi declarations, also indicate that some of the work on the synthesis and identification of pinacolyl alcohol had been done by the Muthanna State Establishment (MSE), the main CW production facility, in cooperation with the Petrochemical Research Centre (PRC). Iraq declared that many attempts to import pinacolyl alcohol in bulk had been made in 1985 and 1988 to 1989. The failure of these attempts, along with the absence of an antidote for Soman poisoning, were cited by Iraq in its FFCD as reasons for stopping work on this agent.

A document from the Haidar Farm that records laboratory reports from 1987 notes that Soman production was easy, except for the preparation of pinacolyl alcohol. It also mentions the fact that atropine does not help in treatment of Soman poisoning – a fact that the report considered to be noteworthy for cases where an enemy possessed large quantities of atropine.

Another document from the Haidar Farm reporting the results of research – it is undated but appears to be from the second half of 1988 – remarks that *"[t]he substance* [pinacolyl alcohol] *was prepared at the lab and pre-industrial* [pilot-scale] *levels and another method is being studied to determine which is the best method in order to design a* [pincolyl alcohol] *production unit."* The 1996 FFCD describes a second method of producing pinacolyl alcohol carried out in 1988 with a purity of only 1-2%.

The other key precursors for Soman are methylphosphonyl dichloride (MPC) and methylphosphonyl difluoride (MPF). About 39 tonnes of MPF that Iraq declared remaining after the Gulf War could not be accounted for by UNSCOM. UNSCOM stated that evidence of destruction of the MPF had been observed but that a proper accounting had not been possible because of the manner of destruction (unilaterally and through aerial bombardment).

In one of the inspections prior to 1994, UNSCOM found an Iraqi document which detailed a meeting (29 July 1990) between Ministries involved in Iraq's CW programme. According to the document, the meeting had been convened to discuss strategies to deal with the acquisition of certain chemicals of a critical character, evidently required for the CW programme. The chemicals were on a list, which appears to be the Australia Group list, and the notations for the penultimate and final precursors unique to Soman production are as follows, *"Substance No28* [pinacolyl alcohol]*: Its use is very limited and it is not used in Iraq..."* and *"Substances...39* [pinacolone] *are not needed."*

Assessment

The information currently available to UNMOVIC suggests that Iraq's declarations on its Soman-related work are not complete. This assessment is based primarily on the fact that one of the Haidar Farm documents reports that a key precursor unique to Soman production, pinacolyl alcohol, was prepared at the *"pre-industrial* [pilot-scale] *stage"*. Iraq has not satisfactorily explained what this work entailed or the quantity or quality of the precursor prepared. Additionally, the laboratory reports of 1987 suggest that Iraq had considered the absence of an antidote for Soman as a military advantage.

Iraq's declarations, documents from the Haidar Farm, and documents submitted by Iraq to support its FFCD and CAFCD, suggest that Iraq could produce pinacolyl alcohol in the laboratory with reasonable success, sufficient enough for it to have attempted to produce it at the pre-industrial (pilot-scale) level. Iraq has not, however, given precise information as to how successful the pilot-scale production trials had been. If the trials had been an outright success, it would be expected that immediate production trials would have ensued, rather than an investigation into another method to see if better results could be obtained. More information is required on this matter.

Production of pinacolyl alcohol from its immediate precursor pinacolone is commonly held to be relatively easy. However, the preparation of pinacolone in industrial quantities from readily available substances such as acetone is not so straightforward. Iraq declared that it could produce pinacolyl alcohol in R&D quantities and there is no evidence of industrial scale production of this chemical in Iraq. However, the extent of Iraq's achievement at the pilot-scale level is unclear.

The precursors pinacolone and pinacolyl alcohol are both on the UN export/import list of normally prohibited chemicals (list B). Additionally, there is very little commercial trade in either of these chemicals – what legitimate trade exists is strictly controlled by national and international agreements.

The other key Soman precursors are MPC and MPF. On the basis of the documents available to UNMOVIC and the observations reported in UNSCOM's inspection reports, there is no evidence of MPC remaining in Iraq. It is noted that the precursor MPF is very corrosive and difficult to store. Iraq destroyed 20 tonnes of MPF under UNSCOM supervision around 1992. Photographs of the cans that contained the chemical indicate that they had been stored under poor conditions and there was evidence of leakage and corrosion in a large number of the cans. There was no evidence that MPF had been specially stored and, accordingly, it can be expected that the 39 tonnes of MPF that could not be accounted for would have become unusable over the past 12 years.

Iraq produced MPC and MPF indigenously using "corrosion resistant" equipment. In practical terms, such equipment is necessary for their production, more so for MPF production than for MPC. Iraq has access to limited numbers of such "corrosion resistant" equipment located at various facilities in the country – facilities that are, to UNMOVIC's knowledge, engaged in civilian/non-prohibited activities. Early-stage precursors (phosphorus trichloride and thionyl chloride) used to produce MPC could not be fully accounted for by UNSCOM, and it is therefore possible that Iraq may have retained the ability to produce MPC in limited quantities. About 300 tonnes of the precursor (hydrogen fluoride) required to convert MPC into MPF was under monitoring in Iraq as of December 2002. Therefore, if Iraq had had the starting materials to produce MPC, it should also have been capable of producing MPF.

Iraq had trouble storing Sarin/Cyclosarin (GB and GF) for long periods of time – most of the agent found by UNSCOM after the Gulf War was of low quality. The quality of Sarin that Iraq produced was such that it would drop to below 40% purity (Iraq's minimum acceptance purity for filling munitions with the agent) 3 to 12 months after production. The same problem would have been encountered with Soman.

Soman is a persistent agent with relatively high toxicity. However, Cyclosarin, an agent that Iraq had successfully produced, has similar toxicity and persistence. Soman has the advantage that it is more difficult to treat in the field than Cyclosarin (because atropine is ineffective against Soman poisoning).

The acquisition of pinacolyl alcohol or its immediate precursor pinacolone would be a serious obstacle for Iraq. This is supported by the comments on pinacolone and pinacolyl alcohol made at the meeting of Iraq's ministries involved in its CW programme suggesting, that, as of July 1990, Iraq had lost interest in the production of pinacolyl alcohol on an industrial-scale and, by extension, Soman.

Actions that Iraq could take to help resolve the issue

- Present any outstanding quantities of phosphorous trichloride, or provide credible evidence that all quantities imported have been consumed, destroyed or spoiled.

- Present documentation or, other credible evidence, on work to indigenously produce pinacolylalcohol at the pre-industrial level.

- Provide credible evidence to support the declared quantities of thionylchloride imported, produced and destroyed through armed action, explaining how more was destroyed by UNSCOM than declared available.

- Provide any additional documentation to support the quantities of chemicals declared destroyed through aerial bombardment. Such documentation may include bills of lading, inventory records, Iraqi reports or memos from the early 1990s that mention the quantities and identity of the chemicals.

g. BZ Analogues (psychoactive compounds)

Introduction

BZ and its analogues, hereinafter collectively referred to as "BZ", are non-lethal incapacitating substances that cause psychoactive effects that prevent those exposed from performing their duties for up to three days. Symptoms of exposure include confusion and an inability to understand and follow orders. These substances are effective at extremely low dosages, usually less than 10 milligrams per individual. Victims cannot recognize their impairment. Detectors for these substances are not common. BZ analogues are solids that can be absorbed by inhalation or ingestion or, when dissolved in a solvent, through the skin. They are stable and can be dispersed as a powder or dissolved in a solvent for dispersal by aerial spraying. Modern protective masks would protect against aerosolized "BZ"

"BZ" would be appropriate for tactical use, e.g. against a field command centre. BZ is regulated and is listed in Schedule II of the Chemical Weapons Convention. It is also included as one of the items prohibited to Iraq under list B of the UN export/import mechanism.

Background

Iraq has stated that it had conducted research on the synthesis of "BZ" type hallucinogens in 1982 and 1986. Iraq also stated that it had imported "BZ" of different types from two foreign sources, and sought to determine the structures of these compounds.

Although Iraq has declared that it had not conducted any toxicological tests, a number of documents from the Haidar Farm suggest the contrary: successful tests on animals, a feasibility study for a new production unit to produce "BZ", as well as studies to weaponize these substances. While these documents point towards Iraq's intent to produce "BZ", UNSCOM did not find any evidence that such production had taken place. UNSCOM concluded that the "BZ" programme required more investigation, given the absence of sufficient information to determine the full extent of Iraq's work with the substances. UNSCOM was unable to fully address this issue before its operations in Iraq were ended.

Assessment

BZ is a stable solid and any remaining quantities would still be viable today. Possible stocks of this material could be easily hidden. However, no evidence has been found which indicates that BZ had been weaponized or produced in other than laboratory quantities. UNMOVIC's assessment is that, given the limited military utility of "BZ", Iraq would have focused its resources on more effective agents for weaponization.

Remaining issues concern what compounds/analogues Iraq studied, apart from the two imported samples it declared, and what compounds it considered for military use - there are many analogues of BZ that Iraq could have selected. Although the documents from the Haider Farm reveal that Iraq extensively studied a number of similar psychoactive compounds, the exact extent of its work on "BZ" is unclear. The documents show, however, that Iraq's declarations have not fully addressed its work in this area. Iraq should be requested to supplement its declaration with additional information that, in particular, relates to the documents on the subject from the Haidar Farm and includes the actual identities of the compounds it studied and selected.

While the precursors for the chemical referred to as BZ are on the UN export/import list, the precursors for many of its analogues are not, and some of those are dual-use items. UNMOVIC assesses that Iraq should be capable of making BZ analogues in pilot or even industrial-scale by importing precursors which are not covered by the export/import mechanism or other international regimes. However, UNMOVIC has no indication of BZ production in Iraq at pilot- or industrial- scale in the past or present.

Actions Iraq could take to help resolve the issue
- Supplement the information provided in the 1996 FFCD and 2002 CAFCD on "BZ", in particular the actual identities of the compounds it studied.

IV. BIOLOGICAL CLUSTERS

a. Anthrax

Introduction

Bacillus anthracis (anthrax) is a spore forming bacteria that is commonly found in the soil and causes disease in cattle, sheep and other animals. Humans are also highly susceptible to certain anthrax strains through inhalation and ingestion of the spores or through infection of cuts or other skin abrasions. By far the most dangerous route of infection is by inhalation and death rates in humans of untreated victims may be 90% or more, depending on the strain. Treatment by antibiotics may be effective if taken early in the course of the disease. Vaccines against some anthrax strains are also available.

Since anthrax is a disease of both animals and humans it has been well studied in a civilian context. The durability of the spores, their ease of production and their effectiveness also makes anthrax highly suited for use as a BW agent and it has, therefore, been researched and developed for military purposes by a number of countries.

Background

Iraq has declared that anthrax production was limited to 20 litres produced at Al Salman in 1989 and 8,425 litres at Al Hakam in 1990 for a total production of 8445 litres. Iraq said that no other facilities were involved and that there was no production of anthrax in 1991.

Contrary to Iraq's assertion that no other facilities had been used to produce anthrax, UNSCOM found evidence of anthrax in two fermenters and a mobile storage tank at the Foot and Mouth Disease Vaccine (FMDV) plant at Al Daura. The strain was said by UNSCOM *"to be consistent with the strain used in Iraq's BW programme"*. Two of the three pieces of equipment that had previously tested positive for anthrax were destroyed in June 1996 pursuant to resolution 687 (1991). A follow up sampling mission to FMDV in November 1996 did not detect anthrax on any remaining equipment.

UNSCOM assessed Iraq's production capability on the basis of two potentially limiting factors: equipment and growth media. UNSCOM assessed that, based on its estimate of the available equipment to the BW programme at that time, and the known capacity of such equipment, Iraq's potential production of anthrax could have been in the range of about 22,000 to 39,000 litres. UNSCOM also estimated that based on unaccounted for growth media, Iraq's potential production of anthrax could have been in the range of about 15,000 to 25,000 litres.

Iraq declared that anthrax had been filled into 50 R-400 aerial bombs and five Al Hussein warheads. In addition, Iraq stated that, just prior to the Gulf War, it had been developing a BW agent spray system by modifying aircraft auxiliary fuel tanks (drop tanks). Initially, Iraq stated that the tanks were to be filled with anthrax and that they were tested with an anthrax simulant, but later said it was possible the fill could have included other agents. Twelve such tanks were planned, but only four were said to have been completed by the end of the Gulf War and the system was said not to have been deployed.

Iraq's account of the number of bombs and warheads filled with anthrax has changed on several occasions. All biological bombs and warheads filled with BW agent were said by Iraq to have been unilaterally destroyed in July 1991. UNSCOM was able to confirm that bombs and warheads were destroyed at the sites declared by Iraq: three intact BW bomb bodies and fragments of 20 others, and a number of destroyed warheads were recovered.

Samples from destroyed Al Hussein missile warheads have confirmed that at least some Al Hussein warheads contained anthrax. However the analysis suggested to UNSCOM that at least seven Al Hussein warheads were filled with anthrax and not five as declared by Iraq.

Iraq declared that all bulk agent, including anthrax, remaining after the filling of weapons, had been stored at Al Hakam and was unilaterally destroyed there in July and August 1991. Laboratory analysis of samples collected by UNSCOM detected live anthrax at Iraq's declared disposal site. However, UNSCOM considered that the evidence was insufficient to support Iraq's statements on the quantity of anthrax destroyed and where or when it was destroyed.

Iraq also declared that no drying of anthrax had occurred. Iraq reiterated this in papers provided, in February 2003, to the Executive Chairman of UNMOVIC.

Assessment

Production

Iraq's declaration that it produced 8,425 litres of anthrax in 1990 is supported by a 1990 Al Hakam annual report, which UNSCOM found to be a credible document. However, there is evidence that contradicts Iraq's assertion that total production for all years, was limited to 8,445 litres.

UNMOVIC has credible information that the total quantity of BW agent in bombs, warheads and in bulk at the time of the Gulf War was 7,000 litres more than declared by Iraq. This additional agent was most likely all anthrax. Iraq has indicated that, after August 1990, anthrax production was given a high priority: up to August 1990 it had produced only 170 litres of anthrax compared with 14,000 litres of botulinum toxin. However, the drop-tank project, which UNMOVIC assesses was for use with anthrax, placed a high demand for the agent. According to Iraq, after the filling of bombs and warheads only about 3,400 litres of anthrax remained. The drop tank project as planned at the end of 1990, involved 12 tanks, each with a capacity of over 2,000 litres, and in total would have required over 24,000 litres of agent.

Iraq's claim that anthrax production ceased at the end of 1990, therefore, does not seem plausible. Indeed, there is evidence to indicate that the agent was, in fact, produced in 1991. The traces of anthrax found on equipment at FMDV suggest this facility was also used for the production of this agent. From the 1990 Al Hakam annual report it is evident that anthrax was not produced at FMDV in that year and, therefore, it seems likely that production actually occurred between 1 and 15 January 1991, prior to the Gulf War. In fact, interview testimony from one senior Iraqi scientist at the plant indicates that, contrary to Iraq's declaration, the fermenters at that site did operate in the first half of January 1991, although the scientist was unable to provide information on what was being produced.

Because of the stated requirement for anthrax, it seems likely that fermenters at Al Hakam also operated in early 1991 for this purpose. Together, the fermenters at FMDV and Al Hakam would have had a capacity to produce about 7,000 litres of anthrax in the first two weeks of 1991. This quantity closely corresponds to the additional amount of agent indicated from other information available to UNMOVIC. The production of 7,000 litres of anthrax would consume about 140 kilogrammes of the growth medium, yeast extract, compared with the quantity (167 kilogrammes) that Iraq declared was lost or stolen.

UNMOVIC's estimate of the quantity of yeast extract unaccounted for is considered further in the clustered issue on bacterial BW agents.

Movement of Bulk Agent

Iraq's statement that all bulk BW agent remaining after the filling of weapons was stored at Al Hakam during the Gulf War, is not convincing. Iraq has declared that *"all dangerous munitions and materials and essential assets"* were instructed to be evacuated from BW programme establishments by 15 January 1991. Accordingly, equipment including fermenters, and materials, such as bacterial growth media, were said to have been removed from Al Hakam facilities. It would have been logical for all bulk agent also to have been evacuated: it was the most valuable item at Al Hakam and could not readily be replaced, it had great strategic significance and anthrax, in particular, was required for the drop tank project. Perhaps, more importantly, if Al Hakam had been bombed, bulk agent and, in particular, anthrax would have posed a contamination hazard possibly even as far away as Baghdad.

Indeed, there is credible information available to UNMOVIC that indicates that bulk agent, including anthrax, was in fact deployed during the Gulf War. Based on this information, UNMOVIC estimates that about 21,000 litres of BW agent was stored in bulk at locations remote from Al Hakam; about half of this (about 10,000 litres) was anthrax.

Destruction

As indicated above, there is persuasive evidence that bulk anthrax was deployed during the Gulf War. The question then arises as to what happened to it after the War.

Iraq declared that the decision to destroy bulk BW agent unilaterally was made in early July 1991, and the actual destruction of the agent was said to have been carried out at Al Hakam in July/August 1991. However, it seems improbable that the bulk agent that had been deployed out in the field would have been returned to Al Hakam for destruction in July 1991. The first UNSCOM CW inspection was conducted at Al Muthanna in early June 1991 and, according to Iraq, Al Hakam was busily being cleaned at that time to remove or cover up any signs of a BW programme. Iraq would have reasonably expected a BW team to arrive at Al Hakam at any time from June 1991 onwards, and to have had any agent there after that date would have posed a high risk of discovery.

It, therefore, seems highly probable that the destruction of bulk agent, including anthrax, stated by Iraq to be at Al Hakam in July/August 1991, did not occur.

Based on all the available evidence, the strong presumption is that about 10,000 litres of anthrax was not destroyed and may still exist.

As a liquid suspension, anthrax spores produced 15 years ago could still be viable today if properly stored. Iraq experimented with the drying of anthrax simulants and if anthrax had been dried, then it could be stored indefinitely.

Iraq should present its stocks of anthrax to UNMOVIC or alternatively provide credible evidence of the fate of the bulk quantities of anthrax it produced and documents or other evidence that may support it. If the agent was unilaterally destroyed at a date later than declared, Iraq should provide proof of this destruction. On the other hand, if Iraq maintains that no undeclared anthrax was produced and that all agent was destroyed, Iraq should then explain: the finding of anthrax in the equipment at FMDV, its contradictory claim that anthrax had not been produced in 1991, the unaccounted for bacterial growth media, and its claim that bulk agent was not deployed. Documentation, such as fermenter records to support its declaration that anthrax had not been produced in January 1991, and any other information to support its account of unilateral destruction of BW agent in 1991, should also be provided. In this regard, the suggestion that Iraq made in papers provided, in February 2003, to UNMOVIC, that investigation of the destruction site could be made using advanced technology, is noted. However, it is uncertain whether such an investigation would resolve this issue.

Iraq currently possesses the technology and materials, including fermenters, bacterial growth media and seed stock, to enable it to produce anthrax. Many of the skilled personnel familiar with anthrax production have been transferred to civilian industries. There does not appear to be any choke points, which would prevent Iraq from producing anthrax on at least the scale of its pre-1991 level.

Actions that Iraq could take to help resolve the issue
- Present any remaining stocks of anthrax or provide evidence for its destruction.

- Explain, with credible supporting evidence:
  - the finding of anthrax in the equipment at FMDV,
  - its statement that anthrax had not been produced in 1991,
  - the unaccounted for bacterial growth media,
  - its statement that bulk agent was not deployed.
- Provide documentation or other evidence, to support its account of unilateral destruction of BW agent in 1991.

b. Botulinum Toxin

Introduction

Clostridium botulinum is a species of spore forming bacteria, which grow in the absence of oxygen, and is commonly found in soil. There are a number of strains of *Clostridium botulinum* each producing an immunologically distinct neurotoxin: letters A through G designate the types of botulinum toxin. Botulinum toxin type A is the most lethal bacterial toxin known per weight of agent and is approximately 15,000 times more toxic than the nerve agent VX.

The most common form of botulinum toxin poisoning in humans is generally associated with types A, B, and E. Botulinum toxin is the causative agent of botulism. It is a food contaminant occurring in low concentrations in some canned foods. Botulinum toxin in very low concentration also has a number of medical applications and is the subject of legitimate civilian research.

Historically, botulinum toxin is well documented internationally as a BW agent: Iraq declared that it produced botulinum toxin type A as a BW agent. The most likely route of infection for this toxin on the battlefield is through inhalation.

Background

Iraq stated that research and development work commenced on botulinum toxin (which it referred to as Agent A) at Muthanna State Establishment (MSE) in April 1986, which drew upon basic research conducted at the Al Hazen Institute in the 1970's. In 1987, the research and development work was transferred from MSE to Al Salman. A small quantity of the toxin was produced for laboratory evaluation during that year. After successful evaluation, Iraq declared that it produced about 800 litres of concentrated toxin between January and October 1988. Iraq also stated that bulk production of botulinum toxin began at Al Hakam in 1989 following the transfer of fermenters from Al Taji and the Veterinary Research Laboratory at Abu Ghraib to the Al Hakam facility at the end of 1988.

In 1995, Iraq declared that, between January 1989 and August 1990, Al Hakam produced about 13,600 litres of concentrated toxin. In addition, Iraq also stated that, in November and December 1990, part of the Foot and Mouth Disease Vaccine (FMDV) plant at Daura was taken over for the production of the toxin and, during this period, produced around 5,000 litres of concentrated botulinum toxin. Total production of the toxin from all facilities, according to Iraq, was about 19,000 litres (concentrated 20 times).

UNSCOM concluded that, while it was possible that large-scale production of botulinum toxin began in 1989 as Iraq had declared, because of incomplete records, the amount of agent produced could not be verified. According to UNSCOM, Iraq could have produced at least double the amount declared.

Iraq declared that field tests with botulinum toxin occurred in March and April 1988 using LD-250 bombs, and, in November 1989 and May 1990, using 122mm warheads. Some documentary and video evidence from the Haidar Farm cache suggest that these tests occurred as declared. Iraq states that about 500 litres of the toxin was used in weapons tests.

Iraq declared that it tested a modified 2,200-litre Mirage drop tank as a method of dispersing BW agents. Tests were undertaken separately with glycerin, potassium permanganate, water and *Bacillus subtilis*, an anthrax simulant, in January 1991. During the Technical Evaluation Meeting (TEM) in 1998, Lieutenant General Amer Al-Sa'adi referred to Iraq not discounting the possibility of using botulinum toxin in modified drop tanks. Prior to this statement, Iraqi officials, when interviewed by UNSCOM, had consistently indicated that they believed that anthrax was the agent of choice for the drop tanks. In its 1997 FFCD and its 2002 CAFCD, Iraq stated that drop tanks were developed for BW agents but never filled with agent and never used.

In its FFCD and repeated in its CAFCD, Iraq stated that one hundred R-400 aerial bombs and sixteen Al Hussein warheads were filled with botulinum toxin between December 1990 and 11 January 1991. Iraq acknowledged that the numbers of bombs it declared filled with particular BW agents were estimates. According to Iraq, these filled munitions were unilaterally destroyed in July 1991 along with 7,565 litres of agent stored in bulk.

UNSCOM assessed that Iraq had provided insufficient information on the production and weaponisation of botulinum toxin. In addition there were inconsistencies between the information provided in its FFCD and testimony by Iraqi officials relating to production and destruction. UNSCOM could therefore not verify the amounts of agent produced and destroyed as declared by Iraq.

The finding of botulinum type B toxin (as opposed to type A toxin) on a fermenter probe at Al Hakam also added to the uncertainty UNSCOM had of Iraq's declarations since Iraq had denied that type B was investigated or produced.

Assessment

With respect to production, Iraq has declared that it destroyed its records. Without such evidence there is very little prospect of verifying the quantities of agent A Iraq may have produced. Although the 1990 Al Hakam Annual Report supports Iraq's statements for the Al Hakam and FMDV production sites for that year, production, especially for 1989 and 1991, could have been much different than declared by Iraq. In this regard, based on fermenter capacity and on available bacterial growth media, production of botulinum toxin could have been greatly in excess of that declared by Iraq.

The significance of the finding of botulinum toxin type B on a fermenter probe at Al Hakam remains unclear. There is no evidence available to UNMOVIC that Iraq imported *Clostridium botulinum* type B strain. Given that type A is more toxic, it is difficult to explain the need for this strain. Contamination from local sources is one possible explanation.

However, UNMOVIC does not question Iraq's statement that botulinum toxin type A was weaponized in the Al Hussein warhead and R-400 bombs. Iraq's inconsistent statements with regard to the numbers of weapons filled and the destruction of agent, together with the lack of documentary evidence for production of agent in 1989 and 1991, makes overall quantitative verification impossible. According to Iraq, the numbers of bombs filled with botulinum toxin are only estimates, and, as such, it is not possible to verify an exact number.

It is significant that a high-ranking Iraqi official at the TEM indicated the drop tank may have been for agents other than anthrax. This is contrary to statements made by lower ranking Iraqi officials.

Any botulinum toxin that was produced and stored according to the methods described by Iraq and in the time period declared is unlikely to retain much, if any, of its potency. Therefore, any such stockpiles of botulinum toxin, whether in bulk storage or in weapons that remained in 1991, would not be active today.

Determining the quantity of botulinum toxin that Iraq produced and the implication that this had on fermenter availability, however, is important as an unresolved disarmament issue. It impacts on the assessment of the quantities that Iraq may have produced of other agents, in particular, anthrax.

A document submitted by Iraq to UNMOVIC in February 2003 relating to the production of Clostridium botulinum toxin, the equipment and media used and the production process involved, restated information available in previous declarations. There was no new information in this document.

Since Iraq produced more botulinum toxin than other agents and it still possesses the expertise and possibly the seed stock, material inputs (such as growth media), and equipment (fermenters), then production at least at the scale of its pre-1991 level could be rapidly recommenced.

Actions that Iraq could take to help resolve the issue

- Present any remaining stocks of botulinum toxin to UNMOVIC.

- Provide complete records of its entire production of botulinum toxin in particular for the period since 1989.

- Provide a detailed declaration supported by credible evidence of the types and total numbers of weapons it had filled with botulinum toxin.

- Provide complete fermenter production records for all of the bacterial agents it had produced, including the periods during which each agent had been produced, in particular for the years 1989 and 1991.

- Explain the occurrence of botulinum toxin type B on the fermenter found at Al Hakam.

Intentionally Blank

c. Mycotoxins: Aflatoxin and Trichothecenes

Introduction

Mycotoxins are naturally occurring toxins produced by certain fungal species.

Aflatoxins, hereafter referred to in the singular, and declared by Iraq and known in Iraqi documents as agent C, is one group of mycotoxins derived from the fungi of the genus *Aspergillus*. They infect crops such as wheat and rice and can occur in foodstuffs such as nuts and cereals. It is known from scientific literature that there is an increased risk of lung and liver cancer among humans continuously exposed to low levels of aflatoxin. High concentrations of aflatoxin can cause acute toxic effects in small animals. The acute toxicity is, however, low in comparison to many other plant, bacterial and animal toxins.

Trichothecenes are another group of mycotoxins, which are derived from the fungi of the genus *Fusarium*. These mycotoxins, which also infect crops such as wheat and rice, have been well studied in a civilian context.

Background

In its September 1997 FFCD and repeated in the 2002 CAFCD, Iraq declared that, in May 1988, the Technical Research Centre (TRC) at Al Salman, the body responsible for managing the BW programme, engaged a mycologist to establish a unit to study fungal toxins for BW purposes. Iraq stated that the research at Al Salman started by surveying local fungal strains with pathogenic effects on crops. The studies centred on *Fusarium* and *Aspergillus* mycotoxins. In 1989, the Director General of TRC approved the mycology unit be moved to another facility at Al Fudaliyah.

Iraq further declared that it produced most of its 2,200 to 2,390 litres of aflatoxin between September 1990 and January 1991, but that it no longer had the actual production records to support these figures. Based on the declared production methodology and time frame, UNSCOM estimated that Iraq could only have produced about half of the amount of aflatoxin of the same concentration that was declared in the FFCD.

With respect to aflatoxin, Iraq declared that it had conducted successful field trials with 122-mm rocket warheads filled with a solution of aflatoxin in November 1989 and May 1990. After three weeks, 100 % mortality of the exposed test animals was reported.

In addition, Iraq declared that it conducted a field test with aflatoxin in combination with wheat smut spores and silica gel. Iraq also declared laboratory tests, which involved using aflatoxin in combination with the teargases CS and CN. The stated aim of the tests with the tear gasses was to see if chemicals would affect toxicity or mask or impede the detection of aflatoxin.

Several times between 1995 and 1997, Iraq changed its declaration of the number of R-400 aerial bombs and Al Hussein warheads it had filled with aflatoxin. Iraq further declared in its 1997 BW FFCD that a total of 1,120 litres had been filled into weapons. It also declared that all munitions and bulk toxin were unilaterally destroyed in 1991. Faced with changing declarations and a lack of documentary evidence, UNSCOM could not verify the amount of aflatoxin produced, placed in bombs or warheads or consumed in tests. UNSCOM questioned whether in fact, aflatoxin was weaponised at all. Iraq repeated the information contained in its FFCD in the 2002 CAFCD.

With regard to trichothecene mycotoxins, Iraq stated that a study of the possibility of producing this agent started in March 1990 and ended in September 1990. According to Iraq, there was no progress beyond laboratory-scale preparation. Iraq declared that it tested the interaction of trichothecene mycotoxins with Mustard agent on laboratory animals but the results produced little added effect. UNSCOM found at the Haidar Farm, a document that indicated research had already begun in late 1987, had involved more personnel and was more extensive than Iraq declared.

Assessment

Doubt remains over the completeness of Iraq's statements with regard its trichothecene mycotoxins research programme, UNMOVIC concludes that the development of the agent did not proceed much beyond the research and laboratory stage. The 1990 Al Hakam Division's Annual Report, which refers to two minor research studies in 1990 and does not mention any production of trichothecene mycotoxins, lends some support to this conclusion. UNMOVIC assesses that the quantity of trichothecene mycotoxins produced was probably quite small and militarily insignificant.

The assertion that aflatoxin was one of the agents investigated by Iraq in its BW programme is supported by the analysis of video tapes of field trials found in the Haidar Farm cache as well as documents and information provided by Iraq. There is little doubt that, as Iraq declared, aflatoxin was designated as agent C for the purposes of research, development and production.

Given Iraq's declared production methods, it is likely that agent C contained mainly organic solvents (chloroform, dichloroethane and triethylamine) with low concentrations of aflatoxin. This would explain the high quantities declared to have been produced. Indeed, the 1990 Al Hakam Division's Annual Report states that 2,200 litres of agent C was produced in that year which is consistent with Iraq's declaration that, in total, 2,200 to 2390 litres were produced. There is documentation to indicate that R-400 bombs and Al Hussein warheads were filled with "agent C" and deployed. There is, however, insufficient information to confirm the numbers of bombs and warheads filled with agent C as declared by Iraq. Resolution of this issue may impact on the material balance of other CBW agents weaponized. Whether weaponised agent C is aflatoxin or some other agent cannot be answered conclusively but UNMOVIC considers that there is a high probability that the weaponised agent C is aflatoxin.

The most puzzling part of Iraq's account on agent C is the rationale for the agent: why did Iraq devote military, financial and human resources to an agent that had such a low acute toxicity and very little, if any, strategic or tactical battlefield utility compared to other biological warfare agents available to it? There may be an explanation, such as the personal ambition and expertise with aflatoxin of the leading scientist who worked on the agent to achieve results, even if ultimately a less than optimal weapon was produced. UNMOVIC should obtain from Iraq further information and explanation to resolve this issue.

Iraq declared that the entire amount of agent was destroyed. Such stocks would have degraded and would contain little if any viable agent in 2003. UNSCOM found fragments of a 50-litre container that Iraq declared aflatoxin was stored in at a pit at Al Hakam. No sampling was performed to verify if the content of the container had been aflatoxin.

The fungal strains of *Aspergillus* and *Fusarium* used in Iraq's BW programme for the production of the mycotoxins aflatoxin and trichothecenes were derived from local sources and were grown on grains such as rice and wheat. In addition, Iraq's production techniques for mycotoxins did not utilize any sophisticated technology. For example, much of the aflatoxin was produced in glass flasks and extracted with common solvents such as chloroform and triethylamine. There is no evidence that Iraq continued to produce aflatoxin or any other fungal agent after 1991. However, small quantities of aflatoxin have been declared by Iraq as being used for research for civilian purposes (in its 2003 semi-annual declarations) at a number of universities and agricultural facilities. Iraq's capability to produce mycotoxins has not diminished, and in fact, the continued research work in this area, may improve skill levels.

Iraq declared that it destroyed documentation relating to its research activities. It would still be useful to enquire whether any laboratory notes concerning mycotoxins are available.

Actions that Iraq could take to help resolve the issue
- Provide a credible explanation for why it had chosen to pursue the development of aflatoxin.

- Provide documentation relating to its work on mycotoxins, such as laboratory notes, etc.

- Provide credible evidence of the types and total numbers of a munition it had filled with aflatoxin.

Intentionally Blank

d. Wheat cover smut

Introduction
Biological anti-plant agents (living organisms that cause disease or damage to plants) can be used to weaken an opponent's economic base by attacking grain production and food stocks. The intention would be to damage an economy dependant on agriculture. Biological agents targeted against agriculture can also be used covertly.

Anti-plant BW agents can be bacterial, viral or fungal. Iraq declared that it had researched and produced a fungus of the genus *Tilletia*, which causes wheat cover smut or bunt. The fungus attacks the inflorescence (flower) of the wheat plant and replaces the developing seeds with masses of black spores, substantially decreasing crop yields.

Anti-crop agents have, in the past, been incorporated into the biological weapons programmes of some countries. From a military perspective, the most efficient way of disseminating wheat smut is by spraying; another efficient method of dispersal is through small multiple dispersion or cluster devices. As wheat cover smut is endemic in areas of northern Iraq, the fungus is easily obtainable and in significant quantities. Wheat smut can be avoided by the planting of resistant strains; the treatment by fungicides and the rotation of cereal crops but these measures still impose costs on a community and would usually occur after a wide infestation of the crop. For a season at least, the effects of wheat smut could be very significant.

Background
Iraq declared that the Scientific and Technical Research Centre (a predecessor of the Technical Research Centre at Al Salman) started research and development work on wheat cover smut (agent D) at the end of 1984, (before the programme under Dr Taha had started at Al Muthanna). According to Iraq, the objective of the research was to find suitable protective measures against the disease and also to investigate its use as a potential BW agent. Iraq stated that two small-scale trials were conducted in 1985 and 1986. According to its 1997 FFCD and the CAFCD, about a 220m by 220m field of wheat was planted in the north of Iraq in 1987 as a pilot production trial. In the following year, Iraq harvested about 5 tonnes of infected and non-infected wheat spikes. Although Iraq's account is partly supported by interview testimony, UNSCOM considered that there was insufficient documentation to confirm Iraq's statements with regard to production.

Iraq declared that no further production of infected wheat was undertaken. Nevertheless, in 1989 some experiments (using infected spikes as a rodenticide) and a field test were conducted. Iraq stated that the field test was the initiative of the head of the fungal group. The test involved using one (perhaps two) 122mm warheads, filled with crushed infected spikes of wheat and silica gel to monitor dispersion patterns. Iraq declared that a second test involving aflatoxin mixed with wheat cover smut and silica gel also occurred to measure the effectiveness of wheat cover smut as a carrier for aflatoxin. With regard to the former test, Iraq declared that the distribution was small and inconsistent and no further tests were warranted: there is no mention of results from the latter test.

Iraq declared that, in April/May 1991, all the wheat spikes, infected and non-infected, were destroyed by burning at Al Fudaliyah. For UNSCOM, the outline of the programme was unclear and it was not possible to confirm the amount of wheat smut produced, consumed or destroyed; nor was it possible to verify the account of the experiment, which was said to have been used wheat cover smut as a carrier for aflatoxin.

Assessment

Iraq's declaration that it had conducted research into wheat cover smut to investigate its potential as an economic weapon is plausible. Iraq found that wheat smut was an ineffective economic weapon and stated that the project was terminated in 1989. It is unclear why the contaminated wheat spikes were stored until their stated destruction in 1991.

There is even less information on the experiment with the spores, silica gel and aflatoxin. The 122mm munition was used to test the dispersion of aflatoxin as an antipersonnel agent, not the distribution of wheat smut as an economic weapon. The test seems to have been the initiative of the head of the fungal section whose responsibilities by 1989 included wheat cover smut. Although from Iraq's declarations and some supporting interview testimony it appears that the experiment with wheat cover smut did not progress beyond a pilot production trial. Some parts of the programme remain unclear. In particular a weapons test with wheat smut occurred and experiments continued with the harvested infected wheat spikes at a time when Iraq portrayed little interest in this agent.

UNMOVIC also notes Iraq's acknowledgement that wheat smut was being considered as a biological agent before the BW programme began at Muthanna; it did not come under the authority of Dr Taha when her team first moved to Al Salman; and was apparently approved and funded separately from her programme. These facts support the observation that Iraq had a separately run and funded BW activity outside of the influence, control and perhaps some parts, even the knowledge of Dr Taha's Al Hakam group.

Examination of Iraq's declarations, other documentation and interview testimony sheds little light on what higher authority was responsible for this activity. UNMOVIC therefore does not have a clear understanding of the background to the decision to test wheat smut as a weapon. Without the knowledge of the mandate and the authority responsible for this activity, it is not possible to determine the scope of wheat smut as a BW agent. This adds to UNMOVIC's uncertainty with respect to other BW agents that Iraq may have considered as suitable to be used against economic targets.

Iraq's account of wheat smut is inadequately supported by documentation; the quantity of agent produced, consumed and destroyed cannot be confirmed. At the same time, if infected wheat spikes had been retained from production in 1988, it is uncertain whether the spores would now be viable. Furthermore, given the ease with which additional quantities of this agent could be produced within the harvest cycles, the material balance question in respect of past production is of little relevance.

Iraq has large areas of arable land, which could be planted with wheat and infected by a fungus for the production of wheat cover smut. The deliberate contamination of wheat to produce this agent would have risked spreading the fungal contamination. Because this agent can be produced with low technology equipment within normal harvest cycles, Iraq's capability to produce this anti-crop agent has not diminished.

UNMOVIC is especially concerned with the broader question of Iraq's intentions with regard to biological agents that could be used as economic weapons.

Actions that Iraq could take to help resolve the issue
-        Provide evidence supporting its declarations on the quantities of wheat cover smut declared produced, consumed and destroyed.

-        Provide a detailed explanation and supporting documentation on the organization(s) and sources of funding for the work on this agent.

Intentionally Blank

e. Clostridium perfringens

Introduction

Clostridium perfringens is a spore forming bacteria, which grows in the absence of oxygen and is present naturally in the soil. After penetrating the body through an open wound or tear in the skin, the bacteria can produce a potent toxin, which causes gas gangrene. As this bacteria causes human and animal diseases it is the subject of civilian research and countermeasures.

Background

Iraq stated that research on the agent was conducted between April 1988 and March 1989, using imported strains as well as local isolates. Iraq declared that research on *Clostridium perfringens* (designated by Iraq as agent G) stopped in March 1989 because some components of the growth medium for this agent were required in high concentrations, were expensive and had to be imported. Iraq stated that production of agent G began on 1 August 1990 using an imported strain and two fermenters (capacities of 150 and 340 litres) and continued until 1 November 1990. According to Iraq, a total of 340 litres of ten times concentrated spores were produced which was stored in a one cubic metre mobile tank at Al Hakam until the agent was destroyed unilaterally in July-August 1991.

UNSCOM assessed that research began earlier than stated by Iraq. This was based on evidence that database searches had occurred in mid-1985, and strains had been imported in November 1986. UNSCOM questioned the reason for the apparent cessation of research work in 1989, given that there did not appear to be a shortage of media components. Further, UNSCOM noted that Iraq had not provided an account of testing of this agent and yet chose to produce it at a time when evidence suggested that priority was on anthrax production. UNSCOM could not verify the quantities of production stated by Iraq, and, on the basis of unaccounted growth media for this agent, production could have been 15 times more than that stated by Iraq. According to UNSCOM, there was insufficient documentation to support Iraq's statements on weaponisation and the amount of agent lost or destroyed could not be verified.

A document submitted by Iraq in February 2003 outlining the production of *Clostridium perfringens*, did not add any detail to previous Iraqi declarations. No evidence to support the declared destruction of the agent was provided.

Assessment

UNMOVIC assesses that research on agent G may have begun earlier than declared by Iraq. A document from the Haidar Farm cache outlined Iraq's BW work plan for 1988. The document referred to Iraq being ready to produce agent G in 1988. An intention to produce in 1988 would indicate prior research, and this in turn is consistent with the 1986 acquisition of the imported strains.

UNMOVIC questions Iraq's declared reason for stopping research. Some of the minor components that Iraq stated were not available and expensive to import are actually commonly available amino acids. For research purposes, only gram quantities would have been required. The cost of these would have been insignificant in the context of the whole research programme and especially compared with the 1.5 tonnes of peptone imported in 1988 which, according to Iraq, was solely for the production of agent G.

Documents from the Haidar Farm, in particular, Iraq's 1988 annual report for the Biological Research Department states that work had started on the production of agent G from local and imported isolates: this contradicts Iraq's statements regarding the timing of production but also confirms that local isolates as well as imported strains were used. On the other hand, the 1988 annual report also refers to research for optimum production parameters indicating research was continuing and perhaps some small-scale production had taken place.

The 1990 annual report for the Al Hakam Division also obtained from the Haidar Farm refers to the production of 340 litres of concentrated agent G, which supports Iraq's declaration for this year. Iraq has declared that agent G was not produced in 1989 and 1991. Iraq indicated some production in its 1988 annual report (above), casting doubt on the 340 litre total. In addition, there is a considerable amount of peptone unaccounted for which gives cause for concern that much larger quantities of agent G had been produced than declared by Iraq. Although agent G spores produced by Iraq in 1990 could still be viable in 2003 if properly stored, Iraq probably has seed stocks and can produce this agent quickly following a decision to do so.

While an Iraqi document indicates that agent G was considered for weaponisation, there is no evidence available to UNMOVIC that weaponisation occurred. There are some indications suggesting that Iraq may have considered agent G as a suitable agent for fragmentation weapons (a munition that produces fragments or shrapnel that can penetrate the body) as well as for use in a possible aerosol-type weapon. Iraq conducted aerosol experiments with agent G using animals: these tests showed that *Clostridium perfringens* spores absorbed through inhalation resulted in the death of the animals.

Iraq had embarked on a programme to produce anti-personnel bombs and also had an interest in CBW agents for cluster munitions. Iraq may have considered this agent to be well suited to a clustered munition, which produces or contains fragments that penetrate a body. Such a device would be well suited to *Clostridium perfringens* spores. If this were the case then 340 litres of agent (which could be diluted) would represent a relatively large quantity. Unlike agents, which are designed to create an inhalation hazard, it would be necessary only to coat the interior of the sub-munition with *Clostridium perfringens* and not fill the sub-munition with a slurry. *Clostridium perfringens* would also be useful for special operations especially for use with darts (a munition similar to a small nail in both size and shape).

The production and downstream processing equipment needed for *Clostridium perfringens* is available in Iraq in the civilian sector such as at vaccine plants. With regard to bacterial seed stock, Iraq has demonstrated that it can obtain local isolates. In addition, Iraq has the capability to produce some of the growth media, such as peptone and tryptone although inspection since December 2002 have not detected any evidence of this.

Actions that Iraq could take to help resolve the issue
- Present any remaining stocks of *Clostridium perfringens*.

- Present documents and other evidence that explain the concept of use, including the types of weapons to be used, it had developed for the agent.

- Provide information with supporting documents – production records – for the quantities of the agent it produced, in particular, for the years 1989 and 1991.

Intentionally Blank

f. Ricin

Introduction

Ricin toxin is found in the bean of the castor plant, *Ricinus communis* (1 to 5 % of total bean weight). It is one of the most toxic and easily produced plant toxins. Although ricin's lethal toxicity is approximately 1,000 fold less than that of botulinum toxin, ricin may have significance as a biological weapon because of its heat stability and its widespread availability as a by-product of the castor oil production process. Ricin is toxic by several routes, although on the battlefield it would most likely be used through the inhalation route. It was the agent used in the 'umbrella assassination' in London in 1978. There is currently no certified prophylaxis and no effective treatment for ricin poisoning. It was investigated for possible use as a toxic agent in World Wars I and II but it is not known ever to have been adopted for military use.

Castor oil can be used as a lubricant and is produced in Iraq where the castor bean tree grows in abundance. The ricin toxin remains in the castor bean residue after the oil has been extracted and the toxin can easily be produced using low technology and readily available materials.

Background

In 1995, Iraq declared that, beginning in 1989, it researched and extracted ricin toxin as an agent. A research team was formed at Al Salman as part of the Technical Research Centre (TRC), which was responsible for managing the BW programme. Iraq stated that, between December 1989 and November 1990, a total of 100 kilogrammes of castor beans had been processed to extract ricin.

UNSCOM assessed that research on ricin had actually begun in 1988 and not 1989 as asserted by Iraq and that it was initiated at the request of an Internal Security official. UNSCOM also assessed, through examination of documents, that the role of the Al Muthanna State Establishment (MSE) had been underplayed by Iraq. There had indeed been extensive collaboration on ricin between TRC and MSE in 1989.

Iraq declared that satisfactory results from laboratory work with animals led to a decision to start field trials and, in November 1990, a static test of four 155 mm ricin filled shells was conducted. Iraq stated that none of the animals in this test were affected by ricin poisoning and that the test was considered a failure, with further work on ricin agent being abandoned.

Iraq's known castor oil extraction plant, located in the Fallujah III complex, was subject to monitoring by UNSCOM. This plant was destroyed by aerial bombardment in December 1998.

Assessment

Iraq's ricin research was initiated not from within the mainstream BW programme, but from a suggestion from an individual in the Internal Security Service. It is possible that the ricin toxin was intended as a special operations weapon and only later became of interest for possible military application.

Several documents relating to the ricin project were recovered by UNSCOM in April 1997. Information in these documents contradicts Iraq's account both in regard to the declared starting date of the project and to quantities of agent produced, raises doubts about the correctness and completeness of Iraq's account. Iraq states that a single static field test was conducted in November 1990, that it was considered to be a failure and that the project was abandoned. While UNMOVIC finds it probable that this test occurred, the project was probably abandoned due to the onset of war rather than the failure of the test. Apart from this static field test using 155mm artillery shells, there is no evidence to suggest that Iraq weaponized ricin for military purposes.

The castor oil extraction plant at Fallujah III was destroyed in December 1998. UNMOVIC inspections since December 2002 have verified that the bombed castor oil extraction plant at Fallujah III has been reconstructed on a larger scale. However, the production seems to have ceased in July 2001. The residue from the oil extraction process is rich in ricin and could be used for the extraction of the toxin. However, Iraq had the capability to produce ricin had it wish to do so even without the reconstruction of the castor oil extraction plant.

If, despite ricin's limitations as a weapon of mass destruction, Iraq pursued ricin toxin as an agent, there would be indications of this proscribed activity, such as large-scale production, and weapons testing and development.

Actions that Iraq could take to help resolve the issue
-       Present any remaining stocks of ricin it had produced.

-       Provide a detailed explanation and supporting documentation on the organization(s) and sources of funding for the work on this agent.

-       Provide credible evidence which shows when it started to produce the agent as well as the total quantities it had produced to date.

g. Undeclared BW agents

Introduction

There are a number of microorganisms and toxins that have been developed as BW agents by several countries, including *Bacillus anthracis* (anthrax), *Clostridium botulinum* toxin, *Yersinia pestis* (plague), *Francisella tularensis* (tularemia), *Brucella* species (Brucellosis) *Coxiella burnetii* (Q fever) and Variola major (smallpox).

Iraq declared that it had produced and weaponized three BW agents: *Bacillus anthracis* spores, *Clostridium botulinum* toxin and aflatoxin. It also declared that it investigated a number of other agents for BW purposes, including *Clostridium perfringens*, wheat cover smut, ricin, and trichothecene mycotoxins.

Background

In 1985, a biological weapons group was established at the Muthanna State Establishment (MSE), Iraq's main CW production agency. Iraq declared that, starting in April 1986, it acquired a range of biological isolates (seed stocks) both locally and abroad for its BW programme.

Iraq stated that after the biological weapons group had moved from MSE to Al Salman (~1987/88), the Technical Research Centre (TRC), which was responsible for managing the BW programme, became interested in other potential BW agents (including viruses and different toxins). It became the policy of TRC to expand the programme into these other fields. Subsequently, Iraq revealed that other agents had been investigated and that in 1990, viral and genetic engineering units were established.

UNSCOM determined from a review of supplier information that Iraq had attempted to acquire more strains of microorganisms than it had declared for its BW programme.

In 1991, the first UNSCOM BW inspection team was provided with a declaration of the number and the types of microorganisms that had been acquired by Iraq as part of its biological research for military purposes. Iraq provided the team with a number of unopened vials of these strains. The only strain not handed to the team, that was said by Iraq not to have been used in the BW programme, was a vial of *Brucella melitensis*. This strain was declared as having been provided to a member of the BW programme for use in a Master of Science (MSc.) project. However, the strain was declared to have been destroyed before it could be used in the project. The validity of the statements concerning the fate of this strain could not be confirmed by UNSCOM.

UNSCOM also expressed concern over the accounting of growth media and its relation to the possibility of undeclared BW agents. UNSCOM stated that it had no information regarding the fate of unaccounted for media. UNSCOM found that *"it is not possible to determine if bacterial or toxin agents other than those stated in the 1997 FFCD were produced"*.

Assessment

This issue relates to the question whether Iraq declared the full range of BW agents it had investigated, produced or weaponized.

While UNSCOM did not find any substantial evidence that agents other than those disclosed by Iraq had been part of the BW programme, there are some indications suggesting an interest in other agents. One of these concerns has been addressed in the virus research assessment, namely smallpox.

UNMOVIC assesses that neither peptone or tryptone soya broth (TSB) growth media have been adequately accounted for by Iraq. It is not possible to be definitive about the amount of peptone and TSB that may be unaccounted for, but the amount would appear to be significant. TSB is particularly suitable for the growth of *"fastidious organisms"* (including gram negative microorganisms such as *Brucella, Yersinia* and *Francisella*). Iraq has not declared that it produced such organisms. It is therefore a matter of concern that Iraq had obtained bulk quanties of such media. In this regard, it is noted that the declared destruction of the *Brucella* isolate which was acquired in 1986 was not supported by evidence, which adds to the concern surrounding the accounting for TSB.

Accounting for the outstanding media, in particular TSB, would greatly reduce the uncertainty surrounding this issue. In the absence of such accounting or verified account of the R&D, production and weaponisation aspects of Iraq's BW programme, questions will remain concerning the possibility that Iraq worked on agents that it did not declare to UNSCOM.

Actions that Iraq could take to help resolve the issue

- Present any remaining stocks of undeclared agents it had produced.

- Provide a comprehensive account, with credible supporting documentation, of the peptone and TSB it had declared imported.

- Provide Annual Reports relating to its BW programme for the years 1989 and 1991. Such reports should exist, as Iraq had provided an Annual Report for 1990 to UNSCOM.

h. Drying of BW Agents

Introduction

BW agents are produced by a process that usually results in a liquid product, for example bacteria in an aqueous suspension, or toxins in an aqueous or organic solution. The storage life of BW agents in liquid form is usually significantly less than in the dried form and, therefore, the agents are sometimes dried. There are also other advantages to drying BW agents, including a reduction in bulk, ease of dissemination and the facilitation of a particle size that would present an optimum inhalation hazard.

There are several methods of drying BW agents. Commercially available dryers, including freeze dryers and spray dryers, may be used for this purpose. Depending on the method used, the drying of BW agents may create a contamination hazard. Special industrial dryers with containment features exist that can overcome this hazard. Alternatively, standard dryers that have been appropriately modified may be used.

Background

Iraq's interest in drying of BW agents appeared to focus on anthrax (agent B). Iraq stated that it was aware of the fact that the persistency of spores in dried form was much longer than in liquid form. To this end, a foreign company was approached in 1989 in an attempt to acquire a special dust-free spray dryer suitable for the safe drying of anthrax spores. Documentation shows that, in 1990, the company could not obtain an export license for the dryer and the order lapsed. Iraq declared that no bulk spray drying was carried out, either of pathogenic or of non-pathogenic bacteria.

Iraq declared that a spray dryer was transferred to Al Hakam, Iraq's main BW production facility, from a civilian facility in 1988. However, Iraq stated that no attempt was made to use this dryer in its BW programme because of the unsuitability of its dust filters and its inability to produce appropriate particle sizes. In addition, Iraq stated that its Al Hakam staff lacked experience in the operation of such equipment.

UNSCOM assessed that Iraq had not fully reported its work on the drying of BW agents and that Iraq's expertise in drying was greater than declared. However, it concluded that it was not possible to determine if BW agents had been dried.

In 1996, three industrial spray dryers were destroyed, under UNSCOM supervision, during the destruction of Al Hakam. Elsewhere in Iraq there were other dryers including industrial spray dryers, drum dryers and freeze-dryers, that may have been suitable for the drying of BW agents; Iraq's interest, however, appears to have been in spray dryers.

Assessment

It is clear that from the start of the BW programme, Iraqi scientists understood the importance of drying BW agents to enhance their long term storability. In 1986, laboratory freeze-drying equipment was obtained and used to preserve laboratory stocks of bacteria. In 1988, a small quantity of anthrax was dried for inhalation experiments. In the same year, Iraq decided that industrial dryers for the large-scale drying of anthrax needed to be obtained.

It is most likely that, as it had declared, Iraq was unsuccessful in 1989/90 in acquiring a special dust-free spray dryer to safely dry large quantities of anthrax.

There was at least one spray dryer present at Al Hakam from 1988 onwards. This dryer would have been suitable for drying BW agent if safety modifications had been made. Whether this dryer, or other suitable dryers that were available in the country, were so modified, and used for drying of BW agent is unknown.

In any event, it seems likely that no bulk drying of agent took place in either 1989 or 1990. Apparently, in 1989, large-scale BW agent production was in its initial phase and Iraq was expecting to obtain from an overseas company a special dryer for its future requirements. Therefore, there seemed to be little reason, at that time, to modify existing dryers to make them safe for BW agent drying. An Al Hakam annual report for 1990 makes no reference to large scale drying of BW agents, implying that no drying occurred in that year either. The annual report, which UNMOVIC considers reliable, indicates that research into the drying of anthrax continued in 1990, but even this ceased for that year when the foreign company failed to supply the special dryer.

It is not certain, however, that no drying of BW agents was conducted in 1991. Given that Iraq then knew it could not obtain the special dryer it had sought, it may have modified existing dryers at Al Hakam, or elsewhere, for this purpose. It is noteworthy that, by 1993, Iraq was successfully drying large quantities of bacterial insecticide (using a non-pathogenic spore forming bacteria related to anthrax) at Al Hakam. Evidently, the technology for drying bulk quantities of spore-forming bacteria had been gained at some time prior to this date.

In December 1998, there were over 20 spray dryers and 70 freeze dryers under inventory control including some of these items that could be used for the drying of bulk BW agent. In addition, there was evidence that Iraq was developing the capability of indigenously manufacturing spray dryers. If bulk agent were available, Iraq would have had the capability after 1991, to process this using available equipment modified to reduce the risk of contamination.

UNMOVIC has no evidence that drying of anthrax or any other agent in bulk was conducted. But given Iraq's interest in drying, the existence of large quantities of liquid bulk agent in 1991, the availability of suitable dryers and the expertise that Iraq had developed, UNMOVIC cannot be certain that Iraq did not dry agent.

In February 2003, Iraq provided UNMOVIC with a paper repeating its arguments that it did not dry BW agents. No new information was disclosed in this paper and, therefore, it does not affect the above assessment.

UNMOVIC should seek further information from Iraq in relation to the drying of BW agents, including the acquisition of dryers and drying materials.

Iraq has available to it many dryers of different types, that with modification could be made safe for the drying of BW agents.

Actions that Iraq could take to help resolve the issue

- Provide more information and supporting documentation on its efforts to dry BW agents, in particular concerning its attempts to acquire specialized dryers from abroad and indigenous modification and production of dryers.

- Provide more information and supporting documentation on the drying of bacterial insecticide at Al Hakam from 1992 to 1995.

Intentionally Blank

i. Bacterial BW agent production

Introduction

Production of bacterial BW agents (e.g. anthrax and botulinum toxin) requires certain equipment, typically a fermenter and down stream processing equipment such as separators and settling tanks. The fermenter is a key item in the production process. It is essentially a tank in which the temperature and other environmental factors can be controlled to promote the growth of bacteria. It is a dual-use technology item and is commercially available for the production of vaccines, beer, yoghurt, antibiotics and other biochemicals. Fermenters may vary in size from a capacity of a few litres to tens of thousands of litres.

Also required for the production of bacterial BW agents are nutrients that are dissolved in water and added to the fermenter. Typically, they will include an energy source such as glucose, and other factors such as protein digests prepared from yeast, milk or meat products, and vitamins and minerals. These are known as bacterial growth media and may be purchased commercially as individual components, or as complete media.

Background

Iraq has declared that it produced three bacterial BW agents: about 19,000 litres of botulinum toxin (agent A), about 8,500 litres of anthrax (agent B) and 340 litres of *Clostridium perfringens* (agent G). In addition, about 900 litres of bacteria as a simulant for anthrax was produced. For the production of these, Iraq declared that it had acquired a number of foreign manufactured fermenters which, with one exception, were obtained from industries within Iraq. Iraq's main production line was acquired in 1988 from a veterinary vaccine plant at Al Kindi and was stated to have been transferred to Al Hakam in the same year. All BW agent production at Al Hakam was said to have ceased in 1990, although one production fermenter was stated to have been operated, early in 1991, for the production of anthrax simulant.

Another production line was established at a Foot and Mouth Disease Vaccine (FMDV) plant at Al Daura in September 1990. Equipment at this site was said to have been used exclusively for the production of botulinum toxin in November and December 1990. Iraq stated that FMDV was not used for the production of BW agent after December 1990.

Clostridium perfringens was stated by Iraq to have been produced, between August and December 1990, in two relatively small fermenters at Al Hakam.

UNSCOM noted that, if Iraq's account on fermenter usage was accepted, then the fermenters used in the programme were under-utilized and, in some cases, had remained idle for long periods of time. UNSCOM noted that this contradicted Iraq's statements that its fermenters had been fully utilized and that priority had been placed on agent production after August 1990.

UNSCOM also commented that, based on the finding of evidence of anthrax on equipment at FMDV, it could not exclude the possibility that anthrax had also been produced at this site.

Iraq has declared that large-scale purchase of bacterial growth media for BW agent production began in 1988, and continued until early 1990. Iraq's 2002 CAFCD omitted a quantity of about 650 kilogrammes of growth media that had been imported in 1988. However, in papers provided in February 2003 to UNMOVIC, Iraq corrected this and acknowledged that this media had been imported, but stated that it *"was counted within the lost quantity"*. Documentation indicates that, in fact, a total of about 43 tonnes of bacterial growth media had been imported; Iraq also stated that some relatively small quantities of media had been acquired locally, although the origin of this material also appeared to be from foreign suppliers.

UNSCOM found that there was a significant discrepancy in the material balance for media. Based on its estimate of the amounts of various types of media unaccounted for, UNSCOM estimated that the quantities of additional undeclared agent that potentially could have been produced were: 3,000 – 11,000 litres of botulinum toxin, 6,000 – 16,000 litres of anthrax, up to 5,600 litres of *Clostridium perfringens*, and a significant quantity of an unknown bacterial agent.

Assessment

The lack of supporting documentation makes it difficult for UNMOVIC to confirm Iraq's figures on the quantities of bacterial BW agent produced. Two approaches to estimating the quantity of agent potentially produced have been made by UNMOVIC. The first is based on fermenter capacity and availability and the second is based on the amount of media unaccounted for and, therefore, assumed consumed in Iraq's BW programme.

With respect to fermenters, there are two annual reports (1988 and 1990), considered credible by UNMOVIC, that appear to confirm Iraq's statements on the utilization of fermenters for those years. However, for 1989 and 1991, there is no such documentation and UNMOVIC is, therefore, unable to confirm whether the fermenters were idle in those years to the extent claimed. UNMOVIC's understanding is that there was a great demand for BW agent towards the end of 1990, and January 1991 in particular, would have been a critical time for production. UNMOVIC, therefore, questions Iraq's statement that all but one fermenter stopped production at the end of 1990. This one fermenter, at Al Hakam, was said by Iraq only to have produced anthrax simulant.

If the fermenters known to be available to the BW programme were not idle to the extent declared by Iraq, but were used to their full capacity in 1989 and in January1991, then a significant amount of additional agent could have been produced. UNMOVIC estimates that the amount of additional agent could be about 7,000 litres of botulinum toxin, as well as 7,000 litres of anthrax (see Clustered Issue on Anthrax) and 1,000 litres of *Clostridium perfringens*. These estimates are maximum amounts and are somewhat interchangeable. In addition, they do not take into consideration unaccounted for growth media.

UNMOVIC has also assessed the amount of bacterial agent that potentially could be produced based on its estimate of the amount of growth media unaccounted for. Any estimation of unaccounted for media is complicated by a number of factors including the fact that about 1400 kilogrammes of "unknown" media components were destroyed under UNSCOM supervision.

Other complicating factors include uncertainty of the quantity of media obtained from local sources and the possibility of other unknown imports of media.

Within a few percent of the total known quantity acquired, there is an approximate material balance of the overall media equation. However, a closer examination of each media component suggests that two media components, peptone and tryptone soya broth (TSB), have not been adequately accounted for and any discrepancy could be of considerable significance. These issues are dealt with in the *Clostridium perfringens* and undeclared agent clustered issues.

With regard to the other media components, even though there is an approximate balance, UNMOVIC cannot exclude the possibility that there may be some relatively small quantities unaccounted for. For most components this may not be significant, but for yeast extract even small amounts can be used for the production of large quantities of anthrax. The implication of this is that UNMOVIC's assessment of the theoretical production of an additional undeclared 7,000 litres of anthrax, based on fermenter availability, would be possible based on media material balance considerations. For example, production of 7,000 litres of anthrax would require only 140 kilogrammes of yeast extract and this is within the margin of uncertainty of accountancy for this media component and less than the quantity (167 kilogrammes) that Iraq declared was lost or stolen.

On the other hand, it seems unlikely that significant undeclared quantities of botulinum toxin could have been produced, based on the quantity of media unaccounted for. Thus the estimate, based solely on fermenter availability, that an additional 7,000 litres of botulinum toxin could have been produced is not supported i.e. the limiting factor for additional botulinum toxin production is not fermenter availability but media.

Fermenter availability and media accountability relate directly to the bacterial BW agent material balance. The undeclared quantities of agents potentially that could have been produced up to 1991 are significant and, at least anthrax and *Clostridium perfringens*, if stored appropriately, could still be viable today. Iraq should, therefore, be asked to substantiate the declared downtimes of fermenters in 1989 and 1991, particularly in relation to anthrax and *Clostridium perfringens* production. Supporting documentation such as fermenter operating logs, maintenance schedules and assignment of fermenter personnel should be sought.

Also in the context of possible agent production, Iraq should provide further information concerning the fate of the media components, peptone and TSB. On the other hand, given the inherent uncertainties in media accountability, further follow up with Iraq on the accountancy of yeast extract is unlikely to result in any greater precision of the balance figures for this media component and is, therefore, unwarranted.

There are several fermenters similar to those used for BW purposes available in Iraq. In addition, there were a large number of other vessels, in the pharmaceutical and food sector, that could be used as fermenters with minor modifications. Iraq also had the capability to indigenously manufacture vessels that could be used for the growth of bacterial BW agents. Other dual use equipment capable of being used in a BW programme was available at sites throughout Iraq.

UNMOVIC cannot discount the possibility that Iraq has developed mobile production facilities or that it has production equipment at other hidden sites. In a letter to UNMOVIC dated 5 March 2003, Iraq claims that it does not possess mobile laboratories for the production of biological agent and has offered to assemble a range of refrigerated and other vehicles for UNMOVIC and IAEA inspection. This offer is being evaluated by UNMOVIC.

Growth media was available in varying quantities at several locations, including over two tonnes of yeast extract in aggregate at two facilities in Iraq.There is no evidence that Iraq was indigenously producing large quantities of growth media although research into growth media production had occurred and continues. Iraq could now have a capability to continue its development of bacterial growth media production, to the stage of being able to supply large quantities of dry or liquid media to a proscribed programme.

Actions that Iraq could take to help resolve the issue
- Provide detailed information with supporting evidence, such as documentation, on fermenter production schedules for the bacterial BW agents produced.

- Provide a credible account with supporting evidence, for the unaccounted for peptone and TSB growth media.

See also Actions in related issues on Anthrax, Botulinum toxin, *Clostridium perfringens*, and Undeclared BW agents.

j. Genetic Engineering and Viral Research

Introduction

Genetic engineering, a process whereby an organism's genetic material is modified, has many medical and industrial applications. Such techniques can also be applied to an offensive BW programme. For example, pathogenic bacteria could be made antibiotic resistant or the virulence or toxin production could be increased.

Iraq stated that its brief viral research programme had focused on three incapacitating but generally not lethal, agents: enterovirus 70, rotavirus and the camel pox virus. Enterovirus 70 can cause severe eye pain, blurred vision, photophobia and sub-conjunctival hemorrhage. The symptoms appear suddenly and recovery can take up to 10 days. The rotavirus causes diarrhea, dehydration and cramps. The effects normally last for about 48 hours and some strains are lethal for the very young and old. The World Health Organization does not rule out the possibility of the camel pox virus being transmissible to humans even though actual cases seem rare. None of these viruses are considered traditional BW agents.

Background

During 1990, Iraq expanded its BW programme to include both genetic engineering and viral research. Iraq declared that two genetic engineering units were established in 1990: one under the authority of the Technical Research Centre (TRC), the main organization controlling Iraq's BW programme, in March and another at the Sera and Vaccine Institute (SVI) under the Muthanna State Establishment (MSE), Iraq's main CW production facility, in October. Although Iraq declared that the former unit had not developed a work plan, Dr Rihab Taha, the head of Al Hakam, Iraq's main BW agent production facility, indicated to UNSCOM that one purpose had been to develop antibiotic resistant anthrax. Iraq stated that MSE's interests were in the medical applications of genetic engineering.

Iraq stated that the activities at both of these units ended in January 1991 and that after the Gulf War, the two units, which were unrelated, were combined and transferred to the Baghdad University for civilian purposes.

By testimonies and documents, UNSCOM was informed of and received a planning document produced in 1990 for a third unit at the Foot and Mouth Disease Vaccine (FMDV) production plant at Al Daura, which appeared to be under the control of Al Hakam. From interviews, UNSCOM assessed that the unit did not proceed beyond the planning stage and that no staff were recruited or equipment acquired.

With regard to its viral programme, Iraq declared that, apart from some basic research at the Al Hazen Institute between 1974 and 1978, no other viral research for BW purposes took place between 1974 and 1990. Following a scientific literature survey in July 1990, research was initiated in September 1990. Iraq produced documentation supporting these statements.

In its 1997 FFCD, Iraq declared that, on 1 December 1990, laboratory work commenced with camel pox virus, infectious hemorrhagic conjunctivitis virus (enterovirus 70) and rotavirus, all of which were locally acquired. Iraq provided UNSCOM with a daily logbook covering the period 1 December 1990 to 17 January 1991 that described Iraq's research on rotavirus and enterovirus 70. Iraq stated that all research work had been terminated on 17 January 1991 and that all viral agent specimens were destroyed. Iraq declared that the objective of the virus research was to study viral agents suitable as incapacitating BW agents.

With regard to the viral research programme, the head virologist stated to UNSCOM that the camel pox virus was chosen in the belief that it would selectively infect "non-Arabs". UNSCOM was told that it had not been pursued as a model for the smallpox virus. In addition, UNSCOM was told that the head virologist had attempted to acquire a 5,000 egg incubator with a view to producing the camel pox virus for weaponisation.

UNSCOM found two foreign scientific publications among the Haidar Farm documents that related to smallpox and smallpox vaccination. These publications referred to production and storage of smallpox vaccine in the 1980s and the storage of smallpox vaccine seed stock. While retention of these publications could reflect legitimate medical concerns, they were considered by UNSCOM to be indicative of Iraq's interest in smallpox.

Assessment

Although in the lead up to the Gulf War, Iraq's BW programme was focused on the production of bulk agents and weaponisation, some attention was given to diversifying the BW programme and making it more robust. In fact, the BW effort was expanding, as evidenced by the establishment of a number of genetic engineering facilities and the commencement of the viral research programme. Although both of these programmes seemed short-lived, and probably achieved little, it does demonstrate intent and commitment to a more diversified and dynamic BW programme.

It is clear from statements by senior Iraqi officials, such as Dr Taha and Lieutenant General Amer al Sa'adi, that the potential for genetic engineering for BW purposes was well understood. There is documentary evidence and testimony supporting the existence of three separate plans to establish genetic engineering units in Iraq in 1990: the TRC unit, the MSE unit and a third unit at the FMDV plant at Al Daura. The 1990 Al Hakam Annual Report provided by Iraq supports its declaration with regard to the starting date of the TRC unit and that minor progress had been made at the unit by the end of 1990.

Iraq's BW genetic engineering programme was in the embryonic stages of development in 1991 when the scientists involved were transferred to Baghdad University. Iraqi declarations and UNMOVIC inspections have confirmed that Iraq has devoted additional resources to improving its civil biotechnology sector in 2002. The creation of three biotechnology or genetic engineering facilities since 1998 and the equipping of these Centres will augur well for an increased future capability. Although there has been no evidence of proscribed activity detected so far, UNMOVIC cannot rule out the possibility of continued research into BW-related genetic engineering.

The direction which Iraq's BW viral research programme took seemed to have been the initiative of the head virologist. His interest in the camel pox virus may have been prompted by a study at the University of Baghdad in the 1970s which mentioned the possibility that *"viruses like camel pox, buffalo pox and monkey pox may establish themselves in a less immune human population"* and cause smallpox-like disease. It is conceivable that this paper may have influenced the head virologist to think that camel pox could be an incapacitating BW agent that could selectively infect *"aliens"* (non-Arabs). Whether the intention was to weaponise this agent remains unclear. However, according to the head virologist, one concept of production, weaponization and use of viruses involved the breeding of vectors for their dissemination.

Whether Iraq was using the camel pox virus as a simulant for smallpox has not been established. While UNSCOM had some concern and there was some related scientific literature in the Haidar Farm cache, there is no evidence that Iraq had possessed seed stocks for smallpox or had been actively engaged in smallpox research. Whether that was the eventual intention cannot be determined as the viral programme was said to have stopped at an early stage.

In the absence of supporting evidence and further explanation, such as instructions covering the viral research plan and the logbook covering the work done for camel pox, the scope of the viral research undertaken by Iraq remains unclear. Scientific literature describing the symptoms and infectivity of the viral agents selected by Iraq confirm that, enterovirus 70 and rotavirus could theoretically be used as incapacitating agents. Despite Iraq's apparent belief that camel pox virus could be an incapacitating agent, this is not supported by scientific literature. Although these viruses are not considered as serious BW candidates in the open literature, Iraq was in the embryonic stages of its research and it is conceivable that more potent viral agents would have been selected as the programme matured.

According to Iraq's declarations, its BW virus research work lasted only 47 days and the logbook provided to UNSCOM addressed work conducted on rotavirus and enterovirus 70 appears to confirm this. Other documentation provided by Iraq also supports the short time-frame for its BW viral research programme. Iraq should provide the logbook and any laboratory notes, which involve pox research and any documents from the senior hierarchy, which relate to plans for the viral programme.

Although UNMOVIC assesses that probably little would have been achieved in Iraq's BW genetic engineering and viral research programme prior to the Gulf War, but, these areas of research identify the possible future directions of a BW programme and should be followed up.

Actions that Iraq could take to help resolve the issue
- Provide information on any work done on smallpox whether for military or civilian purposes after 1972 including vaccinations of civilians and military troops.

- Provide records of destruction of smallpox isolates obtained in 1972.

- Provide documentation, such logbooks, laboratory notes, etc. relating to the research on camelpox as well as documents from other levels of the management hierarchy concerning virus research in connection with the BW programme.

k.   BW Agent Simulants

Introduction

Biological simulants are chemicals or microorganisms that have very similar characteristics and properties to a biological warfare agent. Generally, bacterial simulants are closely related to the BW agent that they are substituting for, but lack the pathogenicity of that BW agent. For example, *Bacillus subtilis* is closely related to *Bacillus anthracis*, the causative agent of anthrax and yet is harmless to humans. The rationale for the use of a simulant is that it can be used for a variety of purposes in a BW programme, such as to accurately assess a variety of production methods, storage conditions, weaponisation parameters and dispersal techniques, without the danger of exposure to pathogens or toxins. However, they are also used for a variety of bio-defence and civilian activities, including at universities and pharmaceutical plants.

Background

In its 1995 BW FFCD, Iraq declared the production of *"bulk"* BW agent simulant at Salman Pak and Al-Hakam between 1988 and 1990. Field tests with simulants were conducted, from February 1988 to January 1991, at several locations. These included tests with LD-250 and R-400 aerial bombs, 122-mm rocket warheads, aircraft drop-tanks modified for spraying and other aerosolisation devices. In addition, Iraq had used simulants to determine the best media cultures, to test production equipment, in scaling up production, to develop spray drying processes, to study the conditions suitable for preserving (storing) microorganisms and the viability of these organisms in aerosol. Iraq also used simulants to design and test all BW munitions and spraying vehicles, study the dispersion and dissemination of agents and for personnel training purposes.

UNSCOM found that the information and documentary evidence supplied by Iraq on its production of BW agent simulants contradicted its statements on the field trials it had conducted. UNSCOM assessed that the quantity of BW agent simulant produced and used by Iraq could not be confirmed, and that several matters related to simulants had not been adequately explained by Iraq.

Iraq constructed and operated what it stated was a bacterial bio-pesticide plant at Al Hakam after 1991. UNSCOM determined through analysis of the bio pesticide product that the strain used did not possess the genes necessary to produce bio-pesticidal proteins and thus did not have any utility as a bio-pesticide. UNSCOM also found Iraqi documents, which indicated that Iraq had been aware that the strain used for production had no pesticide effect. UNSCOM assessed that the Al Hakam bio-pesticide project was an attempt to avoid the destruction of the site and conceal the BW programme. The *Bacillus thuringiensis* bacteria stated to have been used in the bio-pesticide programme had been used by Iraq, in 1989, as an anthrax simulant in drying studies. The entire Al Hakam site was destroyed under UNSCOM supervision in 1996.

Assessment

UNMOVIC's main concern is the adequacy of Iraq's account of its production and use of BW agent simulants.

Iraq used chemicals and bacteria such as the spore-basesd bacteria (*Bacillus subtilis*) as a simulant for different BW agents to model properties of anthrax (agent B) and *Clostridium perfringens* (agent G). It is possible that simulants may have also played a part in Iraq's research on viral BW agents.

Some discrepancies remain concerning the quantities and times of production of simulants, as well as the number and dates of their use as reported in Iraq's 1997 BW FFCD and the 2002 CAFCD. For example, Iraq has provided no account for simulant production in connection with the tests it carried out with a helicopter spraying device, the testing of a 450-litre fermenter and the training of personnel in bulk production using a 1,850-litre fermenter at Al Hakam. Iraq also has not adequately explained the rationale for the production of the bacteria *Bacillus megaterium* at Salman Pak in 1988, the reason for acquiring strains of *Bacillus licheniformis* for the BW programme and the reason for having *Bacillus pumilus* at Al Hakam in 1991. These types of bacteria have utility as BW agent simulants. UNMOVIC cannot exclude the possibility that Iraq's BW programme involved other simulants.

The use of simulants appears to have played an integral part in Iraq's BW programme. Further information from Iraq on its work on simulants could assist in obtaining a technically coherent picture of its BW programme. The quantity of simulant produced is a factor in the consideration of the overall material balance of bacterial BW agents. The production of simulant consumes bacterial growth media and utilizes fermenters that otherwise might have been used in the production of BW agent: the more simulant that was produced the less agent may have been produced and vice versa. The timing of production is also of interest because it may be a pointer to when and how many weapons tests were conducted.

Iraq gained considerable experience in the production of dry bulk bacterial pesticide at Al Hakam. The bacteria used in the process is similar to anthrax and its production and drying could, therefore, be a model for anthrax. The particle size achieved in the drying process for the pesticide was more appropriate for inhalation and would have had little use in agriculture. Some 140 to 160 tonnes of a dry pesticide preparation containing *B. thuringiensis* spores were declared produced in Al Hakam from 1993 to 1995.

Bacteria that were used by Iraq as BW agent simulants, are widely available in Iraq's civilian biological sector, at pharmaceutical and university sites (for example at least 10 sites declared *Bacillus subtilis* in their collection). UNMOVIC inspections and Iraqi declarations confirm that Iraq continues working with organisms (at least in small quantities) that could be used as BW agent simulants. For example, Iraq has acknowledged that research on the development of biopesticides *(Bacillus thuringiensis)*, which may be used as an anthrax simulant, has been ongoing at the Agricultural and Biological Research Centre, Tuwaitha since 1998. Iraq has the capability to work with simulants for spore forming and non-spore forming bacteria, viral agents or toxins.

Actions that Iraq could take to help resolve the issue

- Provide more documentation that details its production and use of simulants, including the locations, quantities and specific timing of production.

- Provide information on the use of all simulants.

Intentionally Blank

UNMOVIC Working document

6 March 2003

APPENDIX
A HISTORICAL ACCOUNT OF IRAQ'S PROSCRIBED WEAPONS
PROGRAMMES

TABLE OF CONTENTS

Intentionally Blank

IRAQ'S PROSCRIBED WEAPONS PROGRAMMES

Introduction

Following the defection of Lieutenant-General Hussein Kamal in August 1995, Iraq provided a large quantity of documentation concerning its proscribed weapons programmes (the Haidar Farm documents). It also disclosed more information about these programmes which lead to new declarations in 1996 and 1997. On 7 December 2002, in accordance with resolution 1441 (2002), Iraq provided a further declaration on its proscribed weapons programmes.

UNMOVIC has assessed these declarations in the light of information available, including the documents from Haidar Farm, UNSCOM and UNMOVIC inspections, and other sources such as import records. The following account is UNMOVIC's understanding of the development of Iraq's proscribed programmes.

The starting point for the following account of Iraq's proscribed programmes is the series of declarations made by Iraq. As earlier mentioned, after the defection of Lieutenant-General Hussein Kamal in August 1995, Iraq provided new chemical, biological and missile declarations. And on 7 December 2002, Iraq provided a further declaration that in essence repeated the information in the earlier declarations.

Little of the detail in these declarations, such as production quantities, dates of events and unilateral destruction activities, can be confirmed. Such information is critical to an assessment of the status of disarmament. Furthermore, in some instances, UNMOVIC has information that conflicts with the information in the declaration. In the following account, the areas where UNMOVIC is reasonably confident of the accuracy of the Iraq's declarations are indicated, as well as the areas of uncertainty, including areas where the Iraqi account is unsupported by evidence or where there is conflicting information. These uncertainties and consequent outstanding issues are discussed in the section on Clusters of Unresolved Disarmament Issues.

The account covers the programmes up to 1991, and then other related activities and capabilities after that date, up to the end of inspections in 1998.

Intentionally Blank

IRAQ'S CHEMICAL WEAPONS PROGRAMME

Introduction

Both in its size and maturity, Iraq's chemical weapons (CW) programme was the most advanced of all its proscribed weapon programmes. The programme started probably in the late 1960s, and progressed steadily from basic research on simple agents, to large scale production of a variety of agents and the design and manufacture of a range of delivery systems. Iraq imported thousands of tons of chemicals and complete chemical plants. It constructed industrial-sized production facilities where CW agents and some of their precursors were synthesized. By the end of the Iraq-Iran War in 1988, Iraq's CW programme had advanced to the point where a variety of chemical weapons, including Mustard and nerve gas bombs, were being manufactured. World attention was drawn to these developments when Iraq used CW against Iranian forces in that war.

Further development continued after the Iraq-Iran War, including the production of the highly toxic nerve agent, Vx, and the design and production of a wider range of munitions. By the time of the Gulf War in 1991, Iraq had amassed a sizable CW arsenal comprising thousands of short range rockets, artillery shells and bombs, and hundreds of tonnes of bulk agent. It had also produced at least 50 special warheads to be filled with nerve agent ready for use with the 650 kilometre range Al Hussein missile.

Beginnings

The beginnings of Iraq's CW programme are uncertain, but it appears to have had its origins in the 1960s. From the beginning of the 1960s, a number of Iraqi army officers were trained overseas in nuclear, biological and chemical (NBC) defence and the first of these were to form the basis of the Iraqi Chemical Corps which was established on 14 January 1964. The primary interest at that time appeared to be in chemical defence but, sometime in the late 1960s, at about the time of a change in the Iraqi leadership, an interest in the offensive aspects of chemicals developed.

Iraq stated that, in 1971, a group of Chemical Corps officers, proposed that research work be conducted on chemical agents. It is not clear to UNMOVIC what the objectives of this work were, nor under which authority it was conducted. However, from the available evidence, it appears that a basic research laboratory was built at Al Rashad village on the north east boundaries of Baghdad and small quantities of chemical agents were synthesized.

Three years later, Iraq's CW efforts became more formalized. Iraq stated that, in response to a rising threat from Israel and Iran, a new scientific organization was established, in 1974, to look at the "*scientific, academic and applied researches in the fields of chemistry, physics and micro-organisms*". The umbrella organization for this was the Al Hazen Ibn Al Haitham Institute. From available evidence, UNMOVIC considers the establishment date may have been a little earlier than Iraq has declared, perhaps 1973. Iraq has stated that, although it was officially under the auspices of the State Security Apparatus, representatives from various government ministries were on its board of directors, and its head was a military officer from the Chemical Corps. Iraqi officials have indicated that its objectives were to gain a familiarization with chemical agents and eventually to develop weapons.

The Al Hazen Institute was organized into three or four divisions, or "Centres", and the laboratories associated with these were scattered around the Baghdad area. The CW development work became the responsibility of the "First Centre" which located its laboratories at the former CW site at Al Rashad. New laboratories were built there and were equipped with modern equipment; according to one scientist at Al Rashad *"no one in Iraq had any better"*. Iraq has stated that, in 1975, further CW facilities were planned at a remote site in the desert near Al Sammara, 85 kilometres north west of Baghdad. Iraq said that beyond laying a foundation stone little construction took place until the early 1980s.

For the next few years, work at Al Rashad flourished. According to interview testimony, the work was divided into four sections dealing with nerve agents, vesicants such as Mustard gas, incapacitants, and defoliants. Iraq has declared that pilot scale production equipment was purchased, and Mustard gas and the nerve agent Tabun, as well as several herbicides, were successfully synthesized in laboratory-scale quantities. Scientists there have said that the advanced nerve agent, Vx, and its precursors, were also investigated at the laboratory-scale at Al Rashad.

Iraq declared that, in 1978, the Al Hazen Institute was abolished because of mis-management and financial fraud, and its director general and some leading staff members were jailed. There is some evidence to support this, but there is also evidence to indicate that the institute continued on, in some form, for at least several years.

Iraq has stated that the State Organization for Technical Industries (SOTI), which came under the authority of Ministry of Industry, inherited the assets at Al Rashad in 1978. However, Iraq has said that SOTI was not responsible for the continuation of the programme and that work ceased in 1978. UNMOVIC has limited information for this period and cannot be sure that work ceased, but some scientists have stated that, at that time, they were assigned to other duties. On the other hand, the then head of the Chemical Corps said that, in 1978, he submitted to the Ministry of Industry a five year plan for a CW programme that envisaged the production of weapons, and some work continued. Iraq has acknowledged that research on chemical agents relating to chemical defence and synthesis studies continued at Al Rashad from 1979 until 1981.

The Iraq-Iran War
Project 922
With the outbreak of the war with Iran, in September 1980, Iraq's CW programme was reactivated. The inability of Iraq to achieve speedy victory, and a series of successful counter offensives by Iran in early 1981, may have been an influencing factor. Thus, on 8 June 1981, under the code-name Project 922, the CW programme came under the control of the Ministry of Defence and assumed a new urgency.

Initially Project 922 was located at Al Rashad while a new site was being sought. Iraq has stated that further expansion of the Al Rashad site occurred and equipment that had been previously acquired, but not used, was installed. Iraq has stated that during that time further research into production methods, including the synthesis of Mustard gas and Tabun, was conducted and pilot scale quantities produced.

Al Muthanna State Establishment

Later in 1981, construction work was resumed on the CW site selected in 1975, near Al Samarra. Initial engineering works started that year and, in the following year, contracts were agreed for the construction of the first four buildings. These buildings were small production facilities that were built underground to protect them from air attack. Included was a laboratory and inhalation chamber where toxic chemicals could be tested on laboratory animals. This was the start of what was to become Iraq's main CW production and research centre. It would eventually become known as Al Muthanna State Establishment (MSE).

In 1982, contracts were signed for the acquisition of production equipment and raw materials. UNMOVIC estimates that, in that year, over 800 tonnes of chemicals were purchased, mainly for the production of Mustard gas and Tabun. Most of the equipment for the plant was ordered from foreign suppliers but, in 1983, immediate requirements were satisfied by the acquisition of second-hand reactors and equipment from Sammara Drug Industries.

Iraq also faced the problem of finding a suitable delivery system for its CW agents: to develop such systems may have taken years. The solution found by Iraq was to purchase bombs designed for white phosphorus (an incendiary and smoke bomb) and then, by simple modification, make them suitable for the delivery of CW agent.

Construction activity, in 1982 and 1983, at Al Muthanna was intense. Five large research laboratories, an administrative centre, and eight large underground bunkers for the storage of chemical munitions were built. By early 1983, the first production buildings were completed at Al Muthanna and equipment installed. Iraq has declared that, in the summer of 1983, the staff and equipment from Project 922 were relocated to the Al Muthanna site. The Al Rashad site closed shortly thereafter.

Mustard Gas

Production began as soon as the first pilot scale plants were completed. Iraq has stated that, in 1983, 150 tonnes of Mustard gas were produced at Al Muthanna; this was in addition to about 85 tonnes of the agent produced in the previous years at Al Rashad. Although UNMOVIC cannot confirm these figures, they would appear consistent with Iraq's capability at that time.

At the same time as Al Muthanna was coming into production, the casualties in the Iraq-Iran war were mounting on both sides. Iran had begun human wave attacks in 1982 and continued with similar offensives in 1983. Iraq was first reported to have used chemicals to counter such attacks in that year. In March 1984, the UN Secretary-General sent a group of specialists to Iran on a fact-finding mission. The UN specialists came to the unanimous conclusion that Mustard gas had been used. This was condemned by the Security Council. The Mustard bombs that the team found were later identified as the converted white phosphorus bombs that Iraq had imported in 1982.

The nerve agent, Tabun

In 1984, further production plants were built and large scale production equipment installed. Iraq stated that production of Tabun began at Al Muthanna in 1984 and, by the end of the year, a total of 60 tonnes had been produced. The use of Tabun by Iraq in its war with Iran was also reported that year and this was also confirmed by the UN specialists.

CW munitions

Iraq also widened the range of weapons it was to use with the CW agents. In 1983 and 1984, large scale purchases of artillery shells, rockets and bombs were made. For example, Iraq has declared that, in 1983 alone, it purchased 40,000 artillery shells and 7,500 bomb casings. Iraq said that, in 1984, contracts were signed for the supply of 20,000 short range rockets which were to be modified for the delivery of chemicals.

To reduce reliance on foreign suppliers, from 1984 onwards, Iraq purchased machinery and components to manufacture its own munitions. The concept was that munitions that it had already imported would be reverse engineered and small modifications made to the design, to make the weapon suitable for CW purposes. Extensive weapons trials were conducted to further develop the design. Eventually, such weapons would form a substantial part of the Iraqi CW arsenal. For example, Iraq declared that, by 1988, it had manufactured 10,000 CW bomb casings based on the reverse engineered white phosphorus bomb it originally had imported in 1982. Also by 1989, Iraq had manufactured 18,500 rocket warheads which were based on designs that had been imported in the early to mid-1980s.

The nerve agents, Sarin and Cyclosarin

With the expansion of the facilities and staff at Al Muthanna, the production of other CW agents became practical. Iraq had been having continuing problems with the purity of Tabun and typically the product was only 50 to 60% pure and contained by-products which, in turn, adversely affected its stability. As part of a policy of diversification, Iraq started to explore the production of other nerve agents. Accordingly, pilot scale production of the nerve agent, Sarin, commenced at Al Muthanna in early 1984. By December, with the completion of new production facilities, larger scale production began. Iraq declared that, in 1985, it produced 30 tonnes but was experiencing problems with the process. According to Iraq, in 1986, only another 40 tonnes were produced and it was not until later that year that the problems were overcome.

Iraq declared that, in 1987, it stopped the production of Tabun, and concentrated on the production of Sarin, which by this stage it said it was successfully producing. About 200 tonnes was produced in that year and 390 tonnes in 1988. UNMOVIC has some evidence to support these figures. However, according to documents recovered by UNSCOM from Iraq, the purity of this product was only 40 to 60% and the stability and storability was not good. The shelf-life of the agent, as produced by Iraq at that time, is assessed by UNMOVIC to be in the order of only several months.

As the production of Sarin increased, so did its use by Iraq in the war with Iran. Reflecting the urgency of the war with Iran, the agent was used almost as quickly as it was produced. The fact that the agent could not be stored for long periods, therefore, was not such an important consideration at the time. Iraq declared that almost all of 1985's production (30 tonnes) was "consumed" that year. In the following years the pattern was similar. Initially, the agent was used in bombs but, later, Sarin filled rockets were used. For example, Iraq stated that, in 1986, about 1,200 Sarin rockets were "consumed". The following year, as more agent became available, consumption of rockets jumped to 15,000.

Sarin, in contrast to Tabun, is very volatile: at high temperatures it disperses quickly in the atmosphere and, hence, is only effective in the open for a short period of time. From the earliest days, Iraq had been researching other nerve agents at Al Muthanna. It settled on an analogue of Sarin, Cyclosarin, for production, probably because the volatility of this agent was more suited to a hot climate and its toxicity, by both skin and inhalation routes, is greater. Furthermore, the production process for Cyclosarin was similar to that of Sarin, requiring just the substitution of one alcohol for another, and the same equipment could be used. According to Iraq's declarations, the production of Cyclosarin only began in 1988. It was often produced in conjunction with Sarin to create a cocktail of agents. UNMOVIC has documentation indicating that Iraq had determined that this mixture of agents was more toxic than either component separately.

The nerve agent, Vx

For Iraq, the epitome of its development work on CW agents was the nerve agent Vx . This is one of the most toxic man-made substances known and, with its low volatility, is also one of the most persistent nerve agents. In a top secret letter, written in 1987 by the Director-General of Al Muthanna to senior government officials, the importance of the agent to Iraq was recognized. In the letter, Vx was compared to a nuclear weapon: *"two tonnes carried by an aircraft compare with a medium nuclear bomb of 20 kilotons"*. The letter continued that its possession *"…ushers us into the* [field] *of armament of advanced countries"*.

Iraq has stated that serious work on the nerve agent Vx did not begin until 1985, although it has acknowledged that some preliminary investigations had been conducted earlier, including at Al Rashad. The above referenced letter stated that the work on nerve agents focussed on Vx after the problems with Sarin production were solved in 1986, and that Vx was considered as an agent to supplement Sarin.

Iraq has declared that it experienced many problems with the production of Vx, both with the equipment and the process for its production. A number of different routes for its synthesis were tried but there is evidence to indicate that, by the end of the Iraq-Iran war, only small quantities had been made. Iraq declared that, in 1988, in five production trials it had produced only 2.4 tonnes of Vx and that this was unstable and had degraded rapidly. Further work on the agent continued after the war (see later).

Research into other agents

From its very establishment, Al Muthanna had an active research programme. One of the objectives appeared to be to diversify the range of agents Iraq had available to it. Novelty was also considered to be important. According to a 1988 Iraqi research paper, *"new highly toxic agents as substitutes for the present agents"* were to be investigated as these would have *"the element of surprise when using them on the battlefront because of the lack of information on the part of the enemy and the difficulty of detecting them".* As a consequence, a range of nerve agents, mostly analogues of Sarin and Vx, were researched, as well as nerve agents such as Soman and Tammeline esters.

More exotic chemicals were also investigated, such as PCP, a hallucinogenic compound known as "angel dust", as well as incapacitants such as BZ and its analogues.

In addition to these agents, Iraq also researched synthesis techniques for better known agents cyanogen chloride, lewisite, nitrogen mustard and adamsite. There is no evidence that any of these were produced beyond laboratory scale.

Efforts were directed towards solving the stability problems of the nerve agents. An approach that was adopted for Sarin was to synthesize an immediate precursor (MPF), that is relatively stable. Immediately before use this precursor would be reacted with the appropriate alcohol to produce Sarin. This was referred to as "binary Sarin". A similar approach was investigated in 1988 for Vx. In addition, stabilizers for nerve agents were investigated.

New Facilities, Al Fallujah

As production increased at Al Muthanna, so did the requirement for raw materials and precursor chemicals. At the start of the programme all the chemicals Iraq required for the production of its CW agents had been imported. Iraq has declared that, in 1985, it decided to reduce this dependency by building three chemical plants outside of the Al Muthanna complex to provide precursors for the CW programme. The plants were near the town of Al Fallujah, 50 kilometres west of Baghdad, and were named Fallujah I, II and III. Iraq said that intention was that the plants would also support the civilian chemical sector in the provision of chemicals. Construction of the first plant, Falljah II, began in 1986 and was designed for the production of the key chlorinating agent thionyl choride, a precursor for the production of Mustard and Sarin.

Iraq stated that Fallujah II was intended to start production in 1987, but equipment problems delayed production until 1988 when, according to Iraq, 70 tonnes of thionyl chloride were produced. UNMOVIC has evidence that actual production was almost twice this amount. The achievement was quite significant because the plant was completely indigenously designed and constructed. However, problems were said to have stopped production in 1988. In 1987, Fallujah III began construction. This plant was intended for the production of precursors mainly for nerve agents, but Iraq said that it did not become operational because of equipment problems. UNMOVIC is unable to confirm this.

International control of chemicals

In 1985, following confirmation of the use of chemicals in the Iraq-Iran War, an international group was formed (the Australia Group) to apply export controls on a range of precursor chemicals. By this stage Iraq had a stockpile of imported chemicals, but it recognized that it could no longer rely on foreign imports.

Attempts to circumvent the Australia Group controls were made by the employment of front companies and intermediaries. In addition, alternative suppliers, not subject to controls, were sought and there is evidence that some success was achieved. Iraq also looked at different production methods that would use chemicals that it had in stock or were readily available. Thus, in 1987, according to Iraq, phosphorus trichloride was substituted for thionyl chloride in the production of Mustard. Thionyl chloride was then reserved for the production of nerve agent.

At the same time as the above measures, Iraq planned a longer term solution to the acquisition of chemicals by producing key chemicals in-country. Al Muthanna had the coordinating role. It is not clear from Iraq's statements whether the decision to build the Fallujah plants was prompted by these controls, but certainly they were built at a time when precursors were in short supply. At Al Muthanna, a number of plants were also built in the mid 1980s, to synthesize precursor chemicals. In addition, other Iraqi agencies, including the Al Qaim phospate plant and Al Qaa Qaa munitions factory, were instructed to provide chemicals.

UNMOVIC's assessment is that Iraq's CW programme, prior to the end of the Iraq-Iran War, was not significantly hindered by international controls: the controls probably came too late and Iraqi stockpiles of raw materials at that time were still quite significant. After the war though, the controls seemed to cause major problems and, in 1990, Iraq set up a ministerial committee to address measures to overcome them.

Reorganization

Project 922 had been set up in 1981, under the Ministry of Defence. In order to disguise the end-user for chemicals and equipment, the cover name for the purchasing arm went under the name of the State Establishment for Pesticide Production (SEPP). Gradually the cover name became compromised and, in 1985, administrative and commercial matters became the responsibility of the Ministry of Industries, under the State Organization for Technical Industries. In effect, the Director-General of Al Muthanna then reported jointly to both Ministers. The purchasing authority then became the State Organization for Chemical Industries, although other fronts were also used, including the State Organization for Refinery and Gas Industries (SORGI).

In 1987, in a general reorganization of government departments, the formal ties between Al Muthanna and the Ministry of Defence were cut. Al Muthanna then came solely under the Military Industrial Commission, which was then headed by the newly appointed Lieutenant-General Hussein Kamal. It was at this time that Project 922 officially became Al Muthanna State Establishment. This was also a time of peak production for Al Muthanna, with the establishment employing a staff of about 1000 workers.

The end of the Iraq-Iran War

The use of CW

The war with Iran ended in August 1988. By this time seven UN specialist missions had documented repeated use of chemicals in the war. According to Iraq, it consumed almost 19,500 chemical bombs, over 54,000 chemical artillery shells and 27,000 short-range chemical rockets between 1983 and 1988. Iraq declared that about 1,800 tonnes of Mustard, 140 tonnes of Tabun and over 600 tonnes of Sarin had been consumed during these years. Almost two-thirds of the

CW weapons used, were used in the last 18 months of the war. In March 1988, unidentified chemicals were also used against civilians in the Kurdish city of Halabja in north-east Iraq.

UNMOVIC has little information to confirm the types and quantities of CW weapons that Iraq declared were consumed from 1983 to 1988. Specialists on UN fact-finding missions, from 1984 to 1988, simply concluded that bombs and rockets carrying Mustard and Tabun had been used. However a document Iraq provided UNMOVIC, in December 2002, indicates that fewer chemical bombs than declared were used. The document, from Iraq's Air Force headquarters, shows that 13,000 chemical bombs were dropped during the War. This is less than that (19,500) declared by Iraq.

Post war activities

Iraq has declared that, after the Iraq-Iran War, the production of CW agents stopped as there was no longer an immediate need for the products: UNMOVIC has some limited information to support this. Also, given the short shelf-life of the nerve agents and the possibility that stock piles of relatively stable Mustard existed at that time, (possibly about 700 tonnes), it is logical that further production did not proceed. The evidence available to UNMOVIC indicates that much of the effort at Al Muthanna, at the end of 1988 and in 1989, was directed towards production to assist the civilian sector. Thus, production was turned to the manufacture of chlorine-based disinfectants and insecticides. Such chemicals still required the continued operation of some of the precursor plants at Al Muthanna. In addition, work continued at the Fallujah sites with the installation of chemical production equipment, including a chlorine plant.

Although Al Muthanna was involved in the production of civilian products after the Iraq-Iran War, the facility was still a military one under the control of MIC. In August 1989, the Director-General wrote to senior government officials that "*research on munitions and chemical weapons are very important in war conditions. We must always be ready and prepared and must follow up every new development in this domain. The other face of the coin is pesticide research.*" In accordance with this edict, development of CW agents and weapons continued. In particular, there is evidence to indicate that, in early 1989, efforts were directed towards the testing of binary Sarin agents and investigating various munitions including "*a binary system for 122 mm rockets*" and a chemical cluster bomb.

The lead up to the Gulf War

On 2 April 1990, President Saddam Hussein stated that, if Israel attacked Iraq, "*we will make the fire eat half of Israel*". There is strong evidence to indicate that the CW programme was reactivated at this time. Iraq stated that the instruction for this came from MIC, headed at that time by Lieutenant-General Hussein Kamal. UNMOVIC, however, cannot discount the possibility that there was not also some renewed activity before this.

One major new project that was started in April 1990, and said by Iraq to be response to the President's statement, was the development of a new CW bomb. This was based on a reverse engineered imported, parachute-retarded bomb and was intended for low-level release from an aircraft. There is evidence to show that engineering drawings were completed by 16 April, and prototypes fabricated in April/May 1990. The first trials of the bomb were conducted on 22 May

1990, and production began soon thereafter. The initial order of 1,000 bombs, eventually designated the R-400, was delivered to Al Muthanna in July 1990.

Another project, initiated in April 1990, was the development of Al Hussein warheads for CW use. Modified warheads, with internal containers for liquid agent, were designed and manufactured. Iraq said that these were tested in two static trials held in April and May 1990. Iraq stated that two flight tests, one using an inert liquid (oil and water) and one using spoiled Sarin, were conducted in April 1990. Iraq declared that, by June 1990, the first batch of "special" warheads had been manufactured and delivered to Al Muthanna, and that 50 such warheads were eventually manufactured for CW purposes. UNMOVIC is unable to confirm this figure.

Clearly, both of the above munitions projects had a sense of urgency. In conjunction with these munitions projects, there were renewed efforts to increase agent production. In a December 1990 report to Lieutenant-General Hussein Kamal, the Director-General of Al Muthanna wrote *"following the tense military situation after 2 April 1990, there arose the importance of finding substitutes to resume nerve agent production"*. The report indicated that Al Muthanna had had some success in overcoming shortages due to international controls on chemicals. Indeed, according to Iraq's declarations, production of Sarin for 1990 was 117 tonnes. Iraq stated that 280 tonnes of Mustard was also manufactured that year.

There is evidence that attention was also focussed on Vx immediately prior to the Gulf War. In fact, in December 1990, Lieutenant-General Hussein Kamal ordered the Director-General of Al Muthanna to *"concentrate on producing the intermediate substances as well as on producing Vx as a final product"*. However, Iraq has stated that it only managed to produce 1.5 tonnes of Vx in 1990.

Iraq declared that the filling of the new R-400 bombs and the Al Hussein warheads began in June 1990 as the first munitions were delivered to Al Muthanna. In all, over 1000 R-400 bombs and 50 Al Hussein warheads were said to have been filled. The agents said to be selected were Sarin and Cyclosarin, either as the agent or in binary form (ie the alcohol only was placed in the munition and the precursor was stored alongside in containers). UNMOVIC cannot be certain of the fill for these weapons but notes that, on some destroyed warheads recovered by UNSCOM, degradation products of Vx were found, implying that at least some of these weapons were filled with that agent. In addition to these weapons, Iraq stated that it filled many thousands of other CW munitions in 1990. For example, in that year, 12,500 artillery shells were filled with Mustard and 8,500 rockets were filled with Sarin.

By 15 January 1991, the CW weapons were dispersed to airfields and other locations. Iraq has stated that its policy was to use these weapons only if Baghdad was attacked with nuclear weapons and then field commanders had the authority to use them at their discretion. UNMOVIC has no evidence to indicate that any CW weapons were used in the Gulf War.

Destruction

The Gulf War started on 17 January 1991. During the bombing campaign the main CW facilities at Al Muthanna and Al Fallujah were heavily damaged. In addition, some of the CW weapons stored at airfields and other locations were also destroyed. However, Iraq had evacuated much of its strategic materials and equipment prior to the war. For example much of the bomb-casing manufacturing equipment from Al Muthanna, had been relocated to a sugar factory at Al Mosul in the far north of the country. Iraq has stated that in 1990, consideration was given to using this equipment to set up an alternative CW bomb factory at this site, although it said this plan was not carried through.

Some of the CW agents were stored in bulk in containers, including large (20 cubic metre) transportable tanks to be buried for safe-keeping. Thus, several hundreds of tonnes of Mustard and Sarin were buried in the desert surrounding Al Muthanna during the war and survived the bombing. The agents was subsequently destroyed by UNSCOM.

After the Gulf War, and the adoption of UN Security Council resolution 687 (1991), of 3 April 1991, UNSCOM began inspections in Iraq. The first site inspected was the Al Muthanna CW plant in early June 1991. It was clear, even from this first inspection, that the site had been severely disabled, but not completely destroyed. The scene was one of smashed production plants and leaking munitions. The air was contaminated for kilometres with a cocktail of gases from the site. In August 1991, the second chemical inspection team visited the precursor plants at Al Fullujah and inspected similar destruction levels. Planning then began on the elimination of remaining CW assets and the safe deactivation of weapons and agents.

Before UNSCOM could begin its work on the elimination remaining CW capabilities, Iraq secretly began its own unilateral destruction. Iraq declared that, in July 1991, under instruction from Lieutenant-General Hussein Kamal, it began the unilateral destruction of selected chemicals and munitions; this activity was not disclosed to UNSCOM at the time. Iraq has stated that the rationale for this activity was not to deceive UNSCOM but that the disclosure of certain items "*would complicate matters and prolong the process with UNSCOM*". It is probable that one of the reasons for this unilateral destruction was an effort to bring what UNSCOM might find more into line with the serious inadequacies in Iraq's initial declaration of its holdings of proscribed weapons and materials. There was said to be no criteria for what was to be destroyed and that there was "*no obvious logic governing the choice of items concealed*". Vast quantities of CW weapons were said to have been destroyed by Iraq in the summer of 1991. In all, Iraq declared the destruction of over 28,000 filled and unfilled munitions, about 30 tonnes of bulk chemical precursors for Sarin and Cyclosarin, and over 200 tonnes of key precursors relating to Vx.

The remaining weapons, materials and equipment declared by Iraq, that could be identified and located by UNSCOM, were destroyed under its supervision, mainly between 1992 and 1994. Thus, over 28,000 munitions, 480 tonnes of CW agent and 100,000 tonnes of precursor chemicals were disposed of. About 400 major pieces of chemical processing equipment and some hundreds of items of other equipment, such as bomb-making machinery, were also destroyed under UNSCOM supervision.

Dual-use capabilities to 1998
Although much of the infrastructure associated with Iraq's CW programme had been damaged by bombing during the Gulf War, other civilian chemical plants had remained untouched. Thus

petrochemical, fertilizer and pesticide production plants remained intact, and continued to operate post-war. Iraq has gradually added to these by expansion or the construction of new facilities. In addition, one of the former CW precursor plants at Al Fallujah was refurbished and configured to produce chlorine for the purification of water. Much of this civilian chemical industry used dual-capable technology and was, therefore, under monitoring by UNSCOM until the end of 1998.

Conclusions

UNMOVIC has a good understanding of the nature and scope of Iraq's CW programme. The areas of greatest uncertainty relate to questions of material balance and whether there may be items still remaining. In this regard, Iraq's unilateral destruction of large quantities of chemicals and weapons, in July 1991, has complicated the accountancy problem. The questions of uncertainty are discussed further in the Clusters of Unresolved Disarmament Issues.

The CW programme itself was impressive in its size and achievements. In 1981, early in the Iraq-Iran War, Iraq demonstrated the ability to rapidly expand its capability when, in a few years, it went from small-scale research, to one of large-scale production of agents and weapons. Up to this point, much of the technology for the programme had been imported by Iraq and simply adapted to its needs. After international controls were applied to the supply of chemicals in the mid-1980s, Iraq demonstrated its flexibility in finding solutions to ensure the continued production of CW agents. Its top chemists were highly skilled, as evidenced by their ability to synthesize, at least on a pilot scale, the nerve agent Vx. Iraq also showed ingenuity and skill in the design, development and manufacture of its own weapon systems. And again, in 1990, just prior to the Gulf War, Iraq showed its capabilities, by rapidly gearing up for war after a latent period.

By some standards, the technology levels achieved by Iraq in the production of its CW agents and weapons, were not high. The agents were often impure and had a limited shelf-life. The weapon designs were not optimized to effect the most devastating dissemination of agent. But, even with these less than optimal weapons, many thousands of Iranians were killed or injured by them in the Iraq-Iran War. It is evident that Iraq's CW capabilities posed a significant regional threat.

Intentionally Blank

IRAQ'S BIOLOGICAL WARFARE PROGRAMME

Introduction

Of all its proscribed weapons programmes, Iraq's biological warfare (BW) programme was perhaps the most secretive. Iraq has stated that knowledge of the programme was kept to a select few officials and that, to maintain secrecy, special measures were taken. This secrecy was maintained after the Gulf War when Iraq went to considerable lengths, including the destruction of documents and the forging of other documents, to conceal its BW efforts from UNSCOM. After intensive investigations by UNSCOM, Iraq disclosed some details of its offensive BW programme on, 1 July 1995. Following the defection of Lieutenant-General Hussein Kamal, in August 1995, Iraq revealed a much more comprehensive BW programme.

Iraq's efforts to conceal the programme, particularly the destruction of documentation and its declared unilateral destruction of BW weapons and agents, have complicated UNMOVIC's task of piecing together a coherent and accurate account of its BW programme. In fact, there are indications that, at various times, there was more than one programme. For example, in 1985, there was a BW programme under the Ministry of Defence and, overlapping this, was another BW programme under the control of the State Security Apparatus. What the connections, if any, between these two programmes may have been, other than through government direction and leadership, is unclear. For the sake of clarity, the account given below, refers to Iraq's BW activities as if they were under a single unified programme.

Origins of a BW programme

The origins of Iraq's BW programme are not readily identifiable. Iraq has declared that its first efforts to initiate a BW programme were made in 1974, following a government decree to look at "*scientific, academic and applied researches in the fields of chemistry, physics and micro-organisms*". The motivation for this work was said by Iraq to be because of the threat from Iraq's enemies.

Iraq stated that the response to this decree in the BW field, was to construct a research facility, the Ibn Sina Centre, at a site on the Al Salman peninsula, 30 kilometres south of Baghdad. The Centre came under the auspices of a newly created organization, Al Hazen Ibn Al Haithem Institute. Iraq declared that construction began in 1974, but, given the sophistication of the design of the Centre, it seems likely that planning for it would have begun in 1973, or perhaps even earlier.

The Al Hazen Institute was ostensibly part of the Ministry of Higher Education and Scientific Research, but Iraq has acknowledged that, in reality, it belonged to the State Security Apparatus. Research at the Centre was stated by Iraq to be basic and that little was actually achieved because of poor direction and management. It is not certain that this was the case and, in fact, from the testimony of some of the scientists at the Centre, it was possible that more was achieved than has been declared.

Iraq has declared that activities at the Centre were terminated, in 1978, when its director and some of the leading scientists were jailed for fraud; Iraq provided documentary evidence to support this. However, it would also appear that the Centre itself did not close and that activities, stated by Iraq to be unrelated to BW, continued for some time into the 1980s. From interview testimony, the actual nature of the continued work is not apparent to UNMOVIC.

The dates of the start and closure of Ibn Sina Centre may not be particularly important, but its objectives and achievements are. The achievements, particularly those that were more military related, could possibly have provided a sound research basis for developments that were to come, and hence shorten the lead-time to the production of biological weapons. In this regard, it is also noteworthy that at least five of the researchers at the Centre went on to make contributions later in the BW programme.

Restart of a BW programme

War with Iran broke out in September 1980, and by mid 1981 Iraq had reactivated its chemical weapon programme to produce weapons to counter Iranian forces. It was in this environment that Iraq's BW programme was restarted. According to Iraq, after the closure of the Ibn Sina Centre, no practical work in the BW field was conducted until 1985. By this time, Iraq had been fighting a war with Iran for four years and both sides were facing mounting casualties.

The 1985 restart of the BW programme was said by Iraq to have taken place after the Director-General of Iraq's CW facility at Al Muthanna State Establishment (MSE) wrote, in the preamble of his 1983 annual report to the Minister of Defence, that his mandate covered both chemical and biological agents. Since the Minister did not dispute this assertion, the Director-General assumed he had authorization to conduct work in the BW field. The Director-General's report also coincided with a 1983 letter from a senior Iraqi microbiologist to the Baath Party, suggesting that Iraq could defend itself from Iran by the development and use of BW weapons.

Whatever the stimulus for the renewed interest in 1983, no action was said to have taken place until early 1985, when the first biologists were recruited. The Director-General of MSE stated that he informed the Minister of Defence, in 1985, that within five years the first biological weapons would be produced.

There is documentation to show that bacterial strains and basic laboratory supplies were obtained in late 1985 and early 1986. According to Iraq, two agents, botulinum toxin and anthrax were selected as candidate BW agents. The basis for their selection was said to be that other countries had produced them for BW purposes and that they were relatively easy to make. Work on these agents, in 1986, was restricted to pathogenicity and toxicity studies, their characteristics, and methods of production at the laboratory-scale.

As a separate stream to the BW activities at MSE, it appears that BW activities were also being conducted under the auspices of the State Security Apparatus at Al Salman. UNMOVIC has no clear understanding of what the stimulus for the initiation of this work was. According to Iraq's statements this work began, in 1984, with the investigation of wheat smut. Initial interest was said to have been to prevent crop infection, but by 1987 the investigations had shifted to the use of the disease as an economic weapon. No other BW activities are acknowledged by Iraq during this period (1984 - 1986) although it is interesting to note that an inhalation chamber was installed at Al Salman, probably in 1984, and was later used in the BW programme.

Programme Expansion: 1987 – 1988

Transfer to the Technical Research Centre

Iraq has stated that, towards the end of 1986, MSE put forward a proposal to scale up the production of botulinum toxin from laboratory to pilot scale. To this end, the takeover of a facility (a former Petroleum Protein Project) at Al Taji was sought. However, before this could occur, a new Director-General of MSE was appointed in early 1987 and, according to Iraq, he considered the expansion of BW activities at MSE to be incompatible with the site and wanted the BW group to move from his establishment. Evidence shows that there was, indeed, a transfer of the BW function from MSE to the Forensic Research Department at Al Salman in the first half of 1987. At Al Salman, the research came under the control of the Technical Research Centre (TRC) which, at that time, was part of the State Security Apparatus.

Senior Iraqi officials have stated that, in early 1987, there was dissatisfaction with progress in the BW field: in its two years of operation, the programme was still involved with basic laboratory research and the promise of weapons in five years seemed unrealistic. Accordingly, following the transfer of staff to TRC, there was an acceleration of the pace the programme. Additional laboratory supplies and equipment were acquired in 1987 and 1988, and new staff was recruited. Iraq has declared that a new building to house a pilot scale fermenter and to allow other expansion, was designed at the end of 1987. Construction of the new building at Al Salman was said to have begun in 1988. The remains of such a building have been inspected by UNSCOM.

Also, some time in 1987, (Iraq has declared from mid-1987), further development work on botulinum toxin and anthrax began. This work involved production of these agents in bench top fermenters and experimentation on a range of animals, including sheep, donkeys and monkeys, to study inhalation and other effects.

Another bacterial agent, *Clostridium perfringens* (gas gangrene) , was added to the research programme, probably in 1987. There is evidence to show that research into certain fungal toxins (trichothecene mycotoxins) also began at the end of 1987. And, in May 1988, a mycologist was recruited for the development of other fungal toxins, in particular aflatoxin.

Pilot scale production

It would appear that the Al Taji facility came under the control of the TRC in 1987. Iraq has declared that the fermenter at that facility was refurbished and botulinum toxin produced there by TRC, from January to October 1988. Although the dates cannot be confirmed there is some evidence to suggest that botulinum toxin was indeed produced at the Al Taji facility, although possibly starting earlier than declared by Iraq.

Weapons developments

The first field trial of a crude BW dissemination device was said by Iraq to have commenced in February 1988, and this was followed by relatively more sophisticated trials of BW bombs (the

LD 250) in April/May1988. UNMOVIC has supporting evidence for at least some of these trials, which were conducted using the expertise of the weapons engineers from MSE .

In addition to the above weapons, there was the development of an aerosol spray device, in 1987 and 1988, at Al Salman. The device, a modification of an agricultural crop-duster, was intended for the spraying of bacteria and was tested with an anthrax simulant.

BW Developments: 1988 – Aug 1990

Iraq has stated that, towards the end of 1987, the head of TRC submitted a report on the success of the BW research work at Al Salman. Iraq has said that, as a consequence of this report, Lieutenant-General Hussein Kamal (then the new head of the Military Industrialization Commission), instructed that the BW programme should proceed towards the production of BW agent. Although Iraq stated that it was the success of the research work in 1987 that stimulated the decision for production, UNMOVIC questions whether very much could have been achieved in the few months the BW team had been at Al Salman. On the other hand, there is evidence that initial preparations for large scale production did begin in late 1987.

At the end of 1987, Iraq placed the first of a series of orders to purchase large quantities of bacterial growth media, the feedstuff for producing bacteria. Eventually, the purchases would total over 40 tonnes. In April 1988, an equipment requirement list, apparently in response to Lieutenant-General Hussein Kamal's instruction, was prepared. The list included three sizeable (5,000 litre) fermenters, two for botulinum toxin and one for anthrax production. Dryers and other processing equipment for anthrax were also specified.

Al Hakam

At about the same time as the enquiries for materials and equipment were being made, the search for a suitable production site was conducted. Iraq has stated that the Al Salman site was considered unsuitable for safety reasons, because of its proximity to Baghdad. A search for an alternative site was, therefore, made in early 1988. According to one account given by a senior Iraqi official, one of the early considerations for production was a mobile facility that could be moved from site to site. This was said to have been rejected as being impractical. Eventually a production site was selected, in March 1988, at a remote desert location about 55 kilometres south-west of Baghdad. Iraqi officials have said that, in commemoration of the date of founding of the site (March 24), it was initially named Project 324. The site later was known as Al Hakam and was to become Iraq's main BW production facility.

Al Hakam was constructed rapidly and in secrecy. Learning from the mistakes made in the building of the chemical weapons plant, MSE, the rule for Al Hakam was that no foreigners were to go to the site. Priority was given to the completion of the production buildings and, by the end of 1988, the first such buildings were said to have been completed and equipment installed. Transfer of staff and functions was stated by Iraq to have begun towards the end of 1988, and to have been completed by late 1990.

Critical to the production of BW agent, was the acquisition of fermenters. In a submission to senior officials, the options available to Iraq for their acquisition were considered. The submission argued that manufacture in Iraq was, at that time, not considered to be technically feasible, and, in any case, it was argued this would take a long time. The recommended action was to purchase fermenters from overseas and, subsequently, several foreign companies were contacted in early 1988. A contract with a supplier for three 5,000 litre fermenters was agreed in July 1988 and, at Iraq's insistence, the first unit was scheduled for delivery later that year. The supplier could not meet the schedule and delivery was postponed to 1989.

Since no foreign supplier was permitted to visit Al Hakam, Iraq modified another facility at Al Latifyah, 50 kilometres west of Baghdad, and presented this to the manufacturer as the plant where the fermenters were to be installed. Iraq also falsified the end-user certificate to indicate the fermenters were for civilian use. Iraqi officials have stated that the plan was that, after the fermenters had been installed and commissioned by the company, they would be relocated to Al Hakam. However, in the end, the supplier could not obtain an export licence and the contract was finally cancelled in late 1989.

However, such was the priority on production in 1988, that another option for fermenters was also pursued. TRC became aware that a line of fermenters was available at the Veterinary Research Laboratories at Al Kindi. Consideration was given to producing botulinum toxin in these fermenters at Al Kindi. Iraq stated that this option was not taken up and instead, Al Kindi fermenters were compulsorily acquired and transferred to Al Hakam in late 1988. UNMOVIC can confirm the acquisition but not the exact date of transfer.

According to Iraq, the fermenter from Al Taji was also transferred to Al Hakam at the end of 1988.

Thus, by the end of 1988, Al Hakam, after a rushed construction and acquisition programme, was ready to produce agent. However, the war with Iran finished in August 1988 and, therefore, it may have been expected that there would have been a slowing of pace. However, the evidence indicates the contrary. In the two years following the end of the war the momentum continued. Activities included BW agent production, new research projects, and weapons-testing and development.

Botulinum toxin production

Production of botulinum toxin was stated by Iraq to have begun at Al Hakam, first in the fermenter from Al Taji, in January 1989, and then in the veterinary fermenter line in February 1989. Iraq has declared that, from the start of production at Al Hakam in January 1989 to August 1990, 13,600 litres of concentrated botulinum toxin was produced.

Anthrax production

Iraq has declared that, in early 1989, Al Hakam did not produce anthrax. However pilot scale production of anthrax was started at Al Salman in March 1989, and continued there for four months. Anthrax production at Al Hakam was said to have started in June 1990. Up to August 1990, total production of (concentrated) anthrax was stated to be 170 litres, a relatively small amount compared with the amount of botulinum toxin produced up to this time.

Aflatoxin production

Aflatoxin production was stated by Iraq to have begun at Al Salman in January 1989 and to have continued there until July 1990, during which time about 400 litres of aflatoxin was produced. UNMOVIC is unable to confirm this.

Research

Research into previously selected agents continued, although UNMOVIC is uncertain of the precise nature, timing and scope of this work. Iraq has declared that, during this period (1988 – August 1990), studies on botulinum toxin, anthrax, gas gangrene and aflatoxin continued. This research included investigation of the best growth conditions, effects on animals and other studies, such as the determination of the optimum storage parameters.

Research into new agents also began during this period. Work on the BW agent ricin (extracted from castor oil beans), was probably commenced in the latter half of 1988. Studies included production and identification of the toxin protein and toxicity effects, including inhalation studies. Iraq has also declared that, in the first half of 1990, research into *Clostridium botulinum* spores (as opposed to the toxin), as a potential infectious agent, was conducted; UNMOVIC cannot confirm this.

A decision to research and develop viruses as potential BW agents was probably made in May 1990, or earlier. In any event, in July 1990, a virologist was recruited to begin work on viral BW agents. Iraq has stated that the laboratories at Al Hakam were considered unsuitable for viral research and actual BW work on viruses only commenced in December 1990 (see the section, *August 1990: Preparations for War*).

In March 1990, a genetic engineering unit was established under the auspices of Al Hakam. A senior Iraqi official said that one aim of the unit was to produce antibiotic resistant anthrax. Another genetic engineering unit, apparently connected to the viral programme, was also planned, but was said not to have been established. UNMOVIC is not entirely clear what the objectives of these BW genetic engineering projects were, but assesses that, in reality, probably very little was achieved.

Other research work during the period included experiments into the drying of anthrax. As noted earlier, spray dryers for anthrax were included on Iraq's equipment requirement list in April 1988. In 1989, Iraq signed a contract for the supply from a foreign company of a suitable dryer for this purpose. At the end of that year, a visit to the company by a senior Iraqi scientist was made, and a small sample of anthrax simulant dried during a demonstration of the company's equipment. UNMOVIC has evidence that, in anticipation of receiving the dryer, Iraq conducted a series of experiments on a laboratory-scale at Al Hakam, in 1990, to determine the best compounds to add to anthrax spores to assist in the drying process. However, in March 1990, the company withdrew from the contract because an export licence for the special dryer could not be obtained. UNMOVIC has evidence that the drying experiments at Al Hakam then stopped (at least for 1990).

Field trials of BW weapons
From documentation it appears that field trials of 122mm rockets as a BW delivery system were conducted, possibly in November or December 1989. No test of any other BW weapon systems is declared by Iraq for 1989.

Presidential speech, April 1990
On 2 April 1990, President Saddam Hussein delivered a powerful speech on the threat to Iraq from Israel. Iraq has stated that, along with other military establishments, Al Hakam was required to respond to this new perceived threat. Consequently, a series of hurriedly organized dynamic tests of 122 mm BW rockets was conducted in May 1990. UNMOVIC has evidence that dynamic firings of such rockets containing botulinum toxin, anthrax and aflatoxin took place at some time in 1990. UNMOVIC cannot identify any other BW activity that might be specifically in response to the Presidential statement.

In summary, the period from the end of the Iraq-Iran War to August 1990, appeared to be an active time in Iraq's BW programme. A new and dedicated facility for BW research and production was completed at Al Hakam, further research was conducted on agents, new agents selected for investigation and field trials of potential BW delivery systems were conducted. However, the focus of the effort for this period was on preparation for large scale production. Large fermenters had been sought (unsuccessfully) from overseas and a production line of fermenters compulsorily acquired from a civilian plant. Large quantities of bacterial growth medium (totalling some 40 tonnes) had been ordered and delivered throughout 1988 and 1989. Production of BW agent had also begun and, by August 1990, Iraq had accumulated a significant stockpile of agent.

August 1990: Preparations for War
After Iraq's invasion of Kuwait, on 2 August 1990, the priorities for Iraq's BW programme changed. Iraq has stated that, after 2 August 1990, Lieutenant-General Hussein Kamal gave instructions to increase BW agent production and to weaponize agents. The programme then, according to one senior Iraqi official, headed down a *"hasty, unplanned and badly conceived course"*. UNMOVIC would not characterize the programme, post August 1990, in this way, but the evidence does indicate that there was a change in direction.

BW Agent Production
UNMOVIC has documentation to show that, between August and December 1990, 5,000 litres of concentrated botulinum toxin and 8,275 litres of concentrated anthrax, were produced at Al Hakam. Thus, for these two agents, the total quantity produced in the last 5 months of 1990 represents more than half of the stated total production for the entire BW programme.

In addition, 340 litres of concentrated *Clostridium perfringens* (gas gangrene) were produced in the latter part of 1990. Iraq has declared that this was the first production in bulk of this agent. There is also documentation indicating that in 1990, 2,200 litres of aflatoxin were produced; Iraq has declared that most of this, about 1800 litres, was produced after August 1990.

To facilitate the increased demand for agent, a new facility was needed. A Foot and Mouth Disease Vaccine plant at Al Daura was compulsorily acquired by Al Hakam for BW purposes in August 1990. A number of fermenters at this facility were modified to make them suitable for the growth of *Clostridium botulinum* and 5,000 litres of botulinum toxin produced there in November/ December 1990. Iraq declared that the plant stopped production at the end of December 1990. However, UNMOVIC has some evidence to suggest that the Al Daura facility continued to operate into January 1991 and that anthrax was also produced there.

The Foot and Mouth Disease Vaccine Plant was also used for the viral research project initiated in July 1990. Iraq has stated that research was confined to three viruses: camelpox, infectious haemorrhagic conjunctivitis (enterovirus 70) and rotavirus, during the period 1 December 1990 to 17 January 1991. UNMOVIC has some evidence to indicate that these viruses were researched, but cannot be certain that this was the limit of Iraq's interest in viral agents.

For the production of aflatoxin, Al Hakam acquired a laboratory at Al Fudhaliyah from the Agricultural Ministry in September 1990. Iraq has stated that this facility was brought into production in September 1990 and operated until 15 January 1991. UNMOVIC cannot confirm the dates of production.

Weaponization

Iraq's approach to BW weaponization changed after August 1990. Prior to that date, Iraq had experimented, apparently successfully, with the LD 250 bomb and 122 mm rockets as dispersal systems for BW agent. At Al Salman, as previously noted, experiments had been conducted to convert crop dusters to BW dissemination devices. Iraq has stated that after 2 August 1990, Lieutenant-General Hussein Kamal instructed that another bomb, the R-400, that had been developed for CW purposes, would now be filled with BW agent. In addition, 25 "special" warheads were manufactured for BW purposes. These were intended for delivery by the Al Hussein missile (an extended range SCUD up to 650 kilometres). Iraq declared that neither weapons system had, at this stage, been tested with BW agents.

It appears that the R-400 biological bomb was tested sometime in 1990, possibly as Iraq declared, in August of that year. This was stated to be a static test limited to two bombs, to determine the optimum burster charge size. Iraq has stated that no other tests of the R-400 bomb took place and that the Al Hussein warhead was never tested as a BW system.

Iraq has declared that, in December 1990, 157 R-400 bombs were filled with BW agent: 100 with botulinum toxin, 50 with anthrax and 7 with aflatoxin. Iraq has also stated that 25 warheads were filled: 16 with botulinum toxin, 5 with anthrax and 4 with aflatoxin. Whilst UNMOVIC has uncertainties regarding many aspects of Iraq's account of the filling of weapons, (including the numbers), there is good evidence to indicate that R-400 bombs and Al Hussein warheads were filled with the agents stated by Iraq.

Iraq has declared that, about a week before the Gulf War, instructions were given to deploy the filled BW munitions. Iraq has stated that the R-400 bombs were sent to two locations and the warheads to another two, where they remained until July 1991; there is some supporting evidence for this. Contrary to Iraq's declaration, there is evidence that bulk agent, remaining after the filling of weapons, was also deployed in the field.

Iraq has stated that, in preparation for the coming war, the development of another BW delivery system was initiated in November 1990. This was a based on an aircraft fuel drop-tank that was modified to enable liquid BW agent to be sprayed. In one Iraqi account (later withdrawn) the concept was that the drop tank was to be filled with anthrax and delivered to the target area by a remotely piloted MIG aircraft. Iraq has declared that 12 such tanks were planned, but only four were completed and the system was not deployed. UNMOVIC has some information that conflicts with the Iraqi account but has evidence that a drop tank project did take place.

The Gulf War and beyond

Iraq has declared that its policy was to use its BW weapons only if Baghdad was attacked with nuclear weapons. Then field commanders had the authority to use them in a counter-attack. UNMOVIC has no evidence to indicate that any BW weapons were used in the Gulf War.

It would appear that Iraq had been successful in keeping the existence of Al Hakam secret. In contrast to the chemical weapons plant at Al Muthanna, and the research facilities at Al Salman, Al Hakam was not bombed by coalition forces during the Gulf War. It was perhaps this fact that encouraged Iraq, initially, not to disclose its BW programme to UNSCOM.

Destruction

Iraq has acknowledged that, in biology, the approach to ending the programme was different to that in chemical and missiles. Iraq has stated that it decided not to declare its BW programme, but to retain all BW associated facilities, equipment and materials. Iraq has stated that Lieutenant-General Hussein Kamal gave instructions to remove any evidence of the existence of a BW programme. Thus a clean-up at Al Hakam and other sites was said to have begun in June 1991and continued until July/August 1991.

Iraq has stated that, although it had decided to retain its BW infrastructure and materials, it decided to destroy, unilaterally, its BW agents and weapons. The decision for this came after the decision to retain the infrastructure was said to have been made at the end of June or early July 1991. Although no documentation relating to this decision is available, the date is consistent with evidence that some of the "special" weapons, although not necessarily agents, were destroyed in mid-July 1991. In 1997, UNSCOM inspection teams found remnants of what appeared to be biological bombs and warheads at the locations declared by Iraq.

The findings of fragments of munitions were insufficient to confirm other aspects of Iraq's account of its unilateral destruction of BW munitions, particularly with respect to the numbers declared by Iraq. Furthermore, there is some information that suggests that some BW warheads were destroyed later than declared by Iraq, the implication being that, if warheads were retained, then there may have been corresponding missiles to launch them. With respect to stockpiles of bulk agent stated to have been destroyed, there is evidence to suggest that these was not destroyed as declared by Iraq.

The first UNSCOM biological team arrived in Iraq, in early August 1991, and inspected the facility at Al Salman that had been destroyed by bombing in the Gulf War. Inspections of Al Hakam, Al Fudhaliyah, Al Daura and other sites followed in September and October 1991.

By the time of its first inspection, Al Hakam had been stripped of any obvious signs of its former role, and had been converted into a civilian facility. Thus, the fermenters that had previously been used to produce BW agents were now producing, or attempting to produce, yeast for animal feed. Other equipment was used for the production of a bacterial insecticide. This latter activity was of particular interest to UNSCOM, because the bacteria used were very similar to anthrax. The product was dried in a spray-dryer by a technique that created particle sizes optimized for an inhalation hazard. The technology had direct application for the drying of anthrax as a BW agent.

Between 1991 and 1995, Al Hakam continued to operate as a civilian complex and, in fact, underwent expansion. In particular, a large fermenter hall was built with the intention of acquiring, either locally or from imports, three 50,000 litre fermenters to produce yeast for animal feed. During this period, it was monitored by UNSCOM and, while no proscribed activity was detected, much of the research and development work at the site was dual-use in nature and would have had application in the BW field.

Iraq disclosed some details of its offensive BW programme on 1 July 1995, and substantially more following the defection of Lieutenant-General Hussein Kamal in August 1995. After that date, any further use of materials and equipment previously associated with the BW programme was prohibited by UNSCOM, and all activities at Al Hakam were frozen. In May/June 1996, all of the facilities, related equipment and materials declared by Iraq as belonging to its BW programme were destroyed under UNSCOM supervision. Thus, the vaccine fermenters at Al Daura that Iraq had declared had produced botulinum toxin were destroyed, as was the entire Al Hakam complex, including all its equipment and materials.

Following the destruction of Al Hakam in 1996, the staff from the programme were reassigned to various biological facilities, including universities, within the civilian sector. These facilities were included in routine monitoring by UNSCOM; no proscribed activities were detected at these sites up to the end of inspections in December 1998.

Uncertainties regarding Iraq's BW programme
Unilateral destruction
The almost complete lack of documentation on unilateral destruction activities in 1991 gives rise to the greatest uncertainties regarding Iraq's declaration of BW activities. Although there is physical evidence that some such destruction took place, it was difficult for UNSCOM inspectors to quantify the numbers and amounts. This, in turn, has repercussions on assessment of material balance and whether all materials and weapons have been accounted for.

Organization and Military Connections
Iraq's BW programme came, at various times, under several different authorities. Some of these changes may have resulted simply from the reorganization of government departments, but others may have reflected a change of direction or priority of the BW programme. For example,

at the rebirth of the programme in 1985, the controlling authority was MSE, which, at that time, came jointly under the Ministry of Defence and the Ministry of Industry and Military Industrialization. Other BW activities, including work on wheat smut and some spray devices, were initiated by TRC, which was responsible to the intelligence services.

Iraq has stated that, after 1987, all of its BW programme came under the control of TRC and, from then on, there were *"no links of any kind to the MOD* (Ministry of Defence)". Considering that the programme's objective was to produce weapons for Iraq's armed services, the lack of any connection to the MOD is surprising.

Another shift in control occurred in 1988, when part of the programme, including production of the agents anthrax, botulinum toxin and gas gangrene, was relocated to Al Hakam. However, another part, including the work on ricin, remained at Al Salman under a different directorship (although still apparently under TRC's control). Because of a lack of documentation, particularly on the Al Salman part of the programme, UNMOVIC cannot be confident that it understands the full scope of the BW programme.

The rationale for elements of the BW programme to be placed under the control of different authorities is also not apparent to UNMOVIC. This in turn gives rise to uncertainties over whether there may have been other activities, or elements of the programme, that have not been disclosed by Iraq.

Conclusions

Much is known about Iraq's BW programme: UNMOVIC has a general understanding of the major sites, equipment, agents and weapons involved in the programme. Iraq's declarations in this regard present an approximate outline of its BW activities. What is not known about the programme is, by its very nature, more difficult to identify and quantify. The issues of greatest importance would appear to relate to agent production, weaponization and unilateral destruction. These are discussed in further detail in the Clusters of Unresolved Disarmament Issues. Iraq would need to provide additional information to support its account on, or otherwise resolve, these matters.

Iraq's BW programme was remarkable for what it achieved in a relatively short time, especially since there appeared to be no foreign assistance involved (except for the equipment and materials used in the programme). After one false start in the early 1970's and another faltering beginning in 1985, the programme flourished and, in the space of five years, went from basic research to the production of thousands of litres of agent and the manufacture of BW weapons.

In the five years from 1985 to 1990, Iraq gained an understanding of the characteristics of a number of BW agents, particularly bacterial agents. It also gained experience in the key technologies of production, dissemination and weaponization.

During the course of the BW programme, Iraq developed some new technologies or adapted existing technologies for BW purposes. For example, it discovered new growth media for the production of BW agents and modified fermenters designed for the production of vaccines to allow the efficient production of bacterial BW agents. That is not to say that the agents and systems that were developed were technically sophisticated, or that the weapons themselves would have been optimally effective. And not all parts of the programme, e.g. viral research and genetic engineering, proceeded to fruition. Nevertheless, the BW capability that Iraq possessed by early 1991 posed a significant regional threat.

6 March 2003

IRAQ'S BALLISTIC MISSILE PROGRAMMES

Introduction

World attention was first drawn to Iraq's ballistic missile programme during the Iraq-Iran War. In the War of the Cities, in 1988, Baghdad launched almost 200 Al Hussein missiles, (an Iraqi modified, extended range SCUD) against Tehran. The programme however had actually started more than 15 years earlier, with the purchase of ballistic missiles and had coincided with other military developments, including the initiation of Iraq's programmes for the production of weapons of mass destruction.

After the Iraq-Iran War, Iraq continued to improve the capabilities of its missiles. Attempts were made to increase the range of the missile and to manufacture more components indigenously. Iraq again launched modified SCUDs in the Gulf War against targets in Israel, Kuwait, Bahrain and Saudi Arabia. It also had ready for use, in that war, special warheads filled with chemical and biological agents.

Following the Gulf War in 1991, Security Council Resolution 687 (1991), ordered an end to Iraq's development and possession of ballistic missiles with ranges greater than 150 kilometres. Accordingly, under UNSCOM supervision, proscribed missiles, facilities and materials were destroyed. However, development of missiles with ranges shorter than 150 kilometres was permitted under the resolution and such activities continued.

Acquisition of an imported missile force

It is uncertain what the stimulus was for Iraq's decision to acquire ballistic missiles, but it coincided with Iraq's interest in WMD in general. The origins can be traced to 1972, in which year Iraq signed contracts with the then Soviet Union, for the purchase of 70 kilometre range FROG-7 missiles, and 300 kilometre range SCUD-B missiles.

The acquisition of the SCUDs was a most significant purchase for Iraq and the missile was to become the cornerstone of Iraq's subsequent ballistic missile programmes. Deliveries began in 1974. Included in the initial purchase was a set of support equipment, comprising 10 transporter-erector launchers (TEL) and one for training. In all, Iraq purchased a total of 819 operational SCUD missiles. Along with the missiles, came standard quantities of fuel, gyroscope instrument sets and spare parts kits. In addition, Iraq was supplied with 15 training missiles, as well as full-scale cut-away models of the complete missile and its engine and Iraqi personnel received extensive operational training.

The Iraq-Iran War

The Iraq-Iran War began in September 1980, and Iraq's missile programme was soon to enter a new phase. Iraq used its SCUDs early in the war, and, by 1985, Iran was retaliating by missile attacks on Baghdad. However, geography put Tehran outside the range of Iraq's SCUDs, and this stimulated a major development programme, to obtain a longer range missile.

Development of an advanced missile system, Badr 2000

Iraq's first attempts to acquire a missile with a longer range than the SCUD began in 1984. In that year, Iraq signed a contract with a foreign country for the acquisition of a very accurate missile having an intended range, initially of 620 kilometre (km) and ultimately 750 km, with a 320 kilogramme (kg) warhead. It was a two-stage missile, known as Badr 2000 in Iraq, with a solid propellant first stage and a proposed liquid propellant second stage. Within the project, the contractor was required to develop the missile to specifications, with the help of a third country. The contract called for the supply of 85 missiles and ancillary equipment and training of Iraqi engineers. The contractor was also to supply the equipment, and associated technical know-how, to enable Iraq itself to manufacture the first stage solid propellant boost motor.

At the end of 1987, following the delivery of equipment, Iraq commenced the construction of three facilities at Yawn Al Azim, Um Al Maarik and Dhu Al Fiqar, for the production of the missile's first stage. However, in 1988, the contractor found itself unable to meet further delivery of contracted items and, consequently, Iraq terminated the contract in early 1989. Iraq, however, continued with the project and, in a reorganization, brought the three facilities under the umbrella name of Belat Al-Shuhada.

Construction and commissioning of the facilities for the Badr 2000 continued until the beginning of 1991 when the three separate plants were bombed by the Coalition forces and suffered substantial damage to buildings and equipment. Further equipment and buildings were destroyed under the supervision of UNSCOM so that, by April 1992, the facilities had become inoperative.

According to Iraq, no first stage composite propellant motors for the Badr 2000 had been produced by the time of the supervised destruction of the facility in 1991-1992. In subsequent years, the facilities were restored to a level where non-proscribed composite propellant developments, subject to UNSCOM monitoring, were undertaken

Extending the range of the SCUD: Project 144 – the Al Hussein Missile

To meet the requirement of a longer range missile for the Iraq-Iran War, a parallel development to the Badr 2000 project was begun. In 1986, a special *ad hoc* group was formed to investigate ways of extending the range of SCUD missiles. The development was later to be called Project 144. This small group conducted the first test flight on 11 February 1987. A standard SCUD missile was fired with a reduced payload: a 250 kg of warhead charge compared to the normal 800 kg. The test was a failure, with the engine shutting off prematurely, after about 30 seconds. After several more failures, and further modifications to the missile and warhead, a successful test was conducted, on 3 August 1987, with the missile achieving a range comparable with its design range of 650 km. This modified missile design was subsequently to be called the Al Hussein.

Iraq declared that, during the Iraq-Iran War, it launched 189 Al Hussein missiles against Iran. This was in addition to 327 standard SCUDs Iraq stated it launched during the same period. UNMOVIC has some documentation to support Iraq's figures.

Post Iraq-Iran War

The Iraq-Iran War ended in August 1988. But Iraq's ballistic missile programme showed no reduction in pace. In fact, a number of missile projects that had been initiated towards the end of the war continued, and new projects started so that the following years saw an overall expansion of activity.

Development of liquid propulsion missiles: Project 1728

After the successful demonstration on 3 August 1987 of an extended range, modified SCUD missile, the Director of Military Industrialisation Commission (MIC), the newly appointed, Lieutenant-General Hussein Kamal, ordered a programme for the domestic manufacture of SCUD engines. The development programme became known as Project 1728.

Project 1728 was established in 1988 at Al Amiriyah, but problems with dust at that site, resulted in its relocation at the end of the year, to Al Taji, to the north of Baghdad. Work continued at Al Taji until 16 January 1991, just prior to the Gulf War.

From 1988 to 1990, a number of items were manufactured locally and others were procured from foreign suppliers. Little success was achieved with locally manufactured items, particularly early on, as they did not meet specifications. The first test of a locally produced item was in August 1989, when an Iraqi combustion chamber and injector head were assembled and tested with an original, imported turbopump.

As Project 1728's mission was to produce engines, a static test facility for liquid propellant engines was required. A foreign firm was contracted, at the end of 1988, to build a static test facility at Al Amiriyah. However, since progress was slow and due to some technical and contractual problems, two temporary test stands were built by Iraq at Al Rafah, and used until the end of 1990.

Iraqi engineers believed that the performance of their engines would be improved by using a more energetic fuel instead of kerosene. Iraq contracted with a foreign firm for such a fuel, and 10 tonnes of the propellant, UDMH, were delivered around October 1989. Iraq sought foreign assistance to set up a production line, but failed in these efforts. Nonetheless, in January 1990, Iraq conducted a static test of an engine using imported UDMH as the fuel at Al Rafah. The test was stated by Iraq to be unsuccessful.

Apart from its major effort directed at producing SCUD engines, Project 1728 was also ordered, in June 1989, to reverse engineer the surface-to-air missile, the Volga (SA-2) and, additionally, as a lower priority, to reverse engineer the motor of an anti-ship missile, the HY-2. Although all design drawings were completed, UNMOVIC assesses that little other progress was made on these either of these system. In August 1989, Project 1728 was further tasked with reverse engineering the SCUD gyroscope, in competition with Project 144. This latter activity continued until early 1990.

Two other significant directives were given to Project 1728. The first of these followed a 1988 decision that MIC should develop a rocket to carry a nuclear device being developed by the Iraqi

Atomic Energy Commission. Thus, in February 1990, Project 1728 was tasked with the design and manufacture of an engine having a 30-ton thrust for this missile. To assist with the task, the project recruited a foreign expert who worked on the design until July 1990. Iraq stated that production of the engine was not started because the designs were not completed. UNMOVIC assesses that this activity did not result in the production of a viable missile system.

The second directive was to prepare designs for a large turbopump to feed four SCUD engines. The intention was that the four SCUDs would be clustered, to form the first stage of a space-launch vehicle which was being developed under the project name of Al Abid (see later). Iraq has stated that no real progress was made in this task. Project 1728 also had a further involvement in the Al Abid project in designing the connection between the first and second stages and in undertaking preliminary work on a spin-motor for the third stage. UNMOVIC also assesses the development of the clustered and multistage activities did not result in the production of a viable missile system.

It is clear that Project 1728 was an ambitious programme and, although falling short of its major goal of fully indigenous production of large liquid propellant engines, it nevertheless established a substantial base.

The development of Al Abbas Missile Programme

Once the war with Iran was ended, Iraq was in a position to push forward aggressively with its reverse engineering effort, and the number of personnel in Project 144 was boosted substantially to nearly 700. Following the success of the Al Hussein missile, a similar approach was adopted to modify the SCUD to extend its range further, to 900 kilometres. This missile was to be called Al Abbas.

The first prototype Al Abbas was test fired, in April 1988, but disintegrated during re-entry with the warhead reaching 760 kilometres. Further modifications were made to the missile, and three flight tests of the new design conducted, in June 1988. However, in all three tests, the missiles broke up in flight, indicating that there was a fundamental flaw in the design.

After several months of analysis and investigation, Iraqi engineers decided on yet further modifications to the missile, including designing the warhead to separate from the body in the final stages of flight. Two comparative flight tests were conducted, on 12 February 1989, one with a warhead to be separated from the missile body by explosive charges and the other non-separable. The one with the normal warhead disintegrated, as usual, upon re-entry, while the one with the separable warhead fell even shorter. The failure of the second missile was believed by Iraqi engineers to be caused by incomplete separation of the warhead.

It was not until 21 August 1989 that there was another test of an Al Abbas, using the same configuration as before, and a similar failure occurred. On 27 June 1990, nearly one year later, another trial was conducted, but, this time, using explosive bolts to achieve the warhead separation. The trial was successful with both the inert warhead and the missile body landing intact, and at the desired range. This success was repeated, on 28 December 1990, with a missile having a live warhead and an Iraqi produced airframe. However, on the same day, a second missile, using some indigenous engine components, exploded shortly after launch. UNMOVIC has no evidence to indicate that there were any further trials of the Al Abbas missile.

Space launch vehicle: the Al Abid Project

In 1983, the Space Research Centre (SRC), was formed as part of the Iraqi Scientific Research Council. However, it was not until the end of the end of the Iraq-Iran War, that funds became available to commence work on the development of an Iraqi space launch vehicle. The project was initially known as Al Taa'er, (the Bird), but later was named Al Abid.

To provide the required thrust to launch a satellite, the launch vehicle comprised three stages. Initial effort concentrated on the first stage, which was to be constructed using five clustered SCUD engines, each burning for more than 100 seconds. This necessitated an extension to the oxidizer and fuel tanks, even greater than that required for the Al Hussein. Designs for the second and third stages of the vehicle were also undertaken but steel mock-ups were used for the first trial.

The first test launch of the Al Abid space launch vehicle took place in December 1989. The initial launch phase was successful. However, the airframe exploded after 45 seconds. Iraqi engineers suspected that the explosive bolts, that were being used to separate the first stage, functioned prematurely. After this failure, further developmental work continued, and a second test was planned for the autumn of 1990. However, with the approach of the Gulf War, this test was not conducted, and the programme came to an end.

Fahad 300 and 500

In June 1988, Iraq attempted to convert an SA-2, surface-to-air missile, into a surface-to-surface weapon. Code-named Fahad 300, the work was undertaken within Project 144 and was one of several programmes involving modification of the SA-2.

The concept was to launch the missile at an inclined angle as if firing at an imaginary air target. Following booster separation, the missile would then align itself with the line defined by its firing radar. Once the radar was shut off from the ground, the missile would then fly in a ballistic trajectory. The intended range was 300 kilometres.

Relatively minor modifications, such as removal of the self-destruct timer, were made to the missile itself. Significantly, the engine had no shut-off valve, so total thrust was dependent on the amount of fuel in the missile. The maximum range achieved was 276 kilometres. Nineteen flight tests were conducted in all. However stability of the system was said not to be good, resulting in unacceptable inaccuracy. The programme was declared to have been a failure, and was said to have been terminated in July 1989.

The Fahad 500 programme was intended to modify the SA-2 for a 500 kilometre range but, because of the failure of the Fahad 300, did not proceed beyond paper studies.

Both missiles were displayed at the 1989 Baghdad Defense Exposition as mock-ups.

Research and development: The Tamouz Missile

Studies for a 2,000 kilometre range missile, the Tamouz, also began after the Iraq-Iran War. Iraq declared that, in May 1989, design work began on the two stage missile. The first stage was to employ an Al Hussein missile, and the second stage an unmodified SA-2 sustainer engine. Iraq declared that the programme did not proceed beyond the early design stage and was terminated, in July 1989, because of problems with the stage separation and guidance system for the second stage.

Project Babylon (Supergun)

In 1988, Iraq embarked on a programme, code-named Project Babylon, to develop a supergun that had a stated purpose of launching a satellite. Iraq has declared that there were three versions of the gun, and that there were also military applications for it. The military aspects have not been fully explained by Iraq. In this regard, it is noteworthy that the project was under the control of MIC, that was responsible for military hardware development, and that the Space Research Centre was said to have no involvement. It is clear to UNMOVIC that the supergun had the potential to deliver chemical or biological warheads over a great range.

Supergun technology is universally credited to the late Dr Gerald Bull. Iraq signed a contract with Dr Bull in March 1988 to develop a supergun of 1000 millimetre (mm) caliber, and the first step towards this was the design and construction of a prototype of a smaller caliber. The prototype was to be a 350 mm caliber gun with a barrel length of either 30 or 52 metres. It was intended to fire a 1.5 metre projectile of about 400 kg to a range of 140 to 490 kilometres depending on which size barrel was used and the type of projectile. It has been stated by Iraq that the projectiles were to have a guidance and control system, but there is no evidence to indicate that anything was achieved in this respect.

Work on the prototype was rapid. By June 1988, contracts had been signed with a number of foreign manufacturers for the fabrication of major components. Minor parts were to be made in Iraq and the final assembly of the system to be done locally. In time, international suspicion over the real purpose of the pipes resulted in some contracted items being blocked.

In spite of difficulties in procuring some of the parts, the 350 mm gun was assembled in a horizontal position in Iraq at Jebel Sinjar. Following some initial experiments on the gun at Jebel Sinjar, it was relocated to Jebel Hamryn, and reassembled on a hillside at an inclination of 45°. At this site, four firings were conducted in June and September 1990. Ranges up to approximately 240 km were achieved, although, if used to its full potential, greater ranges could probably have been reached.

Work on the 1000 mm gun began shortly after the start of the prototype. By 1990, initial design and engineering drawings had been completed and parts had been manufactured overseas, some of which had been imported. Concrete mounts for the gun and other infrastructure work had commenced at Jurf Al-Sakhar. The gun barrel was to be 150 metres long and fixed at an elevation of 45°. Iraq has stated that the projectile was to be 400 mm diameter and 4.3 metre long with a "*maximum desired preliminary designed range*" of 760 kilometres".

Iraq has stated that, following on the death of Dr Bull in March 1990, the supergun project came to a halt. The 350 mm gun, and the components of the 1000 mm gun that had been delivered to Iraq, were destroyed under UNSCOM supervision.

In addition to the prototype and full size supergun, Iraq also planned a 600 mm caliber weapon. In contrast to the other supergun models, the 600 mm gun had design features for elevating and traversing the barrel which would have made it more useful as a weapons system. Iraq stated that the project did not develop beyond "an idea to study the feasibility of having a gun of 600mm caliber". There is no evidence to indicate that any parts for such a gun were imported.

Remote Piloted Vehicle (RPV)

Prior to the Gulf War, Iraq had worked on several Remotely Piloted Vehicles (RPVs), essentially for target practice and reconnaissance purposes. In 1987, under MIC direction, parallel work was being undertaken on RPVs at both the Al Faris factory and the Technical Research Centre at Salman Pak in a competitive mode. However, by 1989, all work on RPVs had been consolidated at Al Faris.

In the lead up to the Gulf War, Iraq began a project to modify a MIG-21 aircraft into a RPV to *"deliver a munition to a target"*. Iraq has also declared that, at the same time as this project started, another decision was made within MIC to convert a Mirage F1 fuel drop tank, to a spray tank for delivery of biological agents. In its initial disclosures of these projects, Iraq stated that they were related i.e. the remotely piloted MIG was to be used to spray anthrax from its modified drop tanks. The target was said to be Israel. Iraq later retracted its statements about the link between the two projects.

Based on available evidence, it appears that the project to modify the MIG began in November 1990. An autopilot from a MIG-23 was installed, together with a remote control system from a foreign country and servos for control surfaces, throttle and brakes. This vehicle was flight tested at Al Rashid Air Base in January 1991. Iraq claims that this aircraft was destroyed in the bombing of Rashid Air Base during the Gulf War.

The Short Al Hussein Programme

After the "War of the Cities", the Iraqi Army pressured Project 144 to improve the accuracy of the Al Hussein missile and to develop firing tables to provide flexibility in range. Learning from the experience of the Al Abbas program, it was determined that increased stability could be achieved by shortening the warhead and the section for guidance and control systems, and by other modifications.

On 2 January 1990, the first flight test of Short Al-Hussein took place. For comparison, two Al Husseins and two Short Al Husseins were tested, in which the effects of additional stiffening to the airframe were also tested. All four missiles failed upon re-entry.

As declared by Iraq, a total of 23 Short Al Husseins were produced. They were not the system of choice for the Iraqi Army, but the lead-up to the Gulf War required that all assets be available for use if required.

Development of missile launchers

In 1987, at the commencement of the Al Hussein project, Iraq possessed ten operational transporter-erector launchers (TEL) for launching standard SCUDs. Since the Al Hussein was a longer missile than the standard SCUD, a new TEL was required. Thus a project was started to design, and construct locally, a suitable launcher. The launcher was to be based on the standard SCUD launcher, and named the Al Waleed.

A total of three different prototypes were developed and tested, but severe problems were encountered, primarily with the pneumatics, hydraulics and launch control electronics. The last prototype, commenced in July 1990, was damaged by air strikes during the Gulf War and later destroyed by UNSCOM inspectors. The ten 25-ton trailers, which had been acquired for this project, were retained by Iraq for future use as standard flatbed trailers.

In mid-1990, following the problems of the Al Waleed project, MIC ordered the design and construction of a less sophisticated mobile-erector launcher. This was named Al Nida'a. Again, severe mechanical problems were encountered in its design. Nonetheless, six Al Nida'a launchers were manufactured, although only four became operational. The Al Nida'a system used separate trucks for the launch control electronics and compressed air equipment.

Indigenous production/modification of warheads

The modification of the standard SCUD into the Al Hussein missile required a reduction of the mass of the original warhead. This required some re-design of the warhead and this work was undertaken by Project 144. Further modifications of warheads for other specific purposes, for example the Short Al Hussein, were also executed by Project 144.

Chemical warheads

Iraq first considered chemical warheads for its SCUDs in 1985 when, in conjunction with the chemical weapons establishment at Al Muthanna, it experimented with the dispersal of liquids from SCUD warheads. The main modification was the incorporation into the warhead of a container to carry liquid agent, and a burster charge to rupture the warhead and disseminate the agent. Iraq declared that, in August 1985, after a series of static tests, a live firing of a SCUD, carrying a modified warhead filled with water, was conducted. The test was said to be successful, but that no further tests were conducted after that. According to Iraq, it was not until March 1990 that Al Muthanna again came to Project 144 with a proposal to use the Al Hussein missile to deliver the nerve agent Sarin.

Following successful static and flight tests with simulant and spoiled Sarin, production of chemical warheads began in May 1990. In all, 75 "special" warheads were produced: 50 for chemical purposes and another 25 for BW purposes. These were deployed to various locations during the Gulf War ready for use. Iraq declared that, after the Gulf War, it unilaterally destroyed 45 of these warheads (20 chemical and all 25 biological) in the summer of 1991. Thirty special warheads were destroyed under UNSCOM supervision between 1991 and 1993.

Nuclear warheads

In 1988, the Iraq Atomic Energy Commission (IAEC) met with MIC to tackle the problem of a nuclear warhead for a ballistic missile. It was agreed that MIC would be responsible for the development of an explosive trigger and the delivery vehicle, while the IAEC would work on reducing the size and weight of the device.

After the invasion of Kuwait, and with war looming, MIC was directed to look at accommodating any future nuclear device within existing missiles, such as the Al Hussein or Al Abbas. The task given to MIC was to fit a spherical device of 800 mm diameter and a weight of 1000 kilogrammes into the warhead. According to Iraq, after some preliminary activity, work on the project ceased, due to the imminent outbreak of the Gulf War.

The Gulf War

Iraq has stated that, during the Gulf War, two missile brigades were responsible for launching Al Hussein missiles. The missile forces had 14 launchers and, between 18 January and 26 February 1991, launched a total of 93 Al Hussein missiles towards Israel and the Coalition forces to the south of Iraq.

Iraq has declared that the 75 "special" warheads, containing chemical and biological agents, were stored separately from the missile bodies, at four locations during the War. Iraq has said that these were only to be fired if Baghdad was attacked with nuclear weapons.

Post Gulf War

Destruction

Under UN Security Council Resolution 687 (1991), all Iraq's ballistic missiles with a range greater than 150 kilometres, and related parts, activities and facilities, were proscribed.

Of the 819 SCUDs declared as acquired, Iraq stated that it unilaterally destroyed 85 in 1991 (83 could be verified by UNSCOM). Another 48 missiles were destroyed under UNSCOM supervision. Iraq has declared that the remaining missiles were accounted for by expenditure in the Iraq-Iran War, the Gulf War, and in training or testing activities. Iraq also declared that it unilaterally destroyed 20 chemical and 25 biological warheads at Al-Nibae in the summer of 1991. An additional thirty chemical warheads were destroyed under UNSCOM supervision in the period 1991 to 1993.

Many of the facilities associated with Iraq's proscribed missile programmes were severely damaged during bombing in the Gulf War, but much equipment and many materials survived. These were later destroyed under UNSCOM supervision. Thus, the buildings and equipment associated with the Badr 2000 project, Project 144 and Project 1728 were destroyed under the supervision of UNSCOM inspection teams so that, by April 1992, these projects had been dismantled. In addition, other equipment, such as launchers and the supergun components, were destroyed under UNSCOM supervision.

Development of non-proscribed missiles

Although ballistic missiles with ranges greater than 150 km were proscribed under resolution 687 (1991), missiles with a shorter range were not. After the Gulf War, Iraq began a variety of activities connected with the development of missile systems ostensibly within the permitted range. Much of this technology, although not-proscribed, would have enhanced Iraq's capability to develop missiles with a range over 150 kilometres, and was under UNSCOM monitoring until December 1998.

Iraq has stated that, in mid 1991, MIC instructed the Ibn Al-Haytham Centre to develop a ballistic missile with a range less than 150 km. Initially it was planned to be a solid propellant missile, but, a few months later, it was decided to also develop a liquid propellant version.

While Ibn Al-Haytham conducted all concept and design studies, responsibility for production of the solid rocket motor was vested in the Al Rasheed Factory and for the liquid propellant engine in the Al Sadiq Factory. The liquid propellant version was eventually to become known as the Al Samoud and the solid propellant version, as the Ababil-100.

Development of a Liquid Propulsion missile, the Al Samoud

The liquid system was based on the SA-2 Volga, which had been in Iraq's inventory as its primary air defence system for some years. Work on this missile began in mid-1991, to modify it into a single stage missile capable of delivering a 300-450 kilogramme warhead to within the permitted 150 kilometre range.

In mid-1992, at Lieutenant-General Hussein Kamal's direction, the design was changed to a two-stage missile vehicle, as employed in the SA-2 system. Six flight tests, and one static test, were carried out between January and April 1993. It was recognized that, using this configuration, the missile would exceed a range of 150 km if the propellant tanks were filled to their normal capacity, so, for these tests, the tanks were only partially filled. Iraq stated that, in the next phase of the project, the SA-2 propellant tanks would be replaced by indigenously produced tanks of a lower capacity to ensure compliance in respect of the range limitation. UNSCOM inspectors viewed some tanks, apparently consistent with this, in February 1996.

In mid-1993, together with a change in leadership of Iraq's missile R&D programme, the liquid propellant option reverted back to the original configuration. In May 1994, a competitive procurement strategy was introduced, with alternative designs being pursued at Ibn Al-Haytham and at Al Karama. In late 1995, Al Karama and Ibn Al-Haytham were re-merged, under a single leadership, and work on the Ibn Al-Haytham design was terminated. From this time onwards, development work continued only on the Al Karama design (the Al Samoud missile).

Iraq's intention was to progressively replace original parts of the SA-2 missile with reverse engineered, indigenously produced components. Up to the end of 1998, some twenty-two static engine tests and seven flight tests were carried out, with varying degrees of success. The first successful static test of a "fully" Iraqi engine was conducted on 12 January 1998. The declared range of the Al Samoud missile is 149 km with a 300 kg warhead.

Ababil-100

Initial design work on the solid propellant Ababil-100 commenced in the third quarter of 1992, and the project progressed very slowly until it was eventually stopped by order of the MIC at the end of 1996. At this time, some hardware components had been fabricated but no propellant grains produced. In the second half of 1997, new funds were provided by MIC and work resumed. During the period January to October 1998, a total of eight reduced scale motors were statically fired, the last two being unsuccessful. By the end of 1998, the project was still only in the research and development stage: the guidance and control system had not been determined and other parts of the missile were still in design. The declared range of the Ababil-100 missile is 120-130 km and the warhead was likely to be 250-300 kg.

Remotely Piloted Vehicles

In a continuation of its pre-gulf War interest in remotely piloted vehicles, Iraq restarted its programme on RPVs in 1995. On 5 October 1995, Udai Saddam Hussein, the President's son, initiated a project for the modification of obsolete jet training aircraft (the L-29), to convert them in to RPVs. The declared purpose was for use as target aircraft. The project subsequently became known as Al Baia'a. An indication of the importance of the project was given, when in November 1995, the President enquired of those in charge: "*Are you capable of pursuing this with the same enthusiasm as Udai? If so, go ahead*".

Iraq stated that work on the conversion of the L-29 began in early 1996, at Ibn Fernas on the northern outskirts of Baghdad. By June 1997, two successful unmanned flight tests had been carried out. The conversion, guidance and control components were taken from other equipment possessed by Iraq.

Iraq has stated that the range of the L-29 RPV, is only 30 to 50 kilometres, because it relies on control from the ground. UNMOVIC, however, assesses that the potential range of the L-29 would be in excess of 150 kilometres, if a system for autonomous flight was developed.

UNSCOM monitored the development of the L-29 RPV until its departure in December 1998.

Conclusions

In a period of 14 years, from 1974 to December 1998, Iraq's missile programmes achieved a reasonable measure of success. Using foreign technology as a starting point and by reverse engineering and adapting systems for its own purposes, Iraq developed considerable indigenous expertise. A wide range of projects were undertaken and some of them, notably the Al Hussein missile project, were very successful, even though they did not achieve a status of total self-dependence.

A number of areas of uncertainty regarding Iraq ballistic missile programmes still exist. Many of these relate to Iraq's unilateral destruction of missile components and propellants. Other areas relate to imports, accountancy and material balance questions. Furthermore, non-proscribed activities, conducted after 1991, complicate assessment. These uncertainties are discussed in more detail in the Clusters of Unresolved Disarmament Issues.

Printed in the UK for The Stationery Office Limited
on behalf of the Controller of Her Majesty's Stationery Office
ID134965   03/03